Treasures of Korean Art

2000 YEARS OF CERAMICS, SCULPTURE, AND JEWELED ARTS

Treasures of
KOREAN ART

2000 Years of Ceramics, Sculpture, and Jeweled Arts

TEXT BY Chewon Kim

DIRECTOR OF THE NATIONAL MUSEUM OF KOREA

AND Won-Yong Kim

PROFESSOR AT THE SEOUL NATIONAL UNIVERSITY

Harry N. Abrams, Inc., Publishers, New York

Library of Congress Catalog Card Number 66-23402
© Copyright 1966 in Switzerland by Office du Livre, Fribourg
All rights reserved. No part of the contents of this book
may be reproduced without written permission
of the publishers, Harry N. Abrams, Incorporated, New York
Printed in Switzerland
Bound in the Netherlands

To Chaihy Lee and Sŏngsuk Yu

TABLE OF CONTENTS

PART IV: GOLD, BRONZE AND LACQUER WORKS

LIST OF PLATES

COLOUR PLATES

BLACK-AND-WHITE PLATES

DRAWINGS AND INK-RUBBINGS

PREFACE

More than forty years have passed since Dr. Sekino wrote the first history of Korean art, and Dr. Eckardt's work on the subject has long been out of date, so we have gladly accepted the opportunity to present to foreign readers an account of Korean art written by Koreans. However, at the suggestion of the publisher, we have agreed to exclude graphic art and architecture, to enable other subjects to be more fully discussed. Although both authors have collaborated closely on the whole work, Chewon Kim is mainly responsible for the text of part II and Won-Yong Kim for the text of parts I, III and IV.

Some of the black-and-white photographs and most of the colour plates are the work of Mr Hans Hinz of Basel, taken while the Exhibition of Korean Arts was being shown at the Ethnographical Museum in Vienna in 1961, but the bulk of the illustrations has been supplied by Mr. Mikihiro Taeda of Japan, who visited Korea for this purpose in the autumn of 1964. Some of the photographs for the Catalogue were taken by Mr. Kyong-mo Lee of Seoul.

The authors are greatly indebted to Mr. Robert P. Griffing, Jr., former director of the Honolulu Academy of Arts, and Pater Richard Rutt of Seoul. Both made useful recommendations which we have gratefully incorporated in the text. Special thanks are due to Mr. Griffing for his invaluable help in the section on ceramics.

CHEWON KIM

Seoul 1965   WON-YONG KIM

Abbreviations:

Pl. i to xxiv: Colour Plates
Pl. i to ioi: Black and white illustrations in the text
Fig. i to ii: Drawings and ink-rubbings
Cat. i to 152: Black and white illustrations in the catalogue

★: An asterisk before a number refers to a textual reference
   in the outer column of the page

PART 1

INTRODUCTION

THE GEOGRAPHICAL SETTING

Korea is a peninsula a thousand miles long, stretching southwards from Manchuria. It forms a land bridge between the Continent and the Japanese archipelago, and is separated from Manchuria by the Amnok (Yalu) and Tuman (Tumen) rivers which flow, one westwards, the other eastwards from the Paektu-san (White-headed Mountain), the highest peak in the country (9,000 feet).

The east coast facing the Sea of Japan is steep and rockbound, but the west and south coasts, with hundreds of small islands lying off them, are for the most part low and shelving. The tide has a span of up to nearly thirty-three feet. The continuous broad strip of plain along the west and south coasts produces most of the rice that forms the main diet of the Korean people.

There are several large mountain ranges, including the famous Kŭmgang-san or Diamond Mountains. The three major rivers are the Taedong, passing the city of P'yŏng-yang, the Han, running through the capital city of Seoul, and the Naktong in the south. Their valleys have been continuously inhabited since prehistoric times. The rivers are shallow and not navigable for large modern vessels, but they have been valuable highways for commerce and communication throughout Korea's history.

The northern half of the peninsula is timbered and mountainous, contrasting with the gentle treeless hills of south Korea. There are, however, some notable gneiss monadnocks in south Korea, such as the peaks of Chiri, Kyeryong and Songni, that stand above the surrounding lowlands. Fir and pine trees are found everywhere, and oak, maple, birch, walnut, hazel and willow are also abundant. Most of the lowland hills, particularly in the south, are now treeless, a condition probably brought about in recent centuries by unplanned felling. The ugly eroded hills surrounding villages and towns have recently been planted once more with trees and shrubs, but it will take another century or so before they return to their original state.

When the forests were thicker, tigers, leopards, bears, and packs of wolves roamed the mountains and hills, and often molested human beings. During the Yi dynasty (1392–1910) it was the custom when there were royal tombs to be constructed to send out bands of skilled snipers to protect the labourers from tigers. During the sixteenth century the invading Japanese forces were so hampered by tigers that the Japanese general Kiyomasa Katō gained more fame from tiger-hunting than from his military successes.

The weather is generally pleasant except in the north, where a continental climate prevails, with severe cold in winter and excessive heat in summer.

The climate is pleasant and dry, and the landscape is peaceful if not spectacular. Mountains are not rugged, streams are not torrential and there are no lofty trees soaring into the clouds. The moderation of their natural environment has certainly affected the art of the Korean people. It is characterized by modesty, sensitivity and a naïve naturalism.

6

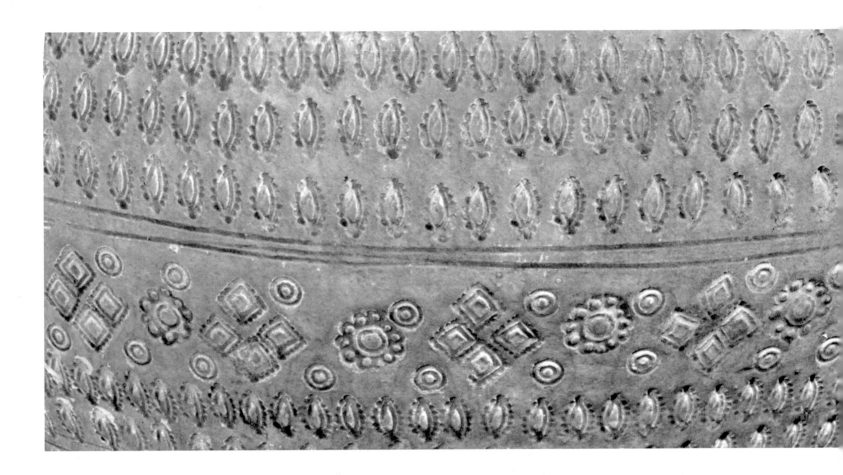

THE HISTORICAL SETTING

PREHISTORIC PERIOD

The legendary founder of Korea is Tangun or the Sandal-wood Prince, who was born to the Heavenly Hwanung and his bear-spouse. The prince founded the Kingdom of Chosŏn (Ch'ao-Hsien) in 2333 B.C., on the third day of the tenth month. Today Koreans celebrate 3 October as National Foundation Day.

This legendary date is of course totally fictitious, but Neolithic Korea probably dates back to the third millenium B. C. At this time bands of people from Siberia came into the coastal regions of Korea. Some of them even crossed to the surrounding islands. They can be recognized by their distinctive 'comb-pattern' pottery. The evidence for previous occupation consists of two sites which have not yet been dated, but which because of the absence of pottery may belong to a pre-ceramic period. These two sites were discovered in 1963 and 1964, one in north-eastern Korea near Unggi, the other in south-central

7

Pl. I Food jar. Celadon glaze without decoration, with inscriptions of cyclical date 993 A.D. H. 1 ft. 2 in. Koryŏ dynasty, 10th century. Coll. Ehwa Women's University Museum, Seoul.

Korea near Kongju[1]. Both have been claimed as 'Palaeolithic', although no definitive analyses of the stone implements or of the geology of the site have yet been completed. The stone implements from Kongju are mostly flakes and small cores of shale and quartzite, and were found together with a considerable amount of waste material. No fossil bones accompanied the artifacts. The tradition of Palaeolithic tool making is certainly seen surviving in the stone implements from the second site. They were recovered from a thick layer of hard, compact clay some twenty-three feet below the present river terrace on the northern bank of the Kŭmgang river. At present these two sites represent the earliest known appearance of human activity in the Korean peninsula. There is as yet no means of telling whether the intrusive Neolithic settlers found a native 'Palaeolithic' population already occupying the land, or whether the 'pre-ceramic' culture had died out by the time they arrived.

The Neolithic comb-pattern pottery of Korea can be roughly divided into two regional types[2]. The first is found chiefly in the western coastal regions, though it also occurs in the south and in some eastern areas. Its main concentration is to the north of the Han river. This western type of comb-pottery is made of a sandy clay tempered with mica, soapstone and sometimes asbestos. It is built up by the ring, or coiling method. It is generally brownish in colour and the shape is predominantly a simple pot with straight neck and a pointed or rounded bottom. The surface of the vessel is covered with horizontal bands of pits or incisions and herring-bone patterns.

The second type is concentrated on the north-eastern coast where it adjoins the Maritime Region of the USSR.

It is characterized by a flat bottom, in contrast to the first type, and the clay is not sandy and is tempered only with grit. Surface decoration, in most cases, is confined to the neck, the lower part of the vessel being left plain. Herring-bone pattern is not used in the decoration, which is mainly limited to horizontal bands of widely spaced sloping pitted lines. There are also vessels with incised meanders and triangular patterns which seem to be derived from similar motifs on south-western Manchurian pottery. This indicates that some aspects of Neolithic culture came from northern China and south-west Manchuria across the Manchurian plain.

About the first half of the first millenium B.C. a new stock of people entered Korea, apparently from south-west Manchuria; waves of these newcomers crossed the Yalu river and pushed southwards to the uninhabited inland areas, where they gradually made contact with the comb-pottery people living on the coasts. Comb-pottery gradually disappeared, and it can be assumed that its makers were in time assimilated or annihilated by the newcomers. These can be identified by their coarse, plain pottery and their intensive use of the adze. Agriculture was not unknown to the comb-pottery people in their most advanced stage, but it was the makers of plain pottery who first cultivated grain extensively.

The plain pottery is hand-made of coarse clay tempered with grit. The typical vessel is a V-shaped pot with a bulbous body and narrow flat bottom. Sometimes the mouth tends to flare out or is narrowed to form a neck. This pottery can be traced across the Tsushima straits and into north Kyūshū, where it developed into the Yayoi pottery of Japan.

Besides this plain coarse pottery there is a type characterized by the treatment of the surface with a coating of red ochre which was burnished. This seems to have been derived from the *hung-tao* ('reddish pottery') of south-west Manchuria, itself linked with the painted pottery of north China.

Unlike the comb-pottery people who lived by the sea or on river banks, the people who made plain pottery lived inland, away from the coasts. They had subterranean pit-houses and they made stone adzes in quantity, and crescent-shaped stone knives. This type of stone knife is the same as the harvesting tool used by the Neolithic Yangshao and Lung-shan peoples of northern China, and its presence in Korea is evidence of the spread of Chinese culture into the peninsula.

The makers of plain pottery built the table-shaped dolmens which are found in great numbers along the river reaches everywhere except in the southern coastal regions. Here a different type of dolmen is found: a large stone exposed on the surface of the ground which covers a subterranean stone cist. The Korean dolmens are believed to be linked via the coastal regions of China to those of South East Asia and India[3].

The people who made the plain pottery were soon followed by a new wave of immigrants, this time probably from regions outside the Great Wall in north-east China. The new immigrants had a bronze culture which can be linked to that of the Minusinsk Bronze Age of the upper Yenisei. All these early inhabitants of the northern part of the Korean peninsula were called collectively Wei-mo ('unclean Tapirs') by the contemporary Chinese, who showed their contempt for all non-Chinese peoples by

giving them names of this sort. The inhabitants of the south, however, they called the Han tribes *(San Kuo Chih,* Vol. 30)—not to be confused with the Chinese Han dynasty.

About the fourth or third century B.C. another wave of immigrants came into north-west Korea from south-western Manchuria. These were the people who introduced the use of iron into the peninsula. They were armed with a distinctive type of bronze dagger and with iron swords, halberds and axes. The success of this iron-using culture culminated in the establishment of a small kingdom, now called Wei-man Ch'ao-hsien, in 198 B.C., with its capital at the modern P'yŏngyang. The new bronze and iron tools were too expensive to be available to the native Koreans, who still lived in a Stone Age setting. They copied the new metal implements in slate and shale and used them as burial gifts.

The Tungusic Wei-man Ch'ao-hsien kingdom was, naturally, hostile to Han China, and seems to have had some relations with the Hsiungnu nomads outside the Great Wall. The (Chinese) Han Emperor Wu-ti regarded this Korean kingdom as a serious menace. In 108 B.C. he sent a huge expeditionary army with marines to north-western Korea to cut off what he called 'the left arm of the Hsiungnu'. The expedition was ostensibly a great success, but a nucleus of the Wei-man fled to the south and settled in the Kyŏngju area of south-east Korea and on the lower reaches of the Yŏngsan river. This river flows into the Yellow Sea at the south-western tip of the peninsula.

This southward flight of the Ch'ao-hsien people caused a rapid spread of iron-using culture in the south, and

stimulated the emergence of powerful new clans within the native social structure.

In north Korea the Emperor Wu-ti established the colonial province of Lo-lang to take over the former territory of Wei-man. Colonial office buildings were erected on the southern bank of the Taedong river across from P'yŏngyang. At this site many roof tiles have been discovered, and the clay seals which were once attached to official documents. Hundreds of Lo-lang tombs are concentrated round the mud-walled enclosure of the colonial headquarters. Koreans and Chinese lived together in the Lo-lang province, ruled by officials sent from the central Chinese government. The expatriate Chinese (called *hua-chiao*) seem to have had their own agency or commissariat to supply them with all kinds of Chinese goods, from lacquer wine-cups to huge wooden coffins. The rich finds of burial gifts in the Lo-lang tombs give an insight into the luxurious life led by these Chinese officials[4].

Chinese material wealth naturally made a great impression on the native Koreans, and even the Han of south

Korea made journeys northward to trade with the Chinese. The chapter on the Han in the *San Kuo Chih* tells how their merchants came to Lo-lang as *soi-disant* envoys, wearing full ceremonial dress decorated with many glass beads. The Han were able to mine and smelt iron, and they traded iron ore to both Japan and Lo-lang by the sea routes. Through such contacts and trading, the 'Unclean Tapirs' of north Korea and the Han of south Korea developed, both culturally and politically.

By the beginning of the third century A.D. the Lo-lang Chinese found themselves forced to establish a new province to the south of Lo-lang in order to maintain Lo-lang itself against the growing national aspirations of the Koreans. By the end of the third century these two colonial provinces were cut off from China and lay virtually defenceless against attack by the Koreans from both north and south. In 313 they were finally overrun by invading Koguryŏ warriors from the north. Many of the Chinese seem to have stayed on, but some fled south, by land or sea, and some even crossed over to Japan.

The fall of the Chinese colonies in the north probably coincided with the formation of two kingdoms in south Korea, Paekche in the south-west and Silla in the south-east. Between the two kingdoms a narrow strip of land along the lower reaches of the Naktong river was occupied by a confederacy of village states called Kaya or Kara. Thus the recorded history of Korea begins in the fourth century with the Three Kingdoms of Koguryŏ, Paekche and Silla.

THE THREE KINGDOMS PERIOD

The *Samguk Sagi* ('History of Three Kingdoms') compiled by Kim Pusik during the twelfth century names 37 B.C., 18 B.C. and 57 B.C. as the dates of the foundation of Koguryŏ, Paekche and Silla respectively. The Koguryŏ had certainly formed a kingdom on the north bank of the Yalu river as early as the first century B.C., but the two southern states cannot be regarded as true kingdoms much before 300. The Paekche dynasty grew from a village state originally located on the south bank of the Han river across from Seoul, ruled by a group of refugees from Koguryŏ. It later extended its rule over all south-west Korea and set up the kingdom of Paekche.

In south-eastern Korea, Silla arose as a true kingdom at about the same time. The foundation of these two southern kingdoms can be dated by the royal tombs around Seoul and Kyŏngju; the burial gifts contained in them are none of them earlier than 300. The history of the three and a half centuries of the Three Kingdoms period (*c.* 300–650) is a confused one of wars fought between the three nations, until Silla finally defeated first one and then the other.

The kingdom of Koguryŏ (37 B.C.–A.D. 668) was at first the strongest of them all; her army twice withstood huge expeditionary forces from Sui dynasty China (581 to 618) before it was finally defeated in 668 by Silla, which had formed an alliance with T'ang China. Buddhism was first introduced into Koguryŏ in 372 by a monk sent from the court of Chin (350–394). The shamanistic kings of Koguryŏ were converted to the Way of the Buddha, and Buddhism rapidly gained ground in the kingdom.

Although Koguryŏ had overthrown Lo-lang in 313 it did not cross the Yalu river and move into P'yŏngyang until 427, more than a century after the victory. Geographically close to China, it is natural that her culture was much influenced by that of China, particularly of the north. It will be shown later that the Buddhist sculpture of Koguryŏ was much affected by northern Chinese sculpture, especially that of the Northern Wei dynasty (386–534).

The Paekche dynasty (18 B.C.–A.D. 660) in south-western Korea, on the other hand, maintained a close relationship with the dynasties of China south of the Yangtze, particularly with the Liang (502–556). Sculpture, and sculptors, architects, painters and potters were sent to Paekche, and the celebrated art of Paekche owes much to these Chinese artisans. Buddhism was first introduced in 384 by a monk from Central Asia, sent by the Emperor Hsiao-wu-ti of the eastern Chin dynasty (317–420). It was received with enthusiasm.

The kingdom of Silla (57 B.C.–A.D. 935) occupied the Kyŏngsang Triangle in south-eastern Korea, separated from the rest of the peninsula by the Sobaek-san mountain range. Secluded from their two neighbours, the people of Silla developed a distinctive culture. Before the formation of the kingdom, important matters of state were decided by a Council of Chiefs, each representing one of the Six Villages. This council meeting resembled the Mongolian *kuriltai;* it was called *hwabaek.* Kings at first were called either *nisagum* or *maripkan. Maripkan* means Great Khan, and here again is an affinity with the Mongols of southern Siberia. As will be discussed later, the gold crown of Silla has affinities with similar head-gear worn by peoples of the steppe.

The strength of Silla was based on the exploitation of the iron and gold found within its territory. The technique of gold mining is thought perhaps to have been learnt from the Chinese refugees who fled southward after the fall of Lo-lang in 313. Whatever its beginnings, the wealth of the gold mines caused Silla to expand rapidly, and her fame as the 'gold-glittering nation' reached as far as the Persian Gulf, where it was recorded in the Itinerary of the famous Ibn Khordadbeh[5]. This wealth is splendidly illustrated in the rich finds of gold ornaments which have recently come to light in Silla tombs. The pride of Silla was also the *hwarang* (Flower Youth) corps, the training ground of the political and military leaders of the Old Silla dynasty. The *hwarang* was formed from sons of the aristocracy, and symbolized the aspirations of the nation[6].

Buddhism may have arrived in Silla as early as the fifth century, but because of Silla's conservative attitude to foreign culture, it did not gain a strong foothold until 528 when King Pophung ('The King of Flourishing Buddhism') sanctioned the public performance of its rites. It is said that white blood gushing from the beheaded martyr Ich'adon finally moved the king to sign the decree of toleration. In spite of this much-delayed start, Silla soon caught up with her neighbours in Buddhist culture. Numerous temples were built at the orders of pious Silla kings, and the stone pagodas with their characteristic Silla features rose up then as electric pylons rise up today in and around the capital city of Kyŏngju.

In 562 Silla defeated the last of the Kaya states on her western frontiers, and this victory resulted in direct contact between Silla and Paekche. For a while the two southern kingdoms had a common enemy in Koguryŏ, who

Bodhisattva. Detail of Pl. 55.

Pl. II Vase. Celadon glaze, incised decoration. H. 9 in., D. at base 3½ in. Koryŏ dynasty, 11th/12th century. National Museum of Korea, Seoul.

frequently attacked their northern frontiers. Silla and Paekche each independently sent envoys to the Sui government asking them to destroy Koguryŏ so that they could set up direct land-contact with China. As already mentioned, the Sui army came twice, but was both times defeated by Koguryŏ. These defeats contributed to the downfall of the Sui dynasty. After the fall of their great ally Silla and Paekche began fighting between themselves; Silla managed to exploit the confused situation to her advantage by approaching the newly established T'ang dynasty.

In the winter of 644 a huge expeditionary army left T'ang China for the east, sacking several Koguryŏ outposts on its way to the Yalu river. But its advance was checked by the heroic resistance of the fort at Anshih in June 645, and the Chinese army was forced to retreat. The T'ang Emperor T'ai-tsung, who personally commanded the besieging army, sent gifts to the victorious Koguryŏ soldiers in recognition of their valour. Two years later the Chinese resumed the attack, but again without success.

In 660 the allied forces of Silla and T'ang China turned south and destroyed the capital of Paekche, thus putting an end to that kingdom. Eight years later the same allied forces successfully attacked P'yŏngyang, and the last king of Koguryŏ came out to surrender.

THE GREAT SILLA PERIOD

The Old Silla dynasty (Ko-Silla) became what is now called the Great, or Unified Silla dynasty (T'ong-il Silla) having unified the entire peninsula under its rule.

The large tumuli of the Old Silla period were succeeded

by much smaller tombs with a square stone chamber, or even merely an urn containing cremated ashes in the Buddhist fashion. Buddhism flourished to such an extent that in 806 King Aejang was driven to issue a ban on the construction of new temples. Buddhist images were engraved on almost every stone and rock of the South Mountain in Kyŏngju. Bronze bells and images were cast in large quantities; Buddhist inspiration brought about the golden age of Korean art that now began.

The Great Silla period lasted for nearly three centuries, from the latter part of the seventh century to the early decades of the tenth century. The main characteristic of this period is the complete sinicization of Korea, both politically and culturally. This process had started during the Three Kingdoms period with the introduction of Chinese Buddhism, but it was the Great Silla period that saw the establishment of the pattern of Korean culture which prevailed during the ensuing Koryŏ and Yi dynasties. The organization of government and legislation followed those of the T'ang dynasty. The Korean language is Altaic, entirely different from Chinese, but they had no script until the invention of the Korean alphabet in the fifteenth century. Until that time Koreans used Chinese characters as phonetic signs for writing their language, according to a system known as *idu*. *Idu* was used in combination with an unmodified Chinese vocabulary. Official documents and other public writings however were prepared entirely in Chinese, and on paper Silla was a Chinese-speaking country. People adopted Chinese personal names consisting of a monosyllabic (rarely disyllabic) surname and one or two first names, much as Koreans do to this day. Place names were also changed into Chinese. This is unfor-

tunate, because the change resulted in the almost complete obliteration of the original meanings of Korean names.

But Koreans in the Silla period had little concern for their national heritage. They were anxious to receive Chinese culture and took no exception to their country being called Little China. Numerous students, many of them Buddhist monks, crossed the sea to study in T'ang China, and most of them were provided for by the T'ang government. Fifty-eight students from Silla passed the Chinese national examination for foreign students, and many of them were given government posts. The T'ang Emperor Hsüan-tsung (712–742) is reported to have remarked that Silla was a country of gentlemen and very well educated (*Samguk Sagi*, Vol. 9).

The *Samguk Sagi* informs us that the city plan of Kyŏngju was copied from that of Ch'ang-an, the T'ang capital, with rows of avenues and streets crossing at right-angles. All the houses within the city walls were roofed with tiles, and the chimneys never smoked because the inhabitants used charcoal instead of firewood for cooking and heating.

The prosperity of Silla began to wane, however, at the turn of the eighth century. The royal family was inbred and degenerate, while the aristocracy, both metropolitan and rural, grew in strength. The last hundred years of the Silla régime were blighted by continual bad harvests, rebellions and banditry. The popularity of Bhaiṣajyaguru, the Buddha of Medicine, is eloquent of the hardships of the common people at this time. Wang Kŏn, the founder of the Koryŏ dynasty, was one of a number of leaders of armed rebellion during the latter years of the Silla régime. The central government gradually disintegrated, unable to control these powerful rebels, while the aristocrats enriched themselves at the expense of the public exchequer they were appointed to administer.

THE KORYŎ PERIOD

Wang Kŏn, lieutenant of the rebel Kung-ye, supplanted his master in 918 in the mountainous regions of east-central Korea. He came from Kaesŏng, an old town of west-central Korea and his aim was to recover the former territory of Koguryŏ across the Yalu river. Declaring himself king of the new Koryŏ state, Wang Kŏn showed both firmness and mercy to the last sovereign of Silla, King Kyŏngsun. In 935 King Kyŏngsun made the long journey to Kaesŏng to surrender, and was thereupon given the eldest daughter of Wang Kŏn in marriage.

Wang Kŏn left a famous will, the *Ten Admonitions*, for his descendants, with instructions on how to maintain the kingdom he had founded. Three of the ten items deal with the encouragement and protection of the already over-prosperous Buddhism, but he also emphasized the need to develop a national culture independent of China.

Surprisingly, however, the *Ten Admonitions* did not encourage his countrymen to win back their lost territory on the Manchurian side of the Yalu river. Instead he insisted that his people should keep away from the northern Khitan, because they were 'nothing but wild beasts who make trouble on the northern frontier'. His hatred of the Khitan was demonstrated in 942 when the Khitan sent fifty camels to him as a gift. Wang Kŏn received them but did not feed them, and they all starved to death. The Khi-tan envoys who had accompanied the camels were deported to remote islands and never returned home.

Exactly fifty years after the death of Wang Kŏn in 943, the Khitan had their revenge. They swarmed into the northern provinces of Koryŏ, and Koryŏ had to send an envoy to negotiate peace. This was only the beginning of trouble. From 993 until the last years of the dynasty, Koryŏ suffered invasion after invasion from Khitan, Juchen and Mongols, either from Mongolia or Manchuria.

Throughout these years of hardship the people of Koryŏ turned to Buddhism for consolation. Buddhism became involved in politics, and kings often paid personal visits to the big temples to witness the important ceremonies. During the Three Kingdoms period Buddhism promised a peaceful after-life for any who knelt in front of the Great Hero, but during the Great Silla and Koryŏ periods it became more and more the centre of resistance and unity against the invasions of its enemies.

In 1232 the government of Koryŏ was evacuated to Kanghwa Island on the west coast, to escape an invading Mongol army, and it stayed there for thirty-nine years, leaving the entire peninsula at the mercy of the Mongol horsemen. In the temporary capital at Kanghwa hundreds of skilled wood carvers worked day and night for more than ten years to complete a set of the *tripitaka* (the Buddhist scriptures), consisting of some 80,000 wooden printing blocks. They believed that this pious achievement would drive the Mongols out of the peninsula. The scheme did not have the desired effect, but today we can be grateful that the world's oldest wooden printing blocks lie intact in the store-houses of Haein-sa in south-east Korea. During these years of humiliation the Koryŏ printers published the earliest editions printed with movable metal type. Some of the best Koryŏ celadon wares also come from Koryŏ tombs on Kanghwa Island.

The last two centuries of Koryŏ history, after the surrender to the Mongols, were a period of intensive Mongolian influence on Korean culture. The Mongols held the Korean navy and ship-building industry in great respect. When they launched their unsuccessful invasion against Japan in 1291 most of their ships were made in Korea by Korean ship-builders. Koryŏ kings were invited to marry Mongol princesses, and many Koreans shaved their heads in Mongol fashion. But this close tie with the Yüan Mongols did not change the fundamental attitude of the Koreans, who by tradition despise and hate the northern Mongols and Manchus. King Kongmin (1352–1374), for example, dearly loved his Mongolian queen Lu-kuo, and indeed her sudden death completely changed his personality; yet he sent his army to attack the Mongols who were retreating before the newly arisen Ming army in 1369. After his death in 1374, however, both the Ming and the retreating Mongols repeatedly sent envoys to Koryŏ, and government officials were split into two groups according

to their attitude to China, some pro-Ming and some pro-Mongol. Times were difficult for Koryŏ: the political situation was not clearly foreseeable; in addition the country had been suffering from Japanese pirates for almost a century. These pirates, some genuinely Japanese, some Chinese masquerading as Japanese, sacked almost every port of any size in southern Korea. The navy and army of Koryŏ were kept busy intercepting the pirates, and General Yi Sŏng-gye gradually won fame and popularity by a series of successful operations against them.

In 1388 the government finally decided to side with the Mongols and sent Yi Sŏng-gye to Manchuria to support the Pei-yüan (Northern Yüan) against the Ming. General Yi led the army as far north as the Yalu river, but he never crossed it. The luck of the Mongols had run out and with it that of the Kaesŏng régime; it was time for a pro-Ming revolution.

Yi returned to Kaesŏng and dethroned the pro-Mongol King Wu, but waited four years before proclaiming himself the founder of a new dynasty, the Yi (1392–1910).

THE YI PERIOD

Yi Sŏng-gye named his kingdom Chosŏn (Ch'ao-hsien). In 1394 he left the old capital of Kaesŏng and moved into his newly built Kyŏngbok Palace in Seoul.

Buddhism, after a glorious history of more than a millenium, received an almost fatal blow from the Yi government, which officially rejected Buddhism in favour of Chinese neo-Confucianism. The occupants of Buddhist temples were expelled from the cities and towns, and retreated deep into the mountains. Buddhist monks were prohibited by law from entering the cities. In 1424 the government reorganized the existing seven Buddhist sects into two, the Kyo (preaching) and the Sŏn (Ch'an or Zen). In 1552 King Myŏngjong even instituted a state examination for monks, with the aim of limiting their number to an authorized few. These measures were intended to curb, if not to suppress, Buddhism, but the faith had deep roots among the masses, and many large temples were patronized secretly by ladies of the court and the wives of the rich.

The kings of the early Yi dynasty were all able and ambitious men. They were sympathetic to Chinese culture, particularly the Way of Confucius, by which they hoped to improve the culture of their own people. Confucian shrines were built everywhere in Korea, as Buddhist temples had been in previous periods. But the most urgent need for the education of an intelligentsia was books. Announcing his plan for casting the dynasty's first bronze movable types King T'ae-jong (1401–1418) declared in 1403 that he wanted to reprint all the books that reached Korea from China 'because the more we read the better we can administer a nation'. The casting of bronze movable type inaugurated by T'ae-jong was enthusiastically continued by his successors, and the extensive use of movable type during the Yi period is one of its most significant cultural achievements.

In 1419 King Se-jong ascended the throne. He was one of the great kings of Korean history, and certainly the greatest of the Yi dynasty. His most important contribution was the invention of the Korean alphabet in 1443. The idea of a Korean script was entirely his own, and he personally guided all the work. The first text book of his

Pl. III Wine cup and stand. Celadon glaze, incised decoration.
H. 3⁷/₈ in., D. 5⁷/₈ in. Koryŏ dynasty, 11th/12th century. National
Museum of Korea, Seoul.

alphabet was published in 1446 under the title *Hunmin-Jŏngŭm* (Teaching the People the Correct Sounds). This alphabet, now called *han'gul*, consists of fourteen consonants and ten vowels which in combination can produce a large number of compound sounds⁷.

The first two centuries of the Yi dynasty were an age of glory and achievement, administered by able, gifted kings, but these were concerned more with culture than politics, and they failed to train a combat-ready army for national defence. One day in the late spring of 1592, the year *imjin (jen-ch'en)*, the Koreans in the southernmost port of Pusan suddenly saw the Japanese fleet approaching, carrying combat-hardened *samurai*. According to the general, Hideyoshi, the Japanese were only intending to pass through the peninsula to attack mainland China, but the Koreans marched against them as soon as they landed and involved themselves in fighting. After two centuries of peace, the Yi soldiers were helpless before the rifles of the invaders. The Koreans had never seen a rifle: it was like men of the Stone Age trying to fight Hallstatt warriors. It took no more than a month for the Japanese to reach Seoul. King Sŏngjo (1568–1608) fled to the Yalu river and sent courier after courier to the Ming court to ask for help. But the Chinese did not arrive until P'yŏngyang had fallen to the Japanese.

The war, called Imjin Waeran ('the Japanese Invasion of the Year Imjin') continued sporadically for seven years until the Japanese were exhausted and confined to the southern coastal regions. Civilian volunteers and monks fought side by side with the army to repel the invaders, whose supply routes from Japan were then cut off by the genius of Admiral Yi Sunsin who commanded the Korean navy. Finally in 1598 the death of Hideyoshi gave the weary Japanese army an excuse to return home.

The invasion dealt a terrible blow to Korean culture. During the Imjin War most of Korea's old wooden buildings, precious libraries and other cultural monuments were destroyed. In addition the Japanese on their retreat took away with them quantities of books, bronze bells and pottery. They even kidnapped many potters who lived in the coastal regions. These potters were made to settle in the Kyūshū area, often much against their will. They became the founders of many famous Kyūshū kilns⁸ and their descendants developed Japanese ceramics into a prosperous industry.

In 1627, and again in 1636, less than forty years after the Imjin War, Manchu hoards swarmed into Seoul. The second invasion came so fast down the Yalu-Seoul road that King Injo's retreat to Kanghwa Island was cut off by the enemy before he could get away. He fled to Namhansan, a mountain fortress south of Seoul, but after two months of cold and starvation he swallowed his pride and came with tied hands to surrender to the Manchus.

All these humiliations at the hands of foreign invaders within the space of a hundred years revived the Koreans' awareness of their identity as a nation. Korean art reflected the new spirit of patriotism by rejecting Chinese tradition in favour of a national style. This is particularly well seen in the field of painting. Gentlemen painters as well as professional court painters started to portray the daily life of Korean people, and went out into the countryside to sketch the Korean landscape. Men and women in Korean dress now appear in paintings in place of the former imaginary figures in Chinese dress in equally imaginary landscapes. Painters like Kim Hong-do, active during the eighteenth century, painted scenes of peasants and craftsmen, the very choice of subject implying a criticism of the upper classes.

Scholars of the so-called *Sirhak* ('Practical Learning') school turned away from unproductive debate on Confucian philosophy in their concern to improve conditions in Korea, studying such practical matters as economics, technology and social customs.

The renaissance of Korean culture was, however, held back by the factionalism rampant in the *yangban* class in Seoul. *Yangban* was the highest social class in Yi society, superior to the three lower grades: *chung-in* (middle people), *sang-min* (commoners) and *ch'ŏn-min* (lowest class). The *yangban* ('two classes'—the civil and military) supplied all the high ranking government officials for state and army. All land other than that owned by the royal family, the government and the Buddhist temples was in the hands of the *yangban*. The *chung-in* were skilled men, such as accountants, meteorological observers, court painters, interpreters and secretaries. Farmers, craftsmen and merchants belonged to the commoner class, and slaves, actors, *kisaeng* (the Korean equivalent of the *geisha*) and Buddhist monks belonged to the lowest class.

The social irresponsibility of the *yangban* in Seoul was extreme. They were split into four rival factions, according to the region of the city they lived in. They were not political parties, since they had no policies, nor were they united by family or clan. Each gathered only for protection from the other factions, or to exercise power as a group against the others. Vituperation and debate occupied them ceaselessly, and continued until one faction was defeated and all its members purged from government posts. It could even happen that a dead man was exhumed to receive post-mortem punishment, if he had supported the defeated faction on an issue of dispute before his death. One example of the kind of controversy which could arouse such fierce partisanship will suffice: the length of time the corpse of the queen-mother should be kept in the palace before burial.

Besides weakening, and ultimately destroying, the Yi dynasty the behaviour of the *yangban* left behind it a tradition of political factionalism. The efforts of King Yŏngjo (1725-1776) to reconcile the factions were unavailing. He erected stone monuments to appease them, without success. By the beginning of the nineteenth century Korea was rotten with inefficient and corrupt government. The country was in no state to take advantage of the new ideas that soon began to circulate in the East. The Japanese were again at the gates, this time armed with the new faith of European imperialism, more ambitious and with more ammunition than during the sixteenth century Hideyoshi invasion. The Manchus regarded Korea as their protectorate since the humiliation of King Injo at the foot of Namhan-san.

In 1863 King Kojong, a young boy, succeeded Ch'ŏljong (1850—1863) who died without a direct heir, and Kojong's father the Taewŏn-gun acted as Prince Regent. The prince cared more for personal splendour than for the welfare of the people: he ordered the complete reconstruction of the Kyŏngbok Palace, deserted since it had been burnt during the Imjin War in 1592. The project severely taxed the nation's economy, and the inevitable debasement of the coinage brought the government into disrepute. In

1866 the Taewŏn-gun executed nine French missionaries who had come from China to spread what the prince regent termed 'malignant thought'. In the same year the US ship *General Sherman* sailed up the Taedong river and was burnt, while French vessels arriving to protest against the massacre of the priests were halted by the Royal Artillery and Rifles stationed on Kanghwa Island. To commemorate this victory and as a warning to his critics Taewŏn-gun erected stone monuments bearing the inscription: 'Foreign barbarians invade. If we do not fight, we have a peace treaty. If we have a peace treaty, we sell our country'. His policy was one of total exclusion of foreigners. But the 'barbarians' kept coming, and in 1894, when the Tonghak Rebels rose in south-western Korea, the Manchus and Japanese fought out their rival claims to the weakened kingdom on Korean soil[9]. The 1894 Tonghak uprising began as a protest against the invasions of Japanese and Westerners, but it turned into a mass movement of peasants against the inefficiency and corruption of the goverment and the extortions of its officials. It was put down with the help of the Japanese army, and the Sino-Japanese war was won by the Japanese. Now it was Russia's turn to challenge Japan's control of Korea. The Russo-Japanese war, started in 1904, was also won by the Japanese. Japan now gained a firm hold on Korea and in 1910 formally annexed the country. The kingdom of Yi, founded by the man who gained his position by his feats against Japanese pirates, was finally lost to the descendants of these same pirates. In 1945, with the end of World War II, Korea became once again an independent nation.

PART II
CERAMIC ART

SILLA POTTERY

ORIGIN AND EMERGENCE[1]

Each of the Three Kingdoms, Paekche, Koguryŏ and Silla, produced distinctive pottery types, though these are obviously interrelated. Only a small number of specimens survive from Paekche, and still fewer from Koguryŏ, from which we can identify with certainty no more than some twenty or thirty examples, all of which betray strong Chinese influence, the natural result of Koguryŏ's proximity to China. We are therefore compelled to deal here primarily with the pottery of Silla, examples of which are abundant enough to enable us to trace its development. Since Paekche pottery bears great similarity to that of Silla, some examples from Paekche will be included in this study.

Cat. 1,2

Following the prehistoric period discussed in the Introduction, two new pottery types emerged in South Korea. The main sites of manufacture were in the Kimhae shellmound area near Pusan. Careful archaeological investigation in recent years has made it possible to study them on the basis of verified data.

The first type is a hybrid of the two prehistoric wares, the plain coarse pottery and the polished red pottery. It is made of comparatively fine clay, is more highly fired than either of its predecessors, and is light or dark brown in colour. The predominant shape is a wide-mouthed pot with a horizontally flattened rim and a narrow flat bottom; vessels with solid, cylindrical feet or hollow conical feet also exist. These were all made on the potter's wheel and show the progress that had been made in ceramics.

The second type shows even more advanced techniques; it is found in abundance at the Kimhae shellmound, and is called 'Kimhae pottery'. This second type is also made of fine clay and is fired at a high temperature. The colour, however, is either reddish brown or grey, with the latter predominating. The differences arise from atmospheric variation within the kiln; the presence of fresh air, producing an oxidizing atmosphere, accounts for the reddish tone, and the grey is the result of a reducing atmosphere (*i.e.* one devoid of oxygen). The dominant form is a large wide-mouthed pot with a sharply everted rim, the edge of which is often grooved along the centre line. Bottoms may be either flat or round, and a horn-shaped handle also occurs. Very frequently the type bears impressed decoration in the form of lattice and cord patterns, both of which seem to have been made by the so-called paddling method, using a beater upon which string has been wound.

It is from this second type, the hard plain grey Kimhae pottery, itself the product of a long evolution going back through Lo-lang to China, that the Silla prototype emerged, which was destined to develop into the ware that dominated the ceramic industry of Korea for centuries to come.

Besides the standard grey pottery, another minor group has also been found at Kimhae. It is made of fine clay, has a light, reddish colour, and is very soft, having been fired at a low temperature. This group, too, seems to have developed from the traditional prehistoric wares, and it is found in the same tombs which have yielded the high-fired grey pots. Since it comprises only a small proportion of the total finds, we shall be concerned here mainly with the grey pottery, and return briefly to this reddish variant later.

Technical considerations connected with the hard grey pottery of Kimhae are of interest. The hardness of the body shows that the ware must have been produced in a much more advanced type of kiln than that used in Neolithic times. No kiln has been discovered at Kimhae itself, but it seems obvious that the characteristic hard body must be the result of firing in a so-called 'tunnel kiln', a development which may be either of Chinese origin or an independent Korean invention.

An example of a tunnel kiln can be quoted from Toksari, near Kyŏngju, to illustrate the general type in Silla. Nearly seventy feet long and eighteen feet wide, it was constructed to follow the natural slope of a hillside—hence it is sometimes called a 'climbing kiln'. Near Puyŏ, the Paekche capital, another slanting tunnel kiln has been discovered, approximately twenty-four feet long and five feet wide, with an angle of inclination of thirty-five degrees. The upper third of the tunnel has been cut out of the natural rock bed, and at its top end is a hole for the smoke to escape; the lower two-thirds contain steps on which to place the pottery to be fired. The fire itself was built within the roomy space provided near the bottom entrance, the natural slope drawing the flame upwards.

All the kilns of Silla (and also of Sue, or Iwaibe, pottery in Japan) were of the tunnel type, and this practice continued throughout the entire history of Korean ceramic manufacture during the Koryŏ and Yi dynasties. Even today, the slanting tunnel kiln remains the most usual type of construction.

CLASSIFICATION

The pottery of Silla can be roughly divided into two basic groups—Kyŏngju and Kaya; the difference between them is less a matter of colour or quality than of shape. Kyŏngju pottery may be considered as Silla pottery proper, and all the wares produced within the territory under the direct cultural influence of the Silla dynasty belong to this grouping. The Kaya group, on the other hand, consists of pottery from the Kimhae, Haman, Koryŏng and Chinju areas—all located west of the Naktong river and members of the Kaya States, a political federation of small regional units contemporary with the Old Silla period. One Kaya state, however, Sŏngju, in the north, produced pottery which belongs not to the Kaya but to the Kyŏngju group.

THE OLD SILLA PERIOD

No one entering the Kyŏngju plain can fail to be impressed by the numbers of huge mounds which dominate the landscape in and around the city of Kyŏngju itself. These mounds are tombs. They have one or more wood-lined chamber covered by stones the size of footballs; these stones, in turn, are covered with a layer of mud. Each is constructed to house the remains of one individual, and has no entrance, so it could not therefore be reopened for a second burial.

All these tombs contain enormous amounts of pottery. Tomb Number 82 of Hwangnamni, for example, yielded 184 Silla pots from its main chamber and an additional chamber at the side. There is a rich variety of shape. These rounded tumuli can all be dated roughly to the period of the Old Silla dynasty, from the fifth to the early seventh century. The refined shapes of the vessels, their elaborate and novel decoration, the advanced technique of firing, and not least the vast quantity produced, combine to make the period of these great tumuli that of the zenith of Silla pottery manufacture. We shall therefore concentrate our study on Old Silla, considering the wares of Great Silla in less detail.

Probably all the ceramic vessels found in the Silla tombs were originally made as objects of daily use, although it is not impossible that a few may have been specially produced for funerary purposes[2].

Pedestal Cup with Cover

Pl. 1, Cat. 3 The pedestal cup with cover—or pedestalled bowl—was the predominant vessel type in Old Silla pottery and always provides the majority of the finds in any tomb excavated.

The cup consists of a shallow bowl with a knobbed cover fitting onto a protruding rim and supported on a conical foot with large perforations. It is elegant in appearance and carefully proportioned. Although it looks as though it might have been designed as a drinking cup, it was in fact used as a container for solid food, as is proved by the frequent discovery of food remains within such cups. In form it bears such a striking resemblance to Chinese vessels of the *tou* type—such as those discovered in the Lo-lang tombs of North Korea—that its derivation presents no problem. This inference is enhanced by the fact that the *tou* also was not used for drinking. The perforations in the conical foot, while ornamental in character,

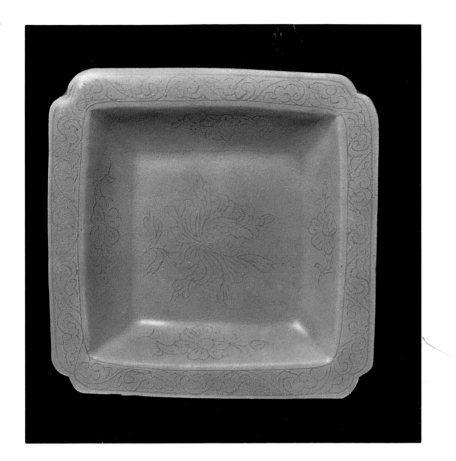

served the practical purpose of decreasing the vessel's weight and protecting it from cracking during the firing process.

Pedestal Cup without Cover

This type is essentially similar to the pedestal cup with cover, except that it lacks the narrow protruding rim. Thus it was evidently not designed to be fitted with a cover but was a drinking cup. The form is not found in many of the most important Silla tombs, and it seems to have enjoyed less popularity than the lidded cup.

Jar with Long Neck

Almost as popular as the lidded pedestal cup, the long-necked jar is characterized by a spherical body terminating in a tall, V-shaped neck. The bottom is either round or slightly indented, a flat bottom being extremely rare. To support such jars, a separate stand was sometimes used, usually with perforations similar to those which we have seen on the pedestal cups; these stands form a sufficiently important group to justify separate discussions below.

The long-necked jar must have been used for food storage or as a water container to be carried on the head, which is still done in Korea. For this purpose a small cushion made of cloth or straw is first placed on the head, the vessel then being set on the cushion. The tall neck keeps the water from spilling while the carrier is moving.

One also finds tall-necked jars with attached foot supports, similar in appearance to the Chinese *chung* type, and quite possibly derived from it. The addition of a foot may indicate a later development, but still within the Old Silla period.

Jar with Short Neck

A round body with a short, wide neck and a round or slightly concave bottom characterizes this type. Some few examples have flat bottoms and an attached foot. The surface is invariably left undecorated, and the edge of the rim ★Pl. 2 is slightly concave in the centre, although not grooved. Such vessels no doubt also served as food storage containers—and probably as cooking pots as well. I have seen similar types of Iwaibe pottery in Japan, discovered in the Heijyōkyu Palace site in Nara, with soot still adhering to the bottom, indicating that the pots were used for cooking. In shape the short-necked jar is finely balanced. This type is found in relatively large quantities in every tomb.

Stand

Originally no doubt designed as a separate pedestal for the round-bottom jar, the stand was also used independently. As a support for another vessel, the form consists of a tall, hollow, conical pedestal, the upper rim of which turns outward in the shape of a small, shallow bowl: it's function Pl. 4, Cat. 6, 7 as a stand is clear. There is a second type, however—a large, deep basin on a large, conical support, useful in itself as a tall bowl. Variations in proportion between the upper Pl. 5 and lower elements of the stand are frequently met with, the lower sometimes being expanded at the base while the bowl has been made so small in relation to it that in shape the whole vessel is like an inverted wine glass. Whatever its form, however, the stand is one of the most imposing forms in the repertoire of Silla pottery.

Miscellaneous Types

The forms described above are those which occur most ★Pl. 3, Cat. 4

*Pl. 8

*Pl. 9

The bowl reproduced must also have been used for drinking. Made of very high-fired clay which gives off an almost metallic sound when struck, it is of thin, light construction and has been provided with a handle.

Another type of vessel is illustrated: a highly developed example, also thin-walled and hard as any porcelain. The long neck flares wide at the rim, and it originally had a spout, which is now lost.

Another most interesting type, believed to have been used as an oil lamp, takes the form of a large bowl on the hollow rim of which small cups have been placed. Small apertures within the bases of the cups lead to the hollow interior of the rim. Below each cup, attached to the outside of the rim, hang ornaments with leaf-shaped finials.

commonly in tomb finds. There are, however, a number of others made for a variety of purposes, which survive from this period. They deserve mention here, however briefly.

One of the most interesting of these is the horn-shaped vessel, doubtless used as a drinking cup, as had been its inspiration, the ox horn itself. That such cups might have stands specially designed for them is proved by an example

Pl. 6, 7, Cat. 8   now in the Kyŏngju Branch of the National Museum of Korea.

Reddish Pottery

We have mentioned earlier that a minor pottery group, soft in texture and light reddish in tone, is found along with the hard grey pottery from the same places. It is fired at so low a temperature that the vessel easily absorbs water and hence becomes extremely fragile, and only the most skilful hand can remove such pots from the tomb intact. The most frequently encountered shape is a small vessel, either shallow or deep, resembling a rice bowl.

Within recent years the National Museum of Korea has acquired a collection of more than twenty examples of this ware, large and small, deep and shallow. They were discovered, however, not in the Kyŏngju area but in the old Kaya region. Two specimens are particularly impressive: the one a steamer with horn-shaped handle, and the other a composite piece consisting of a deep and a shallow bowl. The two elements share a common stand with perforations and are connected in such a way that water can pass from one to the other. Fashioned partly by hand this 'double vase' gives a feeling of perfect balance. This is is the finest example of reddish pottery which has yet come to light.

Pl. 10, 11

Clay Figures

Cat. 10–15 A considerable number of clay figures has also survived, which fall into two categories: those which form an essential part of a vessel or serve as ornamentation for it, thereby creating a combination of vessel and sculpture, and those which are independent sculptural entities in themselves. Most, if not all, are to be dated to Old Silla, and certain kinds of figurines seem to have a restricted provenance within the Kyŏngju area, although some come to us from the Kaya states.

The major source of figure sculpture attached to vessels is Hwangnamni, within the city limits of Kyŏngju, where numerous tombs were uncovered when a new railway station was constructed. Not always, by any means, the products of skilled sculptors, these figurines nevertheless show a gift for observation and expression. Animals, reptiles and birds—rabbit, dog, cow, pig, tiger, tortoise, snake, duck, and even the elephant, with which the potter was certainly unfamiliar, are the favourite subjects, and the essential characteristic of each is caught in an attractive summary manner. These are not the only subjects, however. The human form also plays an important part in the repertoire. Both sexes are depicted engaged in the activities of everyday life, even down to the detailed representation of a man with a *chige* (the traditional Korean carrying-frame used to support heavy loads on a man's back). Erotic, even obscene, representations are also met with, including figures with exaggerated sexual organs.

The free-standing human figures, though crude and primitive in appearance, nevertheless have a humorous charm. A typical example, depicting a male figure playing on a stringed instrument which may be identified as a zither, is reproduced here.

Vessels in Sculptural Form

Every student of Chinese art is familiar with the tradition in that country of animal sculpture in both bronze and clay. The Silla potter did similar work in clay, sometimes with considerable skill. The best known is the pair of vessels in the form of mounted horsemen found in the Gold Bell Tomb in Kyŏngju. In contrast to the Chinese examples, however, these horsemen have been made sep-

arately from their mounts. The horses differ from the Chinese examples in having a spout on the chest and a cup-shaped funnel on the croup: they are not independent figurines but pouring vessels.

One of these horsemen wears a hat and has a more elaborate costume than the other, showing him to be a high-ranking officer; the other is of lower status. In each ✶Pl. 12 case the horse is of a peculiar stocky breed, perhaps related to the Mongolian pony. These figurative pouring vessels Cat. 13, 14 are of great importance, not only in themselves as uniquely important examples of the Silla potter's art, but also archaeologically, for the details of their trappings and accoutrements have been of invaluable assistance in reconstructing the many remains of bronze and leather (the leather always in decayed condition) which have survived from Silla times.

From the same Gold Bell Tomb comes a pair of boat-shaped vessels, set on pedestals with square-cut perfo- Pl. 15 rations. A human figure sits at the stern of each boat, ✶Cat. 11 holding an oar. The importance of the funerary objects ✶Pl. 13 found within this tomb, including one of the three gold crowns found in the area, shows without doubt that the Gold Bell Tomb was made for a royal personage.

Recently several other clay objects of great interest have been discovered. These include another horse-shaped vessel Pl. 16 and a house, reputedly found in Ch'angnyŏng, Kyŏng-sang Namdo, an area which belonged to one of the Kaya states. The horse is hollow and its back forms a large cup. In this instance, the horse stands on a platform, and the trappings are less elaborate than on the horses described above. The whole piece is covered with a brownish, ✶Pl. 14, Cat. 12 natural glaze.

38

Pl. 6 Horn-shaped cup with stand. Grey stoneware. H. 9 5/8 in., D., at base, 4 5/16 in. Old Silla dynasty, 5th/6th century. National Museum of Korea, Seoul.

Pl. 7 Cup. Grey stoneware. H. 3 11/16 in., D., at mouth, 6 1/2 in. Old Silla dynasty, 5th/6th century. National Museum of Korea, Seoul.

Pl. 8 Vessel. Grey stoneware. H. 5 5/16 in., D., at mouth, 5 1/8 in. Kaya States, 5th/6th century. National Museum of Korea, Seoul.

Pl. 9 Lamp. Grey stoneware. Excavated from the Gold Bell Tomb, Kyŏngju. H. 4 3/4 in., W. 4 15/16 in. Old Silla dynasty, 5th/6th century. National Museum of Korea, Seoul.

Pl. 10 Steamer. Reddish earthenware. H. 1 ft. 1 9/16 in., D. 11 1/4 in. Kaya States, 5th/6th century. National Museum of Korea, Seoul.

Pl. 11 Two joined bowls. Reddish earthenware. H. 10 in. Kaya States, 5th/6th century. National Museum of Korea, Seoul.

A similar glaze covers the model of the house, perhaps indicating—although this is by no means conclusive evidence—that the two were products of the same kiln. It has the appearance of a farmyard barn, and the intention seems to have been to reproduce a straw roof protected by clinging vines (or made more secure by the addition of wooden slats). This protection slants downwards to cover one wall of the house, a system often seen in use today in Korean villages. On the roof and at the entrance are small animals, the one at the entrance is certainly a rat, while the one on the roof represents some larger animal. Like the mounted horsemen, the house is a vessel: a cylindrical cup is attached to one side of the roof.

There is a very similar house in the Ogura Collection in Japan. The architectural treatment of the roof is broadly similar, but in the Ogura example the floor has been raised, leaving a storage space below. Over the beam a cylindrical shape projects horizontally, the significance of which is not clear. *Pl. 17

Of great interest too is a vessel in the form of a chariot: two connected cups are mounted on a two-wheeled chariot and set upon a round stand. Again a close parallel is to be found in the Ogura Collection, with the difference that in the latter example the connected cups are horn-shaped. A pottery duck belongs in this category. This piece is especially interesting and most expressive. Pl. 18 · Pl. 19, Cat. 15

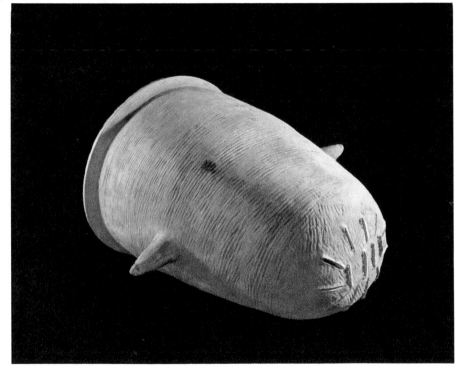

These objects are eloquent testimony to the imaginative and sculptural talents of the Silla craftsman who seems to have been able to create in clay whatever his fantasy conceived. It is interesting that this kind of object is rarely found from the Great Silla period which followed. Its popularity may have waned when Buddhism, reflected in burial customs, became firmly accepted.

THE GREAT SILLA PERIOD

With the unification of the entire peninsula under the Great Silla dynasty, a new type of tomb was adopted. A stone chamber now replaced the earlier one of wood, and a passage was provided to the interior, thereby making multiple burial possible. The tomb became a family grave.

Pl. VI Brush stand. Celadon glaze, reticulated, modelled, incised and underglaze iron decoration. H. 3¹/₂ in., W. 7 in. Koryŏ dynasty early 12th century. Tŏksu Palace Museum of Fine Arts, Seoul.

However, the addition of the passage facilitated robbery and while quantities of pottery identifiable with Great Silla remain to us, very little of it has been obtained under controlled archaeological conditions.

The most important single characteristic of the pottery of Great Silla is its ornamentation, which was produced by the use of stamps engraved with elaborate designs formed of lines, dots, single and double circles, flowers, clouds, and arabesques. Old Silla ornamentation consisted solely of wavy or parallel lines (in exceptional cases with the addition of animals or human figures), always engraved by hand, using pointed tools.

A second development of Great Silla was the use of glaze. Glaze was certainly not unknown in Old Silla, but where it occurs, it appears to be the accidental result of ash falling onto the vessel, or the fusing of imperfections in the clay body during the firing process. Great Silla, on the other hand, developed the technique of deliberate, true glazing. It has been suggested by some that this may have come through Lo-lang, where green and yellow glazes in the tradition of the Chinese Han dynasty wares were not uncommon.

The Urn

No doubt the most impressive as well as the most frequently encountered vessel type of Great Silla is the sepulchral urn. The paste of these urns is very hard; they have thick walls, are always provided with a cover, and are usually ornamented with an overall decoration of stamped designs. Stately in shape and proportion, they seem appropriate vessels for human remains. Their very use reflects an important turning point in Korean history: the introduc-

tion of Buddhism, which dictated cremation of the dead. On the occasional decorated examples the design includes Pl. 20 the lotus, the universal symbol of Buddhism.

The urn reproduced here is covered with a light yellow Pl. 21 glaze, faded in many places. On the shoulder are four Cat. 20 haloed animal masks in relief, used to secure the cord which bound the cover to the urn proper. Stamped designs cover ★Cat. 18 the entire surface. When discovered near Kyŏngju, this urn contained a smaller one, similarly glazed and ornamented. This is the earliest known example of true glazing in the history of Korean ceramics, and represents a marked technical advance.

TILES FROM PAEKCHE AND SILLA[3]

The ornamented tile was used early in both Chinese and Japanese art. In pre-Han China, some tiles were inscribed, while those of Han itself bore animals, landscape, and even figure decoration in addition to inscriptions. The lotus motif, so characteristic of tile decoration under the influence of Buddhism, made its appearance in the Far East towards the end of the Six Dynasties period in China.

In Korea, Koguryŏ tombs near both P'yŏngyang and T'ung Kou have produced inscribed tiles and also some roof tiles with lotus and bracken designs, obviously influenced by northern China. But the tiles of Paekche and Silla show the highest aesthetic quality. Paekche received its influence from south China while Silla was influenced first from both Paekche and Koguryŏ and later directly from T'ang China.

44

Pl. 15   Vessel of boat shape, mounted on a tall conical foot.   Grey
stoneware. Excavated from the Gold Bell Tomb, Kyŏngju. H. 4 15/16
in., L. 8 3/4 in. Old Silla dynasty, 5th/6th century. National Museum
of Korea, Seoul.
Pl. 16   Vessel in the form of a horse.   Stoneware. H. 4 3/4 in. Kaya
States, 5th/6th century. National Museum of Korea, Seoul.

Of particular importance and beauty are six square floor tiles with moulded designs found at the site of an ancient temple near Puyŏ, the capital of Paekche.

Pl. 22   One of these bears a landscape decoration of idealized
*Cat. 21, 22, 23 rounded mountains covered with pine trees. At the top
*Pl. 24, Cat. 24 are cloud forms surrounding a central figure of a phoenix (fêng-huang); a narrow band at the bottom represents water. The figure of a priest may be seen, though scarcely recognizable, near the lower corner at the right, walking toward a building in the centre of the design. Its date in the early seventh century makes the tile a most important document in the development of the representation of landscape in Far Eastern art. The composition is extremely impressive.

Pl. 23   A second tile from the series features a monster mask (kui-myŏn in Korean), resembling in form the t'ao-t'ieh of early Chinese art, a motif frequently found in Silla and frequently appearing on roof tiles in later periods. In this instance, the monster hovers over a landscape which uses the same conventions for water and rock formations as those appearing on the tile discussed above.

Many floor tiles have also been found in Kyŏngju. One which was discovered at the site of Imhae-jŏn, Kyŏngju, has a design of medallions formed in a honeysuckle motif. The edge of this example is adorned with floral designs surrounding two deer.

The tile as a means of popular artistic expression reached its apogee in the simple roof tiles used so frequently throughout the Great Silla period. There are thousands of them from the vicinity of Kyŏngju alone which display a variety and beauty not surpassed by the tiles of China and Japan. They are still to be found, though not always intact,

47

everywhere in the Kyŏngju region, not only at the sites of ruined temples and palaces but even in the barley fields and along the roadsides. They are decorated in relief with innumerable designs drawn from the extensive Great Silla repertoire; their variety and their number is evidence of their makers' ingenuity and of the great popularity of tiles among the people of the time.

The majority of these roof tiles can be divided into two categories. One type is semi-circular in section, sometimes closed at one end with a decorative disk; the other type is flatter, only slightly curved in section, and it sometimes has a decorated rim. The flatter tiles were placed hollow side upwards on the roof, and the semi-cylindrical tiles were set over the joins between the concave tiles (pan-tiling). Tiles with decorated disks or rims were used at the edges of the eaves, to produce a decorated edge to the roof. Less usual shapes, convex with oval end-disks, or concave with two decorated rims, were used at the corners of the roof. All these forms are typical of Great Silla, whereas in Koguryŏ decoration was applied only to the convex end- Pl. 28

*Pl. 25, 26, 27

tiles, never to the concave ones. A comparatively small number of tiles was decorated with particularly fine designs impressed by means of wooden moulds, otherwise all roof tile decoration was made with clay moulds. Decorated roof tiles do not seem to have been used on private houses.

It is of interest to follow the development of the lotus flower design, the most popular of all decorative motifs on Korean roof tiles. After the introduction of Buddhism into Koguryŏ, the lotus on the round roof tile was four-petalled. In Paekche, however, we meet the same lotus in a more developed form, first with six and then with eight petals. The earliest examples from Silla seem to copy the Paekche eight-petalled design, although it is impossible to determine with certainty whether or not this earliest Silla form should be ascribed to Old Silla or to Great Silla. As time progressed, the number of petals in the Silla lotus was increased to sixteen or even thirty-two, often taking on the appearance of a chrysanthemum and evolving ultimately into double-petalled lotus blossom forms. The pattern later became even more complicated by the addition of a kind of honeysuckle motif. The lotus remained the favourite motif throughout the evolution of tile decoration, although motifs from the animal kingdom, real and legendary, such as various birds and the unicorn (*ch'i-lin*), were also added.

Ornamentation on flat tiles differed slightly from that on the round types, owing to the demands made by the shape of the face itself. On flat tiles, running floral designs such as vine-bands were favoured. Other motifs included the *fêng-huang*, the dragon, or the flying angel of Buddhist lore.

Some of these tiles deserve special consideration. One from Koguryŏ is particularly impressive on account of its Pl. 25 size and vigour, and has been moulded in much higher relief than any from Paekche or Silla. Paekche tiles have a characteristic balance and quiet refinement, but they lack the sculptural strength which is the unique contribution of Pl. 26 Koguryŏ. Another Silla tile, said to have been discovered Pl. 27 at the site of Hwangyong-sa temple, Kyŏngju, bears a frog design, derived from Chinese legend. One of the most beautiful left to us from Great Silla is a concave tile; its Pl. 28 decoration of flying angels is so graceful that it is difficult to understand that such designs were employed on tiles placed high on the roof where they could not possibly have been seen and appreciated. In spite of this, the Korean potter spared neither time nor effort in making his splendid, elaborate designs, not only because of the character of the building which the tiles were destined to decorate but also, it would seem, in order to satisfy his own appetite ✳Cat. 25 for creation.

One other type of tile must be mentioned here: the Pl. 29, Cat. 26 demon face used to decorate rafter ends. The same demon mask exists throughout Korean history. It is no doubt intended to ward off evil spirits.

SILLA IN KOREAN CERAMIC HISTORY

This chapter has dealt with the general characteristics of the Silla achievement in Korean ceramic history, and we have described a number of representative examples, including some from Paekche and Koguryŏ as well.

Of all aspects of Korean art, it is the ceramics of this

*Pl. 20 Urn with stamped designs. Grey stoneware. 1 ft. 3¹/₂ in.,
D. 1 ft. 7¹/₄ in. Great Silla dynasty, 7th/8th century. National
Museum of Korea, Seoul.*

period which have been the most neglected. Silla pottery has never been the subject of serious study even in Korea itself. In the opinion of the writer, Silla pottery may very well be the most genuinely indigenous of all Korean art forms, in spite of the formal influences from outside which were brought to bear upon it. It varies from the near-primitive to the sophisticated, but it invariably has about it a natural quality which bespeaks its specifically Korean origin.

The wares of Koryŏ with which we are about to deal are universally praised for their refinement and their beauty of colour; but they reflect to a considerable degree the direct influence of Sung China. Yi dynasty wares were influenced by Confucianism, and owe a similar debt to Chinese inspiration. Silla pottery on the other hand together with that of Paekche, is unchallengeably original and Korean, and is as worthy of admiration and study as the original ceramic contributions of other peoples. Its variety and monumentality is added evidence for the great vitality of Silla, the agency through which the entire Korean nation came to be unified and Korean culture was brought to its highest achievements.

Pl. 22 *Tile with landscape in relief. Grey earthenware. Excavated in Puyŏ. H. 11¹¹/₁₆ in., W. 11³/₈ in., Depth 1³/₄ in. Paekche dynasty, 7th century. National Museum of Korea, Seoul.*
Pl. 23 *Tile with monster and landscape in relief. Grey earthenware. Excavated in Puyŏ. H. 11¹/₄ in., W. 11¹/₈ in., Depth 1³/₄ in. Paekche dynasty, 7th century. National Museum of Korea, Seoul.*

KORYŎ DYNASTY WARES

PRAISE BY CONTEMPORARY SUNG CHINA

Of all the arts of Korea, the ceramics of the Koryŏ dynasty are the best known to the outside world. Praised even by contemporary Sung China, they are still universally considered to be among the most beautiful wares ever made by any people.

A Sung scholar wrote: 'The books of the Academy, the wines of the palace, the inkstones of Huichou Fu, the white peonies of Lo-yang, the tea of Chien Chou, the brocades of Shu, the porcelain of Ting Chou... the secret colour of Kao-li (Koryŏ) are first under heaven[4].'

The passage is significant. The objects enumerated are those which relate particularly to the life of the *beau monde* of highly sophisticated Sung China; what might have appealed to the middle or lower classes has no interest for the writer. It is also remarkable that of the whole range of Sung porcelain of the time, only Ting ware is singled out

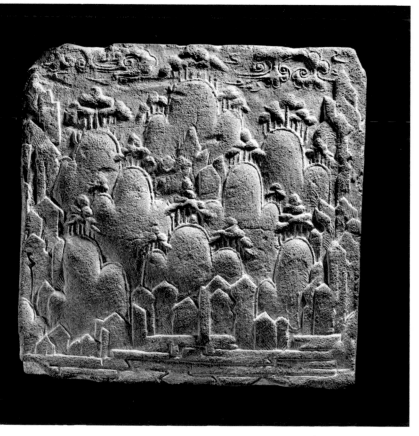

for mention. Finally, as Gompertz has pointed out[5], the Sung writer uses the expression 'secret colour', otherwise reserved for Chinese Yüeh ware, as the chief characteristic of Koryŏ celadon. We have no proof that the wares of Koryŏ were imported by Sung China; nevertheless the likelihood is that some pieces did reach that country, either as official gifts or as goods in exchange. At any rate, the passage makes it clear that Koryŏ celadon was known, at least in certain more or less rarified Chinese circles, and that it was admired especially on account of its beautiful colour.

Even more important praise for the wares of Koryŏ is expressed in the famous travel account of Hsü Ching (1091–1153), a Chinese official who accompanied a Sung envoy to the Koryŏ court in 1123. Hsü Ching, apparently the business manager of the expedition, left China from the port of Ming Chou, in Chekiang province, on the 16th of the 5th month, reaching Koryŏ on the 12th of the 6th month. He remained in the country for thirty days. He wrote a description of all that he had seen and heard on his trip, including detailed reports of the route which his travels had taken. This illustrated compendium, bearing the title *Hsüan-ho Fêng Shih Kao-li T'u-ching* (customarily abbreviated as *Kao-li T'u-ching*), was presented to the Emperor, the author retaining a duplicate copy for himself. Unfortunately both copies were soon lost, and the drawings are irretrievable; but the text survives, presumably more or less intact, in a printed version published in Sung times.

Hsü Ching's account dwells in some detail on the ceramic art of Koryŏ, providing posterity with information of great importance. Chapters 30, 31 and 32 are devoted to a description of 'Wares and Vessels'.

Chapter 32, in which he makes specific reference to ceramics is the most important of all for our purposes. In it he discusses tea equipment as follows[6]:

'The people of Kao-li have become much addicted to tea drinking, and many kinds of implements are made: a black tea bowl ornamented with gold, a small tea bowl of "kingfisher colour", and a silver *ting* for heating water are all modelled after Chinese wares. When a party is held, tea is made in the courtyard and covered with a silver lotus (lid). It is served with dignified step. Only when it is announced that tea is ready does everyone drink; thus it is unavoidable that some should drink their tea cold. In the tea room, the tea things are placed in the centre of a red tablecloth and covered with red silk gauze. Tea is set out three times daily and is followed by hot water. The people of Kao-li regard hot water as medicinal. They are happy every time one drinks the tea. If one cannot drink it, they are unhappy. That is why it is best to drink it.'

Under the heading 'Pottery Vessels' the author continues:

'The pottery wares are green *(ch'ing)* in colour and are called "kingfisher coloured" *(fei-sê)* by the people of Kao-li. In recent years they have been made more skilfully, and their colour and lustre have become finer. There are wine pots of gourd shape with small covers in the form of a duck amidst lotus flowers. They also make bowls and dishes, cups and tea bowls, flower vases and hot water bowls, all copied from the forms of Ting ware, so that they are not illustrated here, but the wine pots are specially shown because they are different.'

The next paragraph, under the heading 'Pottery Incense Burner', goes on to say:

Pl. 25 Roof tile. Reddish earthenware. D. 6⅞ in. Koguryŏ dynasty, 5th/7th century. National Museum of Korea, Seoul.

Pl. 26 Roof tile. Grey earthenware. D. 5⅛ in. Paekche dynasty, 5th/6th century. National Museum of Korea, Seoul.

Pl. 27 Roof tile. Grey earthenware. Found in Kyŏngju. D. 5¹³⁄₁₆ in. Great Silla dynasty, 7th/8th century. National Museum of Korea, Seoul.

'A lion *(suan i)* emits incense and is likewise "kingfisher coloured": the beast crouches on top, supported by a lotus. This is the most distinguished of all their wares; the other resembles the old *pi-sê* of Yüeh Chou and the new kilns of Ju Chou.'

Hsü Ching's remarks deserve comment. First, it is interesting to note that Korea grows very little tea and that Koreans today do not drink tea except in highly intellectual circles. The tea ceremony as practised in Japan was unknown there or anywhere in Koryŏ times. The description secret 'colour' is that classically applied in China to Yüeh ware, from which Korean celadon developed. (The two Chinese characters denoting this colour, *pi-sê*, are pronounced in Korean *pi-saek*, though the meaning is the same.) Hsü Ching's visit took place in the early

58

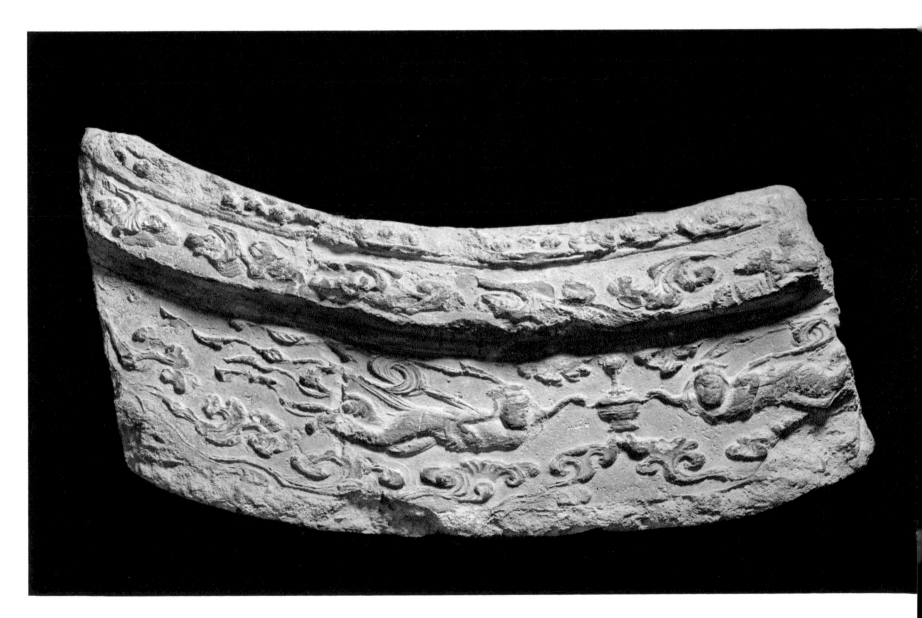

part of the twelfth century, at which time he found that the Koryŏ version of 'secret colour' had made great progress. He was also careful to point out that many types of vessels copied from Ting ware were already in existence, and he goes on to refer to Yüeh and Ju wares as well. An incense burner just as he described it in such detail, still Pl. 36 exists in the collection of the National Museum of Korea. Its cover consists of a lion with one foot resting on a ball, a sculptural type which, according to recent research, was being produced at about the time of Hsü Ching's visit.

The period between the tenth and the fourteenth centuries saw the golden age of ceramic art in both China and Korea. The ceramics of Sung, following on the high achievement of the preceding T'ang dynasty, attained unprecedented perfection. Porcelain—no longer a novelty—was produced at a number of famous kilns including Yüeh Chou, T'ing Chou, and Ch'ing-te-Chen. Because of the frequent intercourse between the two countries, Koryŏ received multiple influences from Sung China, resulting in a Korean product combining classical styles and a remarkable proficiency of technique. The elegant shapes, the rich colour, and the unique use of inlay for which Koryŏ wares are so well-known constitute a major achievement in ceramic history.

In this regard it is worth remembering that porcelain has been made in Europe only for about two hundred years. Even in neighbouring Japan, it was not until the beginning of the seventeenth century that the process of porcelain manufacture became known. It was taken there by Korean potters kidnapped during the Hideyoshi Invasion of 1592, who founded a new ceramic industry in the island kingdom.

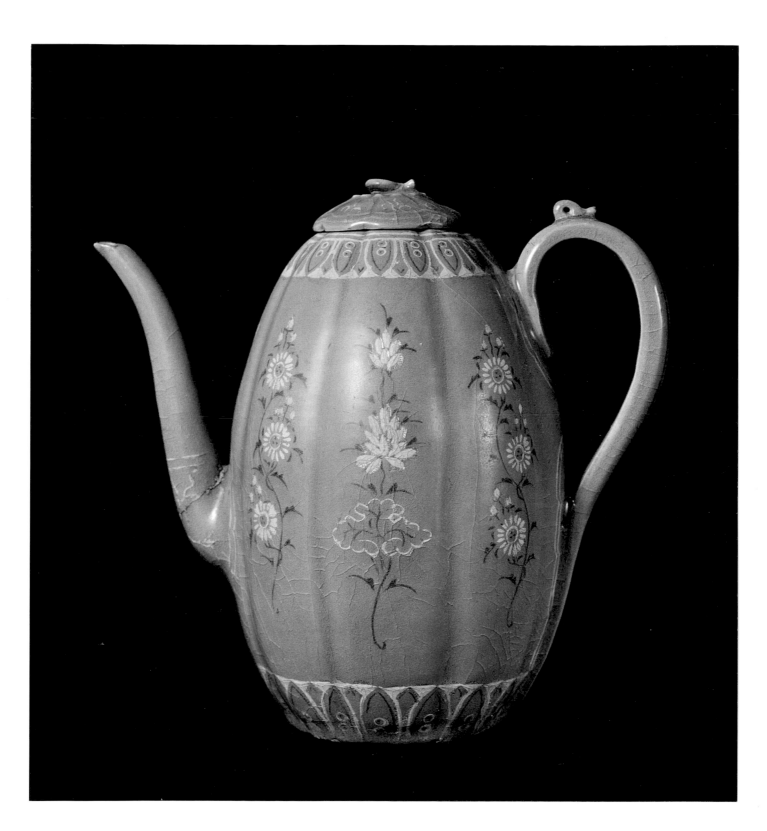

Pl. 30 Vase. Stoneware with natural glaze. H. 6 15/16 in., D., at base, 3 1/8 in. Koryŏ dynasty, 11th century. Coll. Chewon Kim, Seoul.

FOUR PERIODS

The development of Koryŏ ceramics may be divided into four periods, beginning with one of transition and proceeding through one of Chinese influence and one of distinctively Korean trends, with a final era of degeneration.

The first, or transitional, period comprises roughly the tenth century, during which traditional Silla pottery—either unglazed or with low-fired greenish or dark brown glazes—continued to be produced, generally light in weight. We reproduce an example of the former, an unglazed vase known in Korean as a *maebyŏng* (equivalent to the Chinese *mei-p'ing*). However, it would appear that wares of this type were not confined solely to this period of transition, but continued to be made throughout the dynasty for the use of the common people.

Specimens of Koryŏ low-fired glazed wares, on the other hand, are extremely rare, very likely because such Silla-tradition types soon came to be replaced in popularity by high-fired wares based on Sung Chinese examples, which were to become so abundant in Korea.

The second—a period of Chinese influence—had its beginnings at the end of the tenth or beginning of the eleventh century, a time when Sung influence, both in form and technique, became pervasive. This period lasted for approximately a hundred and seventy years or from the reign of King Kyŏngjong (976–981) to that of Ŭijong, who acceded to the throne in 1147.

It is now evident that the most important formative influence in the development of Korean-made celadon was that of the Chinese wares of Yüeh Chou, to which the earliest Korean proto-celadons are so similar in technique, form and glaze that it is often difficult—or even impossible—to be certain whether any particular piece belongs to one or the other group. The most frequently cited case in point is a tall jar with a light brownish body and a light olive glaze now in the collection of Ewha Women's University in Seoul; it has an inscription on the base indicating that it was made to be used in the shrine built to commemorate the founder of the dynasty and with a date that accords with the year 993. It is reasonable to assume that this jar represents contemporary Korean ceramic achievement at its best, and if such is the case we must presume that true, or developed, celadon was not yet being made. The jar has its puzzling aspects, but in the lack of any more precise information or other pottery to associate with a definite date, it continues to stand as the strongest evidence available to us upon which a tentative chronology may be based.

Pl. 1

*Pl. 30

Throughout the eleventh and into the twelfth century progress in the art of ceramics was steady. The glaze colour in particular attained the beautiful, quiet, greyish green tone which is so admired today as typical of Koryŏ celadon. Many of the earliest of these 'true' celadons were left undecorated; others were embellished with incised or impressed designs; still others were modelled in high relief, to produce a sculptural effect. The technique of inlay, if used at all during this second period, could not have been fully developed, since that keen observer Hsü Ching makes no reference to it in his account of 1123. The general form and feeling remained Chinese in character, with strong reminiscences of Ting, Ju and other classical Sung wares.

Hsü Ching's comments are justified by the remaining specimens.

The third period—one of distinctively Korean wares—was ushered in by the reign of King Ŭijong (1147–1170), a time particularly noteworthy in the history of ceramics because of the introduction of the uniquely Korean technique of decoration with inlaid designs. From Ŭijong's reign to that of Ch'ungyŏl (1275—1308), a time span of about a hundred and sixty years, Korean celadon was at its best, and the Korean potter was freed from the restraints of dependence on Chinese precedent. Many of the most beautiful wares decorated with inlaid designs (usually in black and white) come down to us from the reigns of Ŭijong and his immediate successors Myŏngjong (1171 to 1197) and Sinjong (1198–1204). It is an irony of history that this should be so, for this was the very time during which the Koryŏ dynasty entered upon a period of political decline, brought about by the irresponsibility and the luxurious habits of the ruling classes, and by external pressures from the continent. Nevertheless, towards the end of the twelfth century many ceramic masterpieces of surpassing splendour were made, in our own time universally accepted as outstanding achievements in the history of the world's pottery.

The chief product of the period was inlaid celadon, but painted wares, white porcelains, and black wares of different kinds were also made. The most typical designs employed were those which we now recognize as essentially Korean in character—willow trees, swimming ducks, flying cranes and the like, all applied to vessels whose shapes are utterly Korean in feeling. One can only guess at the extent of Hsü Ching's enthusiasm if he had been able to handle the ceramic art of Koryŏ of this period when it reached its most highly developed skills.

The fourth period, extending from the reign of King Ch'ungsŏn (1309–1313) to the fall of the dynasty in 1392, was one of degeneration for ceramics and a sombre era in Korean history. During this time Koryŏ came to be completely dominated by the Mongols. King Ch'ungsŏn did not live in Korea but spent his entire reign in the Yüan capital. In mounting its unsuccessful attempts at the invasion of Japan, Yüan China made Korea its front-line base, and imposed on Koryŏ the duty of supplying both ships and marines. The Mongols were poor seafarers themselves, unable even to invade the small island of Kanghwa, which was for some thirty years the site of the Koryŏ

court-in-exile, although it is less than half a mile off the Korean mainland. The entire burden of the abortive Mongol military and naval forays against Japan fell on prostrate Koryŏ. Not unnaturally, the country declined into a condition of abject poverty, a state of affairs which had its inevitable effect on the manufacture of ceramics. Shapes degenerated, decoration and glaze became rough, even sometimes to the point of crudity; the age of Koryŏ ceramic brilliance was at an end.

The degeneration characterizing this fourth period, is observable not only in the inlaid celadons but also in the painted celadons, the white porcelain, and the black wares. Koryŏ, which had become famous as the producer of some of the most beautiful ceramics in the world, was fast approaching its end, and ultimately had to make way for the new Yi dynasty. Thenceforward, a complete change in the national philosophy caused revolutionary changes in the standards of ceramic manufacture throughout the country.

CLASSIFICATION

It will repay us to review the ceramic achievement of Koryŏ in closer detail, type by type, following roughly the classification according to differences in form, decoration and glaze, made by Nomori Ken, the author of the first important study of Koryŏ ceramics[7]. First, however, a few comments regarding celadon will not be out of place.

Several possible explanations have been advanced for the derivation of the French word *céladon*, none of which need concern us here. Suffice it to say that the word has been in general use since the late seventeenth or early eighteenth century when the type as made in China first attracted widespread European admiration. Ever since that time 'celadon' has been universally applied as the collective term for identifying much of the green, blue-green or greyish glazed wares of Asia.

In Korea, celadon was developed within the framework of a strictly Buddhist society, and many Korean examples are decorated with Buddhist motifs such as the lotus. It is very likely that a great proportion of the finest Koryŏ celadons were manufactured for use in Buddhist ceremonies, but whether that is true or not, the simple, quiet,

greyish-green colour evidently had a special appeal for the Buddhist-dominated Koryŏ aristocracy.

Many commentators have attempted to express in words the particular beauty of Koryŏ celadon, among them Koyama Fujio, who writes: 'The Porcelains of Koryŏ are beautiful flowers brought to bloom in the sad-lonely history of Korea. If we look at the history of Korean ceramics, it seems that such beautiful wares were never made either before or after Koryŏ. There are many excellent and unsurpassed specimens of Koryŏ celadons with which even the ceramics of Northern Sung, the golden age of Chinese ceramic art, cannot compare. Among all the works of art produced in Korean history, it is celadon which has the highest reputation... One wonders how it could have been possible that such beautiful things were produced, since Korea was so often devastated that the minds of the people grew wild, and the ceramics consequently became rough... Koryŏ must have been a wonderful period, with Buddhism flourishing and the people living in prosperity under good government...'[8]

The colour of celadon has often been compared to that of the beautiful Korean sky in autumn, or, using a philosophical analogy, with the 'state of having nothing in the mind', as Uchiyama expresses it[9]. 'Every time I see Koryŏ ceramics', he writes, 'I am led to "zero". This is the source of everything pure, beautiful and deep, and Koryŏ celadons are products of the same source'.

Many Japanese admirers of Koryŏ celadon, including Yanagi Soetsu and Uchiyama, have seen Koryŏ celadon, with its bluish or greyish-green colour, as a reflection of the melancholic state of mind of the Koryŏ people, whose country suffered so bitterly at the hands of invaders. Gom-

67

pertz, however, disagrees with this point of view, pointing out that there were two and a half peaceful centuries under Great Silla, followed by two hundred more tranquil years under Koryŏ before the Mongol invasion[10]. His case is strong; indeed, it is difficult to account for the beauty of form and colour of Koryŏ celadon on the basis of a purely subjective generalization.

If the appeal of celadon to connoisseurs everywhere has been profound throughout the centuries down to the present day, it was equally widespread in its own day, and celadon was by far the predominant product of the Koryŏ kilns. Perhaps it is not too far-fetched to find some relationship between this hegemony of celadon and the fact that the Korean aristocracy of the time was so limited in number, especially in comparison with its counterpart in the Chinese social structure. It may be that this limited group possessed a more uniform taste, by virtue of its smallness, in contrast to the situation in so vast a country as China where a far greater number of intellectuals and a far more numerous aristocracy exhibited a more diversified taste, making possible the development of a much greater variety of ceramic wares.

Proto-celadon

The tall jar in the collection of Ewha Women's University has already been noted as our most important evidence for the beginnings of celadon manufacture in Korea. It is cylindrical in form, with a wide mouth, and is coated with a thin brownish-yellow glaze, slightly tinged with green. Both body and glaze material appear to contain some iron.

The 18-character Chinese inscription on the bottom of the jar may be translated as follows:

'Made in the fourth year of Ch'un-hua, the [cyclical] year of Kuei-szu, for use in the First Room of the Shrine of King T'aejo, by the potter Ch'oe Kil-hoe.' The fourth year of Sh'un-hua, which is a *nien hao* of the Northern Sung dynasty, corresponds to the year 993 of the Christian calendar.

According to the *Koryŏ-sa*, the official history of the Koryŏ dynasty, the shrine built to commemorate King T'aejo, the founder of the dynasty, was begun in 989 and completed in 992. Considering the importance of the monument, it is reasonable to conclude that a vessel made specially for it and identified by an inscription in this way will reflect the highest level achieved by Korean ceramic art of the time.

Developed Celadon

If one follows the somewhat arbitrary classification of Koryŏ celadon into two main groupings—with and without inlaid decoration under the glaze—the latter category may be still further subdivided into four different subgroups as follows: those having no decoration of any kind, those with incised decoration, those with designs in low relief, and, finally, those with modelled or sculptured ornamentation.

Undecorated Celadon.—Two royal tombs of the twelfth century—those of Kings Injong (1123–1146) and Myŏngjong (1171–1197)—have produced examples of undecorated celadon which are of special importance.   *Pl. 1

Four came from Injong's tomb: a vase, a bowl with matching lid, a round covered cosmetic box, and a square 'stand'. The vase is most elegant, shaped like an elongated   *Cat. 28   Pl. 11

68

Pl.31 eight-lobed melon. The 'stand' is a most unusual piece, the exact use of which remains unknown. Its form is not without precedent, however, since another of identical shape, though smaller and almost unquestionably of Sung origin, is to be found in the collection of the Ashmolean Museum in Oxford, England.

*Pl.34 From the tomb of King Myŏngjong we have three bowls without decoration, found together with decorated celadons of various kinds.

The latter find is of particular chronological significance. We know that inlaid celadon was being made at least as early as the reign of King Ŭijong (1147–1170), and consequently there has been, in many quarters, a general tendency to date all non-inlaid celadons to a time before Ŭijong's accession to the throne. Since the Myŏngjong tomb was constructed very near the end of the century, however, the inference would be that the non-inlaid *Pl. III types—including the undecorated category—were not, after all, completely abandoned after inlaid celadon had become popular, but continued to be made over a long period of time. Nomori[11] believes that they were produced throughout the Koryŏ dynasty.

Many undecorated celadons are distinguished for their *Pl. IV serene appearance. A particularly beautiful example is the Pl.32 mallet-shaped wine bottle, a form frequently encountered in Chinese, and later in Japanese, ceramics. Finally, five Pl.33 small dishes in the collection of the National Museum of Korea may be quoted as examples of undecorated celadon of the highest quality, their special claim to admiration lying in the exceptionally even distribution and colour of the glaze, a phenomenon of extreme rarity among Koryŏ *Pl.35 celadons.

Incised Celadon.—Incised celadons, ornamented with designs cut into the body with a pointed tool, are much more plentiful than those which are entirely undecorated. Modelling is often combined with the incision. One incised celadon was discovered in the excavation of the tomb of King Myŏngjong mentioned above.

A majestic example in the incised category is the tall (17 1/4 inches high) vase which is reproduced here, belonging to the Tŏksu Palace Museum of Fine Arts. Its shape is that of the familiar *maebyŏng*, which literally means a vase designed to hold a prunus branch. It is, as we have seen, an adaptation of the Chinese *mei-p'ing* but the Korean version of the form can be distinguished from the Chinese by the more pronounced bulge at the shoulder. In this case, the decoration consists of three lotus blossoms set among leaves and vines. It is widely spread and covers the entire surface of the vessel.

A cup and stand also deserve mention; they are a rare instance of a matching pair, and the colour of the glaze is unusually perfect. The cup is in the shape of a lotus blossom, and the stand is decorated with lotus blossoms and leaves—another indication of the constant influence of Buddhism on Koryŏ ceramic ornament. A small square dish with an incised peony design in the centre is especially delightful. It is very flat, and the rim is decorated with an incised arabesque of vines and leaves.

Celadon with Designs in Low Relief.—Our third sub-group comprises the large body of celadon-glazed vessels whose decoration projects slightly from the surface, an effect achieved by the use of an impressed mould. A typical example is a bowl on which such a mould has been applied

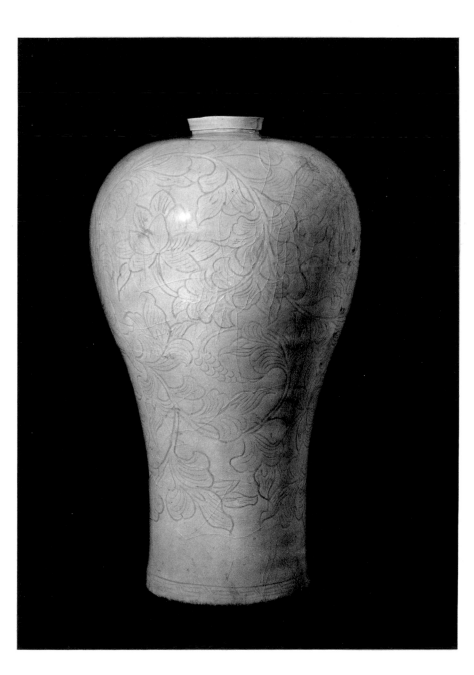

to the interior only; the design is a scene of children playing by a pond on which geese and mandarin ducks are swimming amid lotus and reeds. Another bowl, on which the same mould seems to have been used, is in the collection of the Museum of Fine Arts, Boston. The two differ only in the degree of clarity of various parts of the impressed design.

Among the most interesting of all Koryŏ celadons are the decorated roof tiles which also properly belong in this grouping. The first of these to be discovered—a flat tile—came to light as recently as 1914. Fourteen years later a beautifully ornamented fragment of a similar flat tile was purchased by an official of the Government General Museum. It is embellished with an arabesque pattern in low relief and is fine enough in quality to justify its attribution to the period of the finest Koryŏ celadons. This fragment created a sensation when its existence became known; it is indeed extraordinary to consider the extravagance of a ruling class which could use celadon as a roofing material.

In this connection, the *Koryŏ-sa* records an episode of 1157, in the reign of Ŭijong as follows:

'More than fifty of the people's houses were destroyed and the T'ae-p'yŏng-jŏng (a pleasure pavilion) was built. The Crown Prince was ordered to inscribe a tablet to hang on it. Famous flowers and exotic fruit trees were planted; rare and beautiful objects were arrayed on the right and on the left. To the south of the pavilion a pond was made and a pavilion named Kwallan-jŏng was built beside it. To the north another pavilion was built, named Yang'i-jŏng, roofed with celadon tiles.'

This is the sole known literary record of the use of these sumptuous tiles; it is probable that all the celadon tiles that survive were in fact made for King Ŭijong's one luxurious pavilion: he was notorious for his extravagance.

In the autumn of 1964 an excavation conducted by the National Museum of Korea in Tangjŏnni, Kangjin, located the kiln site at which these celadon tiles were made eight centuries ago. The finds included an intact tile of the flat type and many fragments of flat tiles, all decorated with a tree peony motif, and some magnificent semi-cylindrical tiles as well, also exquisitely ornamented in low relief, with arabesque designs. Both the flat and the semi-cylindrical tiles are glazed on the top only. Some tiles of inferior colour are probably to be explained as rejects which the authorities did not accept as suitable. Some of the fragments were of excellent colour, appropriate to the usual quality of the era of King Ŭijong.

This discovery brought some interesting facts to light. The flat tiles are of varying shapes and sizes, in contrast to the uniform pattern in which tiles are made today. It is the twentieth-century practice to chip off sections of the tile as may be necessary to conform to the shape of the particular roof under construction. Clearly it would be impossible to treat celadon-glazed tiles in this way, so before firing, the various shapes and sizes were plotted out and produced in the exact dimensions required. ★Cat. 40, 41

It is also noticeable that the round tiles of celadon which have been found are smaller than Silla tiles. The building for which they were designed must have been relatively small, and the tiles would fit a pavilion such as is described in the *Koryŏ-sa*.

Celadon with Modelled Decoration.—The Koryŏ potter achieved some of his most ingenious and interesting effects by three-dimensional modelling, a device which so impressed Hsü Ching in the twelfth century that he described one such vessel in detail, writing '… the beast crouches on top [of the vessel] supported by a lotus. This is the most distinguished of all their wares…'

Several of these sculptures still exist in the collections of the National Museum of Korea and the Tŏksu Palace Museum of Fine Arts, and one of them, an incense burner, is precisely of the type described by the Chinese traveller. Pl. 36 The 'beast' is a lion modelled in full relief on the cover, its mouth slightly open for the passage of the incense smoke. The fur and features employ a combination of modelling and incision, and the eyes have been emphasized by painting in underglaze iron. This Korean lion crouches slightly to one side instead of in the centre of its platform and the

asymmetry lends the piece a spontaneity which is not without humour.

A mythological beast, the *ch'i-lin* (unicorn), decorates the cover of still another incense burner in the Tŏksu Palace Museum, similarly designed to allow the passage of the incense smoke through the open mouth of the animal. The bowl of the vessel is ornamented with incised designs.

A third incense burner is more complicated in form. The cover is modelled in the shape of a reticulated ball, and is mounted on a foliate base equipped with a central hole which allows the smoke to be dispersed upwards through the apertures in the ball itself. The piece is supported by three feet carved in the form of miniature rabbits, modelled with most appealing sensitivity.

One of the most delightful of all Koryŏ sculptured celadons is a water dropper in the form of a seated monkey holding its baby in its arms in the collection of Hyung-pil Chun. The water dropper is a familiar form in Korean ceramics, hundreds of them surviving from Koryŏ and Yi times. It was indispensable to the scholar for the preparation of Chinese ink for writing, and it remains a favourite collector's item today, illustrating as it does so well the high degree of sophistication characteristic of the Koryŏ scholar. The example under consideration is unique among known specimens on account both of its expert modelling and of the superb quality of its glaze. The eyes and noses of both animals have been marked with spots of under-glaze iron; apertures in the heads admit and dispense the water.

The brush stand, like the water dropper, is a utensil for the scholar's desk. The example illustrated here is an especially distinguished one, ornamented with panels of

reticulated arabesques of lotus leaves and blossoms, from both ends of which spring the heads of carp-dragons. Again the eyes have been painted in underglaze iron, and the whole is coated with a splendid even glaze. ★Pl. 37

The Koryŏ predilection for elaboration in modelling sometimes produces effects which the ceramic connoisseur of today is inclined to condemn as over-complicated. An example of this is the water pot shown here, which com- ★Pl. v; Pl. 38 bines reticulation with modelling and incision. Though it may be criticized by some as a mere *tour de force* of the potter's art, it nevertheless deserves a prominent place in the history of Koryŏ ceramics as proof of the extraordinary versatility of the Koryŏ potter. It is double-walled, the inner pot being the container, while the reticulated outer 'shell' with its design of boys climbing among flowers is purely decorative. The inner bowl, or holder, is flower-shaped with three tiers of incised petals in relief on the exterior.

Inlaid Celadon.—The Korean potter's most important single contribution to ceramic history is undoubtedly the technique of inlay, a decorative device invented in Korea and used so widely and effectively that it is responsible for the world-wide fame of Koryŏ wares throughout the centuries. Before we turn to specific examples, there are certain technical considerations to be discussed.

In the case of the non-inlaid celadons, the clay mixture, containing a sufficient amount of kaolin to enable the piece to resist high kiln temperatures, was of course first thrown on the potter's wheel until the desired shape was achieved. When dried the vessel was coated with glaze ★Pl. vi and fired at a temperature of not less than 1200 degrees

Centigrade. If modelling or incised decoration was desired, such ornament was added to the object before the glaze was applied, when it had reached the stage in the drying process known as 'leather-hard'.

In the case of inlaid wares, the desired pattern was incised or carved away either by means of a pointed tool (the usual method) or, less frequently, a mould. The incisions thus made were then filled with white or reddish-brown clay, after which the surface was carefully wiped with a cloth or cut with a special tool in order to remove any excess of inlay material which might still adhere to the surface. The piece was then ready for glazing and firing, the white clay retaining its whiteness, the reddish-brown being transformed into black by the heat in the kiln.

Experts differ as to whether Koryŏ celadons were fired only once or whether they first received a biscuit firing, followed by a second firing after the glaze material had been applied. In the case of the inlaid wares at least, a double firing would seem to have been the most likely technique followed, and kiln site investigations have, in fact, revealed fragments of inlaid celadon which have obviously received a biscuit firing. The same generalization may also hold for incised and modelled vessels, but positive evidence is lacking. Present day practice involves double

*Pl.39   firing, and I am inclined to the belief that such practice
*Cat.44 was traditional in Koryŏ times as well.

The final factor governing the ultimate appearance of Koryŏ celadons was, of course, the glaze, the exact composition of which was the Koryŏ potter's secret. However, modern Korean potters have come close to reproducing Koryŏ celadon glaze, and the problem of celadon glaze in general lies outside the scope of the present discussion.

Many of the inlaid celadons left to us from Koryŏ times possess great beauty of glaze as well as decoration of very high quality. But it is noticeable that a large amount of the ware—otherwise of great refinement—is less distinguished for its glaze colour than for its decoration, perhaps implying that as the potter concentrated more and more on the intricacies of ornamentation, he lost interest in achieving that perfection of glaze colour which had so distinguished the earlier work.

Yet this is probably too sweeping a statement, because it is certain that inlaid wares of the finest quality were manufactured at the same time as the finest of the non-inlaid celadons. The problem of deterioration is less likely to be directly related to the technique of inlay than to the gradual degeneration which was to result in the final dismal period of Koryŏ ceramic manufacture.

Hsü Ching made no mention of inlaid wares in his account of 1123. This may have been accidental, but it is more likely that inlaid wares were not yet being made in Korea.

Up to the present our best evidence for dating the invention of inlay is provided by two vessels discovered in a tomb. The tomb contained a stone casket with an epitaph bearing a date corresponding to 1159, which falls in the middle of King Ŭijong's reign. One of these vessels is a bowl, decorated on the interior with an elaborate design in white consisting of a formal chrysanthemum head surrounded by floral arabesques, executed in so-called 'reverse inlay'. On the exterior the inlay method followed is of the more usual variety.

The term 'reverse inlay' has been coined to describe those designs in which the decorative motifs are retained in

75

Pl. 36   Incense burner.   Celadon glaze, modelled, incised and under-glaze iron decoration. H. 8¹/₂ in., L. 6⁷/₁₆ in. Koryŏ dynasty, 11th/12th century. National Museum of Korea, Seoul.

Pl. 37   Incense burner.   Celadon glaze, modelled, incised and under-glaze iron decoration. H. 8³/₈ in., W. 6⁷/₁₆ in. Koryŏ dynasty, 11th/12th century. Tŏksu Palace Museum of Fine Arts, Seoul.

celadon colour, the *background* being cut away and filled with inlay. Reverse inlay is certainly a more complicated technique than the usual direct inlay, and its appearance would seem to indicate an advanced stage of development. The logical inference is therefore that inlay as such must have been introduced before this bowl was made, which is to say prior to 1159, and the discovery of the bowl in Ŭijong's tomb makes it fairly certain that the introduction of inlay must have taken place at some time in the interval between Hsü Ching's visit in 1123 and 1159.

Let us now turn to an examination of individual exam-
Pl. VII ples of inlaid celadon. The water sprinkler illustrated here is one of the finest. Refined and delicate in form, it is decorated with typically Korean designs of willow tree, bamboo, reeds, mandarin ducks and lotus, inlaid (except for the eyes of the ducks which are black) in white.

A notable and splendid example of the technique is
Pl. VIII provided by a wide-mouthed water container of exceptionally large size, provided with handles. A large peony motif, noble in its simplicity, ornaments the side of the
Pl. IX pot. A wine pot of the familiar eight-lobed melon shape has alternate lobes decorated with an inlaid pattern of white chrysanthemums with black stems and leaves. In spite of a repair to the handle, it is still a splendid specimen and in a surprisingly good state of preservation, for long spouts and large handles are seldom found intact.

One of the most monumental of all remaining celadons
Pl. 40 is the *maebyŏng* popularly known as the '*Thousand Crane Vase*', decorated with an overall pattern composed of forty-six ascending and twenty-three descending cranes flying amid clouds. The cranes are drawn within roundels outlined in double rings of white and black. Still another

Pl. 38 Water pot, cover and bowl. Celadon glaze, reticulated, modelled and incised decoration. Pot, H. 7 in., D., at base, 6⁹/₁₆ in. Bowl, H. 3⁹/₁₆ in., D., at mouth, 7³/₁₆ in. Koryŏ dynasty, 12th century. Tŏksu Palace Museum of Fine Arts, Seoul.
Pl. 39 Bowl. Celadon glaze, incised and inlaid decoration. H. 2³/₈ in., D. 6⁵/₈ in. Koryŏ dynasty, 12th century. National Museum of Korea, Seoul.

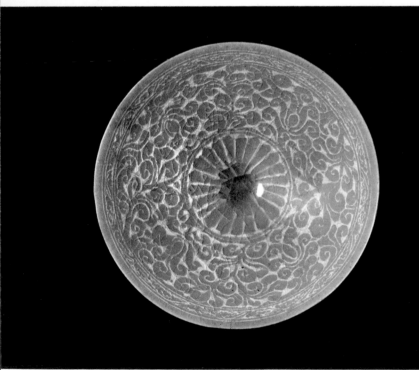

maebyŏng bears a decoration of three large peonies (two blossoms and one bud) on the main body of the vase. In this case the design is distinctive because the edges of the white flower petals have been painted in underglaze copper red. Pl. x

These two *maebyŏng*, together with the other inlaid vessels briefly described above, characterize inlaid celadon at the peak of its achievement, and are probably to be dated somewhere between the late twelfth century and, at the latest, the latter part of the thirteenth century, well before the period of degeneration had set in. Good quality inlaid celadons were seldom produced during the succeeding fourteenth century.

Gilded Celadon

A few inlaid celadons survive which have additional decoration in the form of gilding, usually badly eroded by time so that only faint traces of the original appearance remain. Such gilding seems to have been applied after firing, in order to accentuate special details of the design.

Of the few examples of the technique remaining to us, a fragmentary jar in the collection of the National Museum of Korea is outstanding. In its present condition it measures ten inches in height and eight in width. While its thin glaze is by no means of the best quality, the date generally agreed upon for its manufacture is during the reign of King Kojong (1214–1259), when celadon of good quality was still being made. Floral arabesque designs decorate the body of the jar, to which gilding has been applied following the contours of the leaf, blossom and stem sections of the pattern. In the central part of the main portion of the vessel as we now see it, a monkey holding a peach is depict- Pl. 41

ed sitting under a tree at the side of a lake or pond, all inlaid in white except for the leaves and the animal's eyes which are black. The design itself is framed within an ogival cartouche with two borders of white inlay and one in gold.

The other side of the jar is even more badly damaged; here we find a rabbit, also seated under a tree by water, again in white inlay and also within a similarly outlined cartouche. Flakes of gold are still visible here and there.

Enhancement of the design by means of this gilded overlay strikes the modern eye as over-elaborate and ostentatious; it was considered an extravagant luxury in Koryŏ times as well.

A well-known anecdote from Korean history illustrates this. Cho In-gyu, a minister during the reign of King Ch'ungyŏl, presented a gilded ceramic vessel to the Yüan Emperor Kublai Khan: 'In-gyu once presented a gilt porcelain [to the Emperor]. The Emperor asked whether the gold could be removed and used a second time. Cho In-gyu replied, "The porcelain is easily broken, and then the gold is also broken. How could it be used again?" The Emperor said that he understood. He then ordered that porcelain should not be decorated with gold again and no-one should present him with any more porcelain of that sort.'[12]

Celadon with Underglaze Copper Decoration

On rare occasions underglaze copper was used by the Kŏryo potter in order to add red to some details of the decoration of inlaid celadons. One such example has already been mentioned. As with early Chinese experiments in the use of copper, the results were by no means always crowned with success. The copper sometimes turned

Pl. 40   Vase.   Celadon glaze, inlaid decoration. H. 1 ft. 4³/₈ in.,
D. 9⁷/₈ in. Koryŏ dynasty, late 12th century. Coll. Hyung-pil Chun,
Seoul.

brown or even green in the firing. On the other hand several specimens were conspicuously successful and these, some round cosmetic boxes in particular—are highly valued treasures of the Tŏksu Palace Museum Collection today.

Painted Celadon

The designation 'painted Koryŏ' is generally applied to those celadons which have an underglaze decoration in brownish-black (iron), white, or sometimes red (copper). This type was inspired by contemporary Chinese T'zu-chou ware, and had its origin at least as early as the beginning of the twelfth century. This is proved by the discovery of shards of painted celadon at Tangjŏnni, Kang-jin, together with a great many other shards of non-inlaid celadons, the glaze colour of which points to a date earlier than that of the period when the finest celadon was produced. The majority of the specimens which survived intact, however, betray characteristics which would place them in the early or middle part of the thirteenth century.

The *maebyŏng* illustrated here is a good example of mid-thirteenth century painted Koryŏ. Its decoration consists of three separate peonies, each with one blossom and one bud. The piece is evidence of the strong partiality in Korea for celadon glaze, even when the colour was imperfect, a consideration to which we will revert later on. The green in this instance is rather dark in tone.

A rare variant of painted Koryŏ adds still another ingredient—embossing—to the technical repertoire of the Koryŏ potter. This type can be illustrated by a wine pot of melon shape decorated with peony design in raised white and black lines on each side of the vessel. Its

probable date is also in the thirteenth century, contemporary with the *maebyŏng* mentioned above.

Other Types of Koryŏ Ceramics

While the celadons are the wares for which the Koryŏ dynasty is best known and which were the favourite of the Koreans themselves, other ceramic types were made which deserve some attention.

White Koryŏ.—White porcelains as well as celadons have been found from time to time in Koryŏ tombs ever since they were first looted, though not in comparable number. Nevertheless, their discovery is important for our understanding of the Koryŏ ceramic achievement and has aroused interesting and continuing discussion among scholars.

For a long time, all the white wares found in these tombs were assumed to be of Chinese origin, since the finds contained so many pieces demonstrably of Chinese Ting or *ch'ing-pai (ying ch'ing)* manufacture. Widespread though it is, this assumption can no longer stand, even though ★Pl. xi the Korean whites admittedly bear a great resemblance to those of China and, indeed for the most part, owe their inspiration directly to them. The discovery of white porcelain shards on South Korean kiln sites has demonstrated once and for all that white porcelain was made in Korea during Koryŏ times.

The site of Puan on the south-west coast of Korea is known to have produced Koryŏ celadons of the highest quality. Some years ago a Japanese resident of Chŏngŭp, in North Chŏlla province, collected an impressive number ★Pl. 42 of shards from Puan which are now in the collection of

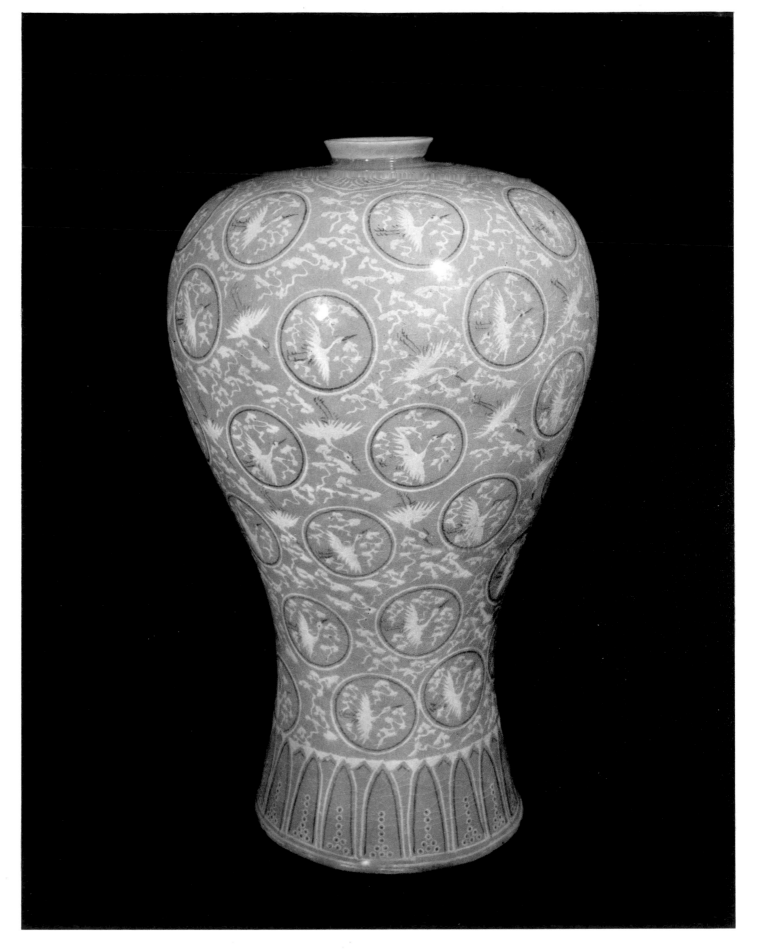

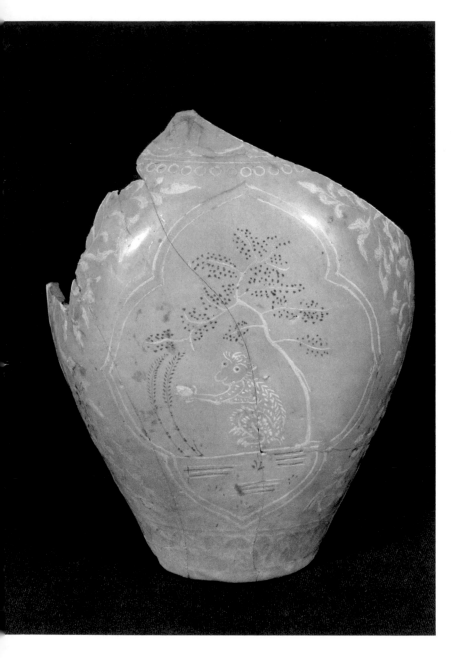

Ewha Women's University. Among them was a considerable quantity of white examples, including beautiful specimens with designs inlaid in black in the typical Korean fashion. Again, when the excavation in Tangjŏnni, Kangjin was carried out by the National Museum of Korea in 1964, about thirty shards of best quality white porcelain were found.

Koyama has divided Koryŏ white wares into three stages of development[13]: a period of imitation of the Chinese prototype, a period of distinctly Korean characteristics, and a period of transition from Koryŏ to Yi. Koyama attributes to his first period all those specimens which in form, design and feeling differ very little if at all from *ch'ing-pai* and Ting wares of the Sung dynasty, and dates them to the first half of the twelfth century. The examples may be of relatively soft clay coated with a translucent glaze with a general, overall crackle pattern, or they may have a hard grey body, also coated with translucent glaze but without a fine surface *craquelure*. Surviving pieces are rare, and the place of their manufacture remains unknown.

In the second period—corresponding roughly to the time of the manufacture of inlaid celadons—Koyama places those white porcelains which have a fine hard body coated with a translucent white glaze tinged with brown, and which correspond in shape, design and feeling with their contemporary counterparts among the inlaid celadons.

Koyama's third period is characterized, as one might predict, by general degeneration similar to that which we have observed in the celadons.

Nomori, on the other hand, classifies Koryŏ white wares in accordance with their design into three groups: those which lack decoration, those with incised designs, and those which have been inlaid. The combined evidence adduced by these two scholars must certainly dispel any lingering doubt as to the independent existence of 'Koryŏ white' and its general evolution along lines similar to that followed by Koryŏ celadon.

Pl. 43
*Pl. 44

The best known example of Korean white porcelain is the *maebyŏng* in the Tŏksu Palace Museum of Fine Arts. It has six celadon panels which are decorated by both incision and inlay in black and white. These panels are lozenge-shaped, with scalloped edges; each one is embellished with a different design utilizing peony, reed, egret and willow-tree motifs. A chrysanthemum petal collar surrounds the neck, while a band of lotus petals around the base completes the decorative scheme. The white ground has a light bluish cast.

Cat. 55

A bowl found in the Diamond Mountains and bearing an inscription with a date corresponding to 1391 may be considered a typical example of Koyama's third period. It was discovered together with three other white bowls, a miniature gilded silver pagoda, a bronze bowl and a white porcelain incense burner, all of which had been placed on a mountain top by Yi Sŏng-gye, who in 1392 was to become the official founder of the Yi dynasty. The bowl has a rough body coated with a bluish-white glaze, but its shape lacks the elegance of the finest quality Koryŏ ceramics.

Black Koryŏ.—Often referred to as 'Koryŏ temmoku', Koryŏ black wares may also be classified into three groups, in this case according to the technique employed, known as iron black, black glazed ware, and iron glazed ware.

*Cat. 56

The first of these, iron black, is made of the same greyish clay as the celadons and is actually a variant of celadon in which a celadon glaze has been applied over a pigment or slip of high iron content. Different specimens may be undecorated, incised, inlaid, or even painted in underglaze white. The type is still further proof of the Korean predilection for celadon even though the resulting colour was no longer the lovely bluish-green associated with the classic types. Very few examples remain to us, one of the best being a *maebyŏng* in the National Museum of Korea, on which a design of ginseng leaves has been lightly incised into the iron-coated body. White slip was then brushed into the incised design before the final coating of celadon. On the evidence of its shape this *maebyŏng* can be assigned to the thirteenth century.

The black glazed ware differs from the iron black in the omission of a celadon glaze coat, the iron glaze on the grey body being directly responsible for the ultimate appearance of the vessel. In colour it is usually a subdued, matt black which may, however, have a greyish-black appearance if the glaze material has been thickly applied. A considerable number of bottles, jars or water pots belong in this category.

Iron glazed ware, on the other hand, is reddish-brown in colour. Some examples are undecorated, while others are ornamented with designs made by scraping away the background, and then filling in the areas thus exposed with white slip.

Miscellaneous Wares.—In addition to the types mentioned above, marbled and lacquered wares were also produced by the Koryŏ potter. The former is evidently a direct imitation of a familiar Chinese prototype of Sung manu-

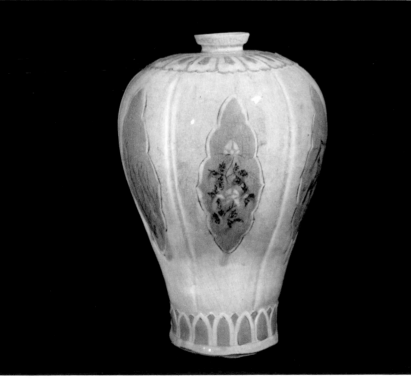

facture based on T'ang models. The pots were made of red and white clays and coated with a celadon glaze, but surviving examples are extremely rare.

Koryŏ lacquered ware is equally scarce; the Tŏksu Palace Museum of Fine Arts, for example, possesses only one specimen of the type.

Koyama also writes of 'mud glazed' and 'candy glazed' Koryŏ wares, the former using a combination of ash and mud as the glaze material. The 'candy glazed' ware has the colour of Japanese *ame*, a wheat gluten of dark greenish tone. Although we have no reliable data at all regarding the manufacture of either, it would seem that these two rare types must be dated towards the end of the dynasty.

To summarize, the predominant taste of Koryŏ was for celadon, though some white and black wares and a few other less important categories were also produced. Only the celadon, however, was consistently manufactured in wide variety throughout Koryŏ times. Indeed, it was so greatly in vogue that it was even applied over an iron slip.

Tomb finds have provided us with the most eloquent evidence of Korean partiality for the ceramics of Sung China, which have been discovered in variety and abundance in Korea. An important trade may therefore be assumed, implying profound admiration for Sung ceramics in all their variety. It is difficult therefore, to account for the fact that Koryŏ, in its own ceramic industry, concentrated so overwhelmingly on celadon alone. Whatever the reasons, this concentration, which began as imitation and progressed to a level of uniquely distinctive achievement, stands as a dazzlingly brilliant chapter in the history of ceramic art.

YI DYNASTY WARES

GENERAL CHARACTERISTICS

With the change of dynasties from Koryŏ to Yi, a transformation took place in Korean ceramics, the result of a drastic shift from Buddhism to Confucianism and the substitution of a bureaucracy for the aristocratic, religiously-oriented society of Koryŏ. Although the Koryŏ tradition was not abandoned *in toto* overnight, from the early years of the new dynasty the potter's products lacks the delicate craftsmanship typical of his Koryŏ predecessors. Koryŏ delicacy, refinement and subtle beauty of colour give way to a direct, unsophisticated approach which produces simpler forms, free and robust.

Among these Yi wares, two varieties predominate: *punch'ŏng*—a development of celadon—and white porcelain, which seems to betray the dual influence of Koryŏ white wares and Chinese white porcelain of the Ming dynasty in China. Both types were produced concurrently from the beginning of the period, but it is demonstrable that *punch'ŏng* enjoyed its heyday in the earlier part of the dynasty, and later disappeared, while the white porcelain alone survived into the later centuries. Different though they are, *punch'ŏng* and white porcelain both exemplify the new Yi ceramic art, one of the most striking features of which is the lack of the brilliant colour which characterized Koryŏ ware; where colour is important in the Yi repertoire, as in the case of the decorated white porcelains, it is an additional and not an essential element, achieved by

85

the use of underglaze painting in cobalt, copper or iron applied purely decoratively against a white ground.

Following Koryŏ tradition, the Yi government established a special office known as *sa'ongbang* (later renamed *sa'ongwŏn*) to administer the manufacture of ceramic wares intended for court or ceremonial use. At its head was a government official of ministerial rank; under him a chief administrative officer exercised direct control over the working potters.

In this connection a passage from the *Yongjae Ch'onghwa*, written by Sŏng Hyŏn (1439–1508), has special interest: 'For white porcelain one must use white clay. Only after careful baking can it be put to use. In the provinces there are many places where porcelains are made, and those made in Koryŏng are the best, but they cannot match the best wares produced in Kwangju. Every year officers of the *sa'ongwŏn* are sent out in two groups to visit villages on the left and right sides of the Kyŏng-an-ch'ŏn river in the Kwangju district. Each group, accompanied by a scribe, supervises the potters making ceramic wares to be brought to the court from spring to autumn. Merit is noted in order to award prizes to the best potters.'

The particular beauty of Yi ceramics was discovered and praised very early in Yi times by the Japanese, who found their simplicity of form extremely appealing, an attachment which continues to the present day. Koyama, for example, has written[14]: 'Yi dynasty wares have something of deep sorrow and loneliness [about them] which one cannot rightly express in words alone. They are not scrupulous about trifles, and nothing is more enchanting than Yi pottery, to which one can only feel attachment. Those who discovered the beauty of Yi ceramics were all

Japanese; in olden times Shuko, Sho-o and Rikyu discovered the beauty of the Korean tea bowl and in modern times Yanagi and Asakawa have again highly praised the beauty of Yi wares. Those ceramics which only the Japanese ceramic experts understood with their simple and natural *(wabi)* and mysterious *(yugen)* expressions are all wares of the first part of the Yi dynasty.'

The Japanese words *wabi* (simple and natural) and *yugen* (mysterious) are difficult to translate, *wabi* can mean something like simple and natural or loneliness, and *yugen* profound and mysterious. Their use indicates a philosophical attitude and a feeling akin to mysticism, which is peculiarly oriental.

Yi bowls reached Japan very early in the period, and even if they had been badly fired or were misshapen, they were highly esteemed by Japanese tea masters, who professed to discover in them a unique kind of aesthetic quality. Such is the force of tradition in Japan that even today a broken Yi tea bowl, when it is known to have been used by a well-known Japanese tea master in the past, may still command an enormous price on the art market, often quite beyond the comprehension of anyone outside Japan.

Again and again the unintentional, unsophisticated simplicity and spontaneity of Yi pottery has been praised by Japanese lovers of ceramics, some of whom have been tempted to account for these characteristics by referring to the 'hard, dark life' of the Korean people in Yi times. This is not the place to debate whether or not this explanation is justifiable, and it is wiser to avoid too much speculative generalization in discussing the ceramic art of Korea.

By the end of the dynasty the Korean people themselves seem to have lost their appreciation for fine ceramics, for decadence characterizes the latest Yi wares. Confucian scholars and the Yi élite, however, were deeply attached to ceramics, and innumerable poems have come down to us from them written in praise of the beauty of porcelain.

An historical episode concerning the great statesman and general Kim Chong-sŏ, victor over the Juchen during the reign of Se-jong (1419–1450) and later executed by King Sejo (1445–1468), is pertinent. It occurs in Kim Chong-sŏ's biography as written by his son Chong-jik: 'In the cyclical year *ulhae* [probably 1455] I met Kim Yun-dŏk (*hao*: Namhae) at the guest house of Chŏngdo, and we talked in the evening. Kim Yun-dŏk said, "When I was in Koryŏng, Kim Chong-sŏ came to our *hyŏn* as Inspector General, and I sat with him at table. Kim pointed to the plain white porcelains on the table and said, "The porcelains of your *hyŏn* are so wonderful, wonderful." He said this repeatedly, so that I did not know what he meant but only replied, "Yes, yes." Later in Seoul he often told people how uneducated I was. I heard so, many times.'

It is difficult to draw precise dividing lines between different periods of ceramic development within the dynasty, especially in the case of those wares which were products of private enterprise in countryside kilns, as opposed to those made in kilns operated by the government. Ceramic manufacture in the private kilns was a tradition handed down through generations from father to son, with little changes in technique. Still today one may see ceramics being made in Korea just as they were made some two or three hundred years ago.

There have, nevertheless, been attempts in this direction. Asakawa, for example, divides Yi manufacture roughly into three periods[15]. According to his scheme, the first hundred years of the dynasty constitute the timespan during which the greatest number of *punch'ŏng* wares were made, the most notable kilns being those of Kyeryong-san, Koryŏng, Sangju and Chinju. In addition, plain white porcelain, white porcelain with underglaze blue (and also underglaze red) decoration, and some black glazed wares were produced during this period.

Asakawa's second period extends from the reign of Prince Yŏnsan (1495–1506) to that of King Hyŏnjong (1650–1659), and is characterized by the manufacture of high-fired white porcelain and blue-and-white wares, together with some black glazed types and others with underglaze iron decoration.

His third period, lasting about two hundred years (1659 to 1868), is that which saw the full bloom of blue and white, *punch'ŏng* being made only in poorer quality and in country districts. Finally, the last fifty years of the dynasty comprise a time of degeneration, with porcelains decorated in underglaze blue or red beginning to disappear from the ceramic scene.

Asakawa's study is most valuable; however, the most compelling factor in the historical situation was the Hideyoshi Invasion, an event which drastically disrupted Yi ceramic development. As a result of this incursion the country was devastated: palaces and temples were reduced to ashes, traditionally known kilns were utterly destroyed, and potters isolated from their workshops or even removed in person to Japan to be put to work in the land of the enemy. The technique of white porcelain manufacture managed to survive this disaster, but *punch'ŏng* was never again to reappear in its original form. It would seem wiser, therefore, to postulate two main divisions in Yi ceramic

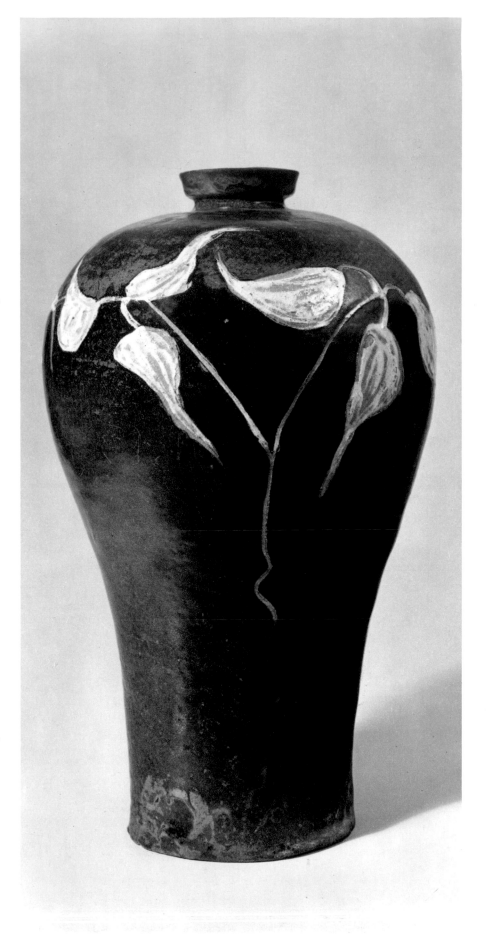

history, with the Hideyoshi Invasion as the line of demarcation.

In such a classification, the first period, lasting approximately two hundred years from the late fourteenth to the end of the sixteenth century, was a time of steady progress in ceramics and is especially notable for the production of *punch'ŏng* in large quantities and a wide variety of types. These are referred to by the names given them by Japanese connoisseurs: *mishima, hori-mishima, hakeme, e-hakeme, hori-hakeme, kohiki,* for example.

The development of Yi ceramics was then interrupted by the invasion, and, according to Yi dynasty annals, more than three hundred kilns were closed down. *Punch'ŏng* was never made again except as an export for the Japanese market. The situation created by the invasion was, in fact, so desperate that the Yi rulers had difficulty in finding kilns where pottery could still be made for court use. A large government kiln was therefore established for this purpose at Kwangju, near Seoul, in the seventeenth century. It was at this Kwangju kiln and its successors in the same district and elsewhere throughout the country, that the plain white and blue-and-white porcelains were made which characterize the second, post-Hideyoshi, period for about three hundred years. In 1883, due to the financial embarrassment of the government, the administration of the Punwŏn (Kwangju) kilns was turned over to a private company, a circumstance which only hastened the already rapid decline of the Yi ceramic tradition.

PUNCH'ŎNG

Even in early Yi times, white porcelain was always favoured for use in ceremonies and by the court, and this state of affairs lasted throughout Yi history. *Punch'ŏng* was a different matter. Although it too was sometimes made for official purposes, it holds true as a generalization that *punch'ŏng* was a popular ware.

The word *punch'ŏng* is an abbreviation of *punjang ch'ŏng sagi*, written with five Chinese characters meaning 'powder, dressing, green, sand, vessel' (dressed blue-green pottery). The last two characters form a word commonly used in Korean for ceramic: *sagi*. The first and third characters taken together form *punch'ŏng*, literally translatable as powder green—in other words, dressed celadon. (The same two characters become, in Chinese, *fên-ch'ing*, but this term is used in connection with Chinese pottery of a type which has nothing in common with Korean *punch'ŏng*.)

Punch'ŏng is made of the same clay as Koryŏ celadon; its texture, however, is noticeably coarser. Its surface may be partially, or even wholly, covered with a white slip. The Japanese have classified the ware into several groups under the general designation of *mishima*.

The simplest *punch'ŏng* is that which has tiny floral designs or rows of simple dots stamped into the surface (perhaps a reminiscence of the technique of stamping used in Great Silla times). These designs are then filled in with brushed white slip in the same way as Koryŏ inlaid celadon. Occasionally designs were incised instead of stamped, and later they also were sometimes filled in with brushed slip of the desired colour. The ware is, then, evidently a development of Koryŏ inlaid ware, despite its changed appearance. It was first manufactured at the end of Koryŏ itself, or in the early years of Yi, and flourished in the early fifteenth century, continuing in production of good quality for approximately a hundred and fifty years, its peak era coinciding roughly with the reign of King Sejong (1419–1450).

The bowl here illustrated is a beautiful and typical example of *mishima* type *punch'ŏng*. On the interior a design of chrysanthemums has been stamped, above which are the so-called 'rope curtain' designs, terminating in a band of 'grass marks' about the upper lip. A celadon glaze has been applied over the whole—further proof of the debt *punch'ŏng* owes to Koryŏ inlaid celadon. Although certainly a hasty method of inlaying (and by Koryŏ standards inferior to the classical technique), the results, as in the case of the bowl under consideration, are nevertheless uniquely beautiful. This piece dates from the early years of the Yi dynasty when *punch'ŏng* was still fairly close to Koryŏ tradition. Later on, *punch'ŏng* was to rely for its effect more on brushed white slip, growing further and further away from earlier practise.

As we have pointed out, in the great majority of *punch'ŏng* ware the body is of coarse, poor quality, and the stamped decoration, and especially the white slip used in later examples, was frequently employed in order to hide this defect. Where slip has been used, in many instances it has been applied with swift strokes of the brush on both interior and exterior of the individual vessel, this 'careless' brush work being precisely the feature which the Japanese tea master found so admirable. The bottle reproduced here illustrates the type, treasured in Japan and known there as *hakeme*.

Pl. XII
Cat. 59
*Cat. 57, 58
Pl. 45

Several variations on this general theme were employed by the Korean potter, one of which is illustrated here. In this case the surface was first incised with designs which were later filled in with brushed white slip. The incised portion—and also some of the background—was then cut away prior to being glazed, a technique known in Japan as *hori-hakeme*. A wine flask and a wine bottle exemplify this category of *punch'ŏng*. Coated with white slip, the decoration has been effected in *sgraffito* style by cutting away portions of the slip to leave a white peony design against a dark ground, the dark colour stemming from the use of a dressing of iron oxide which has turned greenish-black in the firing process, and lends prominence to the main decorative motif.

Still another variant of *punch'ŏng* is the type called by the Japanese *e-hakeme*, decorated with designs of flowers, grasses, animals and so forth painted in iron over a brushed white slip. It is no doubt influenced, as the painted celadons of Koryŏ had been, by Chinese T'zu-chou ware. A pear-shaped wine bottle with a narrow neck illustrates the type: a decoration of painted fish and lotus blossoms has been applied over the white slip with a broad brush, producing a very free effect. The bottle is known to have come from a kiln at Kyeryong-san, in Ch'ungch'ŏng Namdo province. Another specimen, this time a food jar, comes to us from the same kiln, its bold decoration painted in iron, typical of all Kyeryong-san wares. Kyeryong-san had no monopoly of the manufacture of this type, however, some surviving examples having been produced far to the south in Chŏlla Namdo province.

The final glaze applied to *punch'ŏng* was frequently celadon, the clearest indication of the Yi potter's famili-arity with Koryŏ tradition. The results, however, cannot compare with the products of the earlier dynasty. Clearly the Yi potter's major interest lay less in achieving a beauti-ful glaze colour than in experimenting with the new tech-nique of white slip and stamped or inlaid designs. *Cat.61

The reader will recall that *punch'ŏng* literally signifies pottery coated with white powder, and most of the exam-ples so far alluded to conform to this definition, having been coated with white slip (powder) applied with a brush. The results are often pleasing. But brushing was not the only means of coating the vessel. Still another sub-group of *punch'ŏng* was dipped directly into the slip material. Known as *kohiki* to the Japanese, the type was produced only in a limited area of South Korea, and surviving specimens are rare. *Pl.46, Pl.xiii

BLACK WARES

Before proceeding to a discussion of white porcelain, it must be noted that black wares commonly called *temmoku* in Japan, were also made by the Yi potter. Flattened wine bottles, small wine bottles of more usual shape, jars and tea cups were the typical forms, manufactured in a great many kilns throughout Korea. The glaze is usually matt, without lustre. A bottle represents this variety. It is of a common form, usually thought to be a container for wine. *Pl.47
*Pl.48; Pl.49

WHITE PORCELAIN

If celadon with its grace and colour seems to symbolize the taste of the aristocratic Buddhist society of Koryŏ—per-haps a somewhat feminine beauty tinged with sentiment—

Pl. 46 Wine flask. Punch'ŏng ware, celadon glaze, incised decoration, background cut away and painted with iron oxide combined
with ash which looks deep green under the glaze. From a kiln probably located in Muan district. H. 3¹/₂ in., D. 9 in. Yi dynasty, 15th
century. Tŏksu Palace Museum of Fine Arts, Seoul.

Pl. 47 *Wine bottle. Punch'ŏng ware, decorated with white slip applied with a broad brush and painted in underglaze iron. H. 1 ft. ⅜ in., D. 6⅜ in. Yi dynasty, 15th/16th century. Coll. Hong-keun Yi, Seoul. (For detail see p. 11.)*

the later white porcelain may equally well be thought of as symbolic of the scholarly, bureaucratic, Confucian society of Yi: vigorous, orderly, and essentially masculine in tone. Certainly it was white porcelain which was invariably preferred by the court and the upper classes and which was best suited for use in official ceremonies, always strongly oriented along Confucianist lines. According to the *Yongjae Ch'onghwa*, white porcelain was much the favourite ware in the court of the famed King Se-jong (1419–1450), inventor of the Korean alphabet and progenitor of the new Korean culture, and also in Prince Kwanghae's (1609–1622) court. The role of *punch'ŏng* was more to serve the purposes of the conservative elements among the aristocracy and the daily requirements of the common people.

According to a record surviving from the reign of Sejong, in the whole of Korea at the time 185 kilns were engaged in the manufacture of *punch'ŏng* while 136 produced white porcelain. Of the latter, the government-operated kilns of Kwangju were responsible for the finest of all the white wares which even became widely enough known to attract the interest of the Ming Emperor. In 1424 he expressed a desire to be presented with porcelain from Kwangju. Obligingly, the Korean court made him a present of sufficient services to supply ten tables, in total, some two hundred pieces of varying shapes. It is noteworthy that Korean porcelain should have been found so pleasing even in high places in Ming China, the home of blue-and-white porcelain manufacture. No doubt Chinese influence on the Korean potter was strong; the beginnings of the Yi dynasty coincided with the early Ming period in China, a time when Chinese blue-and-white porcelain had

*Pl. 48   Food jar.   Punch'ŏng ware, decorated with white slip ap-
plied with a broad brush and painted in underglaze iron. From a kiln
located at Keryong-san, Ch'ungch'ŏng Namdo. H. 6³/₁₆ in., D. 2⁵/₈
in. Yi dynasty, late 14th/early 15th century. National Museum of
Korea, Seoul.*

reached an unparalleled state of perfection, to which the Korean craftsman was naturally sensitive. The incident of the official gift must have been exceedingly gratifying to the Yi potters.

The preponderance of Yi white porcelain was undecorated, principally because 'Mohammedan blue', the cobalt required in the manufacture of blue-and-white porcelain, was so precious and obtainable only as an import from China. Even though friendly relations existed between the two countries, the export of cobalt from China could not always be counted on, since China herself was forced to import the raw material from western Asia. One can easily understand the statement in the *Kyŏngguk Taejŏn*, therefore, to the effect that the common people of Korea were not permitted to use blue-and-white porcelain. This explains the large quantity of *punch'ŏng* made for the masses in the early part of the dynasty. The high cost of cobalt and the difficulty of obtaining it also helps to explain why blue was used so sparingly on the white porcelain of early Yi. When used at all, it was with a thin and almost dry brush for the grass, flower, insect and bird designs which decorate only a limited surface area of each vessel.

Again from the *Yongjae Ch'onghwa*: 'During the reign of King Sejo (1445–1468) different kinds of painted ceramics were used for miscellaneous purposes. Mohammedan blue was brought from China to paint *tsun*, *lei*, cups and drinking bowls. The wares thus produced were not different from Chinese wares. But Mohammedan blue was precious, and even in China not to be found in great quantity. Thus the government discussed [the matter of] how it came about that even in poor families in remote villages of China everyone used painted vessels; how could

Pl. XV Food jar. Cream-coloured porcelain, painted in underglaze iron. H. 1 ft., D., at base, 6¹/₂ in. Yi dynasty, 17th/18th century. National Museum of Korea, Seoul.

they be painted with Mohammedan blue? There must be something else to paint with. They inquired in China and received the reply that it was, indeed, native cobalt. But this native cobalt could not be easily obtained either. That is why there are so few painted wares in our country.'

In 1464 it was reported that the much coveted cobalt had at last been found within the Korean peninsula, but either the quality was poor or the quantity insufficient, for few examples remain to us painted with the native material, at least from the earlier period. It was only towards the later years of the dynasty that blue came to be commonly used, the surfaces of some large pieces being entirely covered with it. This was probably the result of an increase in the supply available from China, with a consequent lowering of the price of cobalt. In the years after 1883 when the government-operated kilns of Kwangju had fallen into private hands, it was cobalt imported from the western world which met the demands of the ceramic industry. With this change, the charm of traditional cobalt painting was lost for ever.

The Kwangju kilns deserve special attention. Scattered over an immense area of some eighty by twelve kilometres, more than sixty separate kiln sites are still identifiable within the Kwangju region. All these kilns were constructed near the confluence of the Han River and its tributary, the Kyŏng-an-ch'ŏn, nearly twenty-five miles from Seoul. Water transport was an important consideration in order that the fragile porcelain might travel by boat, obviating much of the risk entailed in overland transportation. An equally important consideration in choosing a kiln site was the availability of firewood in sufficient quantity and, if possible, of good clay as well.

Enormous quantities of wood were required by these kilns, and as a particular source became depleted, the kiln was moved to where a good supply still existed, a process repeated constantly over the centuries. Still today in the Kwangju district, thousands and thousands of shards attest to the huge quantities of porcelain made in the region, all of them important for the study of Yi ceramics. Among other things the study of them shows that some Koryŏ celadon types and *punch'ŏng* were also made in the area.

The name of the village in which the largest of the Kwangju kilns was situated is Punwŏn, a place-name familiar as the centre of manufacture for the finest of all Yi white wares. Punwŏn literally means 'Branch of the *sa'ong'wŏn*', the local headquarters of the Office of Ceramic Administration. No trace of the original Punwŏn kilns themselves remains.

White porcelain has a wide tonal range including greyish white, milky white and bluish white as well as 'pure' white. For the ceramic connoisseur, each shade has its own charm, depending upon its fitness to the form of the particular vessel. The large undecorated porcelain food jars of greyish white or milky white owe their grandeur and impressive dignity to their 'colour' as well as their form. The Koreans seem to have a special predilection for white and a heightened sensitivity to it, and have developed a special taste for its various tones. They are particularly partial to white clothing, and indeed are frequently referred to as 'the people of the white clothes'.

Whether the white porcelains of Yi were intended for ceremonial use or for more mundane purposes, they are always essentially simple in form. Upright, sturdy and even rigid, they have a character quite unlike the cur-

vilinear, feminine grace of Koryŏ celadons. For their makers, the exigencies of practical usage superseded any possible considerations of elegance. It is precisely the simplicity and lack of pretension inherent in Yi white wares which has attracted the ceramic lover in all parts of the world.

Plain White Porcelain.—Throughout the dynasty from beginning to end, the plain or undecorated ware was, as we have seen, the predominant type of white porcelain. Except for a short period in the earliest years of the dynasty when *punch'ŏng* too was used in important Confucian ceremonies, white was the only ware associated with such rites.

Korea is rich in clay suitable for white porcelain manufacture, and that used in Yi times is said to have come

from deposits in Kwangju, Yanggu, Chinju and Konyang, each site producing the raw material in quantity, although somewhat different in composition from site to site. Apart from the principal kilns at Kwangju, plain white wares were also made in provincial areas such as Yanggu in Kangwŏn province, Kimhae, Hadong and Namwŏn in Kyŏngsang province, and Koksŏng in Chŏlla province.

According to our own study of the kiln sites of the Kwangju district, Usani in T'oech'on-myŏn on the right bank of the Kyŏng-an-ch'ŏn (one of the many tributaries of the Han River), was the first centre of manufacture for the undecorated white porcelains and blue-and-white wares. Gradually, the focus of the industry moved towards Ch'owol-myŏn and Tochŏk-myŏn, the latter being especially well-known as a source of fine clay. It was at Tochŏk-myŏn that many of the excellent white ceremonial wares for court use were produced in the middle years of the dynasty. A kiln in Tomari village in the Ch'owol-myŏn area on the left bank of the Kyŏng-an-ch'ŏn seems to have made use of clays from various parts of Korea; fine ceramics both plain white and blue-and-white were produced there in the 1530's. The major centre of ceramic activity in the later years of the dynasty, so far as the plain white wares are concerned, was Kŭmsari, close to the Han River, where blue-and-white porcelain was also made. From Kŭmsari the kilns were moved once again to what is known today as Punwŏn, the location of the final and most important government kiln.

A few specimens have been selected to illustrate undecorated white porcelain here. The first, a large food jar, is outstanding both on account of its monumental size and the remarkable dignity of its formal simplicity. Another

bowl is unusual in that it bears a surface decoration remi- Cat. 67 niscent of Chinese bronze design; the tone is bluish, the original use probably ceremonial.

Blue-and-White Porcelain.—White porcelain with designs painted in cobalt under the glaze is known in Korea as *ch'ŏnghwa paekcha* or *ch'ŏnghwa sagi*, *ch'ŏnghwa* meaning 'blue painted', *paekcha* 'white porcelain', and *sagi* simply 'ware'. According to the short passage from the *Yongjae Ch'onghwa* quoted above, it would appear that the type was first made in Korea about the time of King Sejo or shortly afterwards. Although undecorated white porcelain was made in a number of places, the production of blue-and-white seems to have been restricted to a smaller number of kilns. We have already noted that its use was forbidden to the common people; sometimes, however, the upper classes were permitted to use it, but only for such special purposes as the serving of wine, an occasion which every Korean gentleman considers to require ceramic vessels of the finest possible quality. Generally speaking, the porcelains used by the scholar-officials of the upper class are distinguished by the potter's free employment of his creative talents, in contrast to the greater severity of those vessels made for court use for which strict court-promulgated regulations had to be obeyed.

Most of the finest blue-and-white porcelain was also made in the government-operated kilns of the Kwangju district. Ch'ŏngsong in Kyŏngsang Pukdo province was the only kiln outside Kwangju to have been engaged in the manufacture of outstanding examples of the type. Less *Pl. 50 distinguished wares were produced in a variety of local kilns, such as those at Hich'ŏn (P'yŏngan Pukdo), Yŏng-

Pl.XVI   Food jar.   Greyish porcelain, painted in underglaze iron, dragon designs. H. 1 ft. 2¼ in., D. 1 ft. 2¾ in. Yi dynasty, 17th/ 18th century. Tŏksu Palace Museum of Fine Arts, Seoul.

hŭng (Hamkyŏng Namdo), Sŏngch'ŏn (P'yŏngan Namdo) and Koch'ang (Chŏlla Pukdo); their forms are, generally speaking, clumsy, the painting poor in quality, and the blue colour so inferior as sometimes to take on a dark greenish tinge, no doubt the result of employing impure local cobalt. The output of these provincial kilns is not to be compared in quality with the production of Punwŏn.

Many of the blue-and-white wares—jars, wine bottles, flat dishes, water-pouring vessels, and bowls with or without cover—were intended for everyday use in the preparation and serving of food. A special category, however, consists of water containers, brush washers, brush stands and other utensils, all indispensable to the scholar's desk. Made in wide variety, these latter are vivid documents of the sophisticated taste of this section of Yi society.

Themes for the decoration of blue-and-white porcelain are rich and diverse: animals, insects, fish, the so-called 'four gentlemen' (plum blossom, orchid, chrysanthemum and bamboo), flowers, wild grasses, and, of course, landscape. The 'ten longevities' of old Korean folklore (moon, sun, mountain, cloud, pine tree, water, bamboo, crane, deer, and miraculous plants) also provide the elements for decorative designs, but seldom appear all on one vessel. A typically abbreviated design consists of a deer with miraculous plants (guaranteeing immortality) shown beneath a pine tree, the moon and sun painted overhead and water running at the bottom of the design. On occasion the painting is of such high order that it is impossible to regard it as the work of a simple potter. In fact noted painters were frequently dispatched to Punwŏn by the Office of Art to decorate white porcelain for court use.

A vase is especially outstanding, with unusually bold Pl. xiv and spontaneous strokes. It shows a youth fishing in a stream, two ducks, orchids and rocks.

An unusually large wine bottle, pride of the National Pl. 51 Museum, has a dignified shape and a fine painting of peach blossom. The probable date is seventeenth or eighteenth century. A bowl has fine quality and the painting of flow- Pl. 52 ers and butterflies is certainly professional.

There are given in the Catalogue many more fine pieces Cat. 73–84 of blue-and-white wares.

Underglaze Iron Decoration.—A considerable group of Yi porcelain is decorated with designs painted in underglaze ★Cat. 72, 73, 74 iron, a material known as *ch'ŏlsa* or *sŏkkanju*, a reddish clay containing a high proportion of ferrous oxide. Vessels decorated with this material have usually been fired in an oxidizing atmosphere.

The use of *ch'ŏlsa* may be traced back to the early years of the dynasty. Two different methods can be distinguished. One consists of using *ch'ŏlsa* as a filler in designs which have first been incised into the body of the pot—a variant, in other words, of inlay technique but with the difference that the incised parts are usually depressed, unlike those on inlaid celadon or even on *punch'ŏng*.

The other and more usual technique is to paint in *ch'ŏlsa* directly onto the untreated surface of the vessel, in the tradition of painted Koryŏ. It is an obvious substitute for the use of cobalt blue. Blue was in such short supply that in 1754 (the twenty-ninth year of King Yŏngjo's reign) the government decreed that cobalt might not be used except for 'dragon *tsun*' (an important type of ceremonial vase), *ch'ŏlsa* or copper to be employed instead.

The decree is said to have been effective until 1803, the third year of King Sunjo's reign, but vessels of dragon *tsun* shape, decorated with both *ch'ŏlsa* and cobalt, survive from the period of this proscription.

A great many fine white porcelains with *ch'ŏlsa* designs under the glaze have come to us from the Kwangju district, again often the work of professional artists dispatched to the kiln by the Office of Arts. Some good examples of the type were also produced in provincial kilns, such as those of Mokch'ŏn and Koe-san (Ch'ungch'ŏng Namdo), Sŏngch'ŏn (P'yŏngan Pukdo), and Pong-san and Haeju (Hwanghae-do). The most remarkable of all the *ch'ŏlsa* wares, however, are the products of Keryong-san in Ch'ungch'ŏng Namdo. They have designs consisting of ★Cat. 87 fish or grass patterns, which seem to have been the work of Buddhist monks.

Large sized *ch'ŏlsa*-painted vessels such as tall jars, bottles, and even bowls are frequently encountered, flat dishes almost never. Earlier examples have a warm, egg-white tonality; the majority of the later examples are either greyish or bluish white in tone.

Pl. 53   We illustrate here one of the white porcelains with underglaze iron decoration. The jar is grey-bluish white in tone and is incised and inlaid, in the first method of *ch'ŏlsa* decoration mentioned above. It is one of the earliest examples of grey-white porcelain, and can be dated as early as the fifteenth century.

Pl. xv;   Another jar is probably the most beautiful one of this ★Cat. 88, 89 category. The body is decorated with grapes and leaves and a small monkey swinging on a vine. It is probably of the seventeenth or eighteenth century.

Pl. xvi   One jar has a wide mouth and was probably used as a food container. The body is decorated with a very abstract pattern of a dragon and clouds painted in underglaze iron. The chemical action of the iron appears to eat into the glaze.

Underglaze Copper Decoration.—Ceramics decorated in underglaze copper are known in Korean as *chuchŏm sagi* or *chinhong sagi*, literally meaning 'red-painted porcelain'. The 'copper' is, in reality, a malachite containing copper oxide, an ingredient most difficult to handle successfully. It is extremely susceptible to atmospheric variations within the kiln, and seldom produced the red colour desired by the Yi potter. Unless fired in a reducing atmosphere, the malachite had a tendency to become green. Some vessels survive on which designs have been drawn in both copper and cobalt.

Copper oxide had been used in Koryŏ times; it would be only natural therefore to assume that the technique must also have been in use in early Yi. The surviving examples, however, all seem to be of much later date; nor can they compare in quantity either with the wares decorated in underglaze iron or with the blue-and-whites. The type usually consists of bottles and jars, flat dishes—as in the case of *ch'ŏlsa* painting—being most exceptional. Again it is to Kwangju that one must look for the provenance of the majority of the type; some, however, are known to have been made in Yŏnghung, Hamkyŏng Namdo.

We include two more jars of this type in the Catalogue.

PART III
BUDDHIST
SCULPTURE

THE THREE KINGDOMS PERIOD

The Koreans apparently produced no sculpture before the fourth century A.D., and when Buddhism first came to Koguryŏ in 372, they evidently found some difficulty in producing the images prescribed by the Buddhist tradition. There were at least three Buddhist temples in Korea during the last decades of the fourth century: according to the *Samguk Sagi* (History of the Three Kingdoms), King Sosurim (d. 383) of Koguryŏ had two temples built at P'yŏngyang in 375, and ten years later Paekche built a temple at Han-san, south of the Han River. These earliest temples were built for the visiting missionaries who had come from China a few years before.

The exact nature of the Buddhist images installed on the altars of these first temples cannot now be known, but any figures other than small statuettes must have been made locally of either clay or wood. No large-sized Buddhas from this period are extant today, but a small bronze statuette, probably brought into Korea by foreign missionaries, has recently been discovered in the eastern outskirts of Seoul. It is a seated bronze Buddha of the type made in north-western China around 400[1]. The Buddha, in the *dhyāna mudrā*, is seated on a solid square throne with two lions depicted in relief on its front panel. The drapery folds are rendered by symmetrical U-shapes executed in the simple manner of the famous seated bronze Buddha dated 338 in the Brundage Collection. This tiny Buddha from Seoul, only two inches high, is the earliest evidence of Buddhist practice in Korea, and it is certainly one of the early Chinese models used as a basis for Korean Buddhist sculpture.

Pl. 55 Bodhisattva. Gilt bronze. From Puyŏ, south Korea. H. 4¹/₂ in. Paekche dynasty, ca. second half of 6th century. National Museum of Korea, Seoul. (For detail see p. 14.)

However, the earliest Buddhist images made by Koreans and preserved today, date from the first half of the sixth century. They are small altar pieces made of bronze, clay or, rarely, stone. A Śākyamuni from Ŭiryŏng, south-east Korea, nearly seven inches high, is the earliest dated Koguryŏ Buddha in existence. This gilt bronze Buddha Pl. XVII with a large boat-shaped mandorla is a solid piece made in a single casting. The upper part of the mandorla is almost severed, but the statue preserves its pale-gold gilding in perfect condition. It was apparently cast in north-west Korea but was discovered, in 1963, in a gravel pit near Ŭiryŏng, south-east Korea, by a woman of the village. The identity of the image is clearly indicated by an inscription of forty-seven characters incised on the back of the mandorla. A translation of the inscription reads as Fig. 1 follows:

'In the seventh year of Yŏn-ga [Yien-chia], the year of Kimi [Chi-wei], the head priest of the East Nangnang [Lo-lang] Temple of the Kingdom of Koguryŏ wishes to cast and distribute one thousand Buddhas, of which this is the twenty-ninth.'

'Yŏn-ga' seems to be a lost *nien hao* of Koguryŏ and its seventh year may be 479, 539 or 599. As is shown later, 539 seems most likely. The head of the Buddha is crowned by a tall *uṣṇīṣa* and the snail-curls of the hair are depicted by simply incised lattice-like patterns. The face is slender and oval with a hint of a smile around the mouth. The monastic robe covering both shoulders falls at the front in ripple-like ridged folds arranged slightly off-centre so that the side-hem of the robe can be hung over the left arm. The lower hems of the *sanghāti*-skirt project sideways like fins pointing downward. The body below the

neck-line is completely covered by the heavy voluminous garment, except the feet and hands, which are in the *abhaya* and *vara mudrās*.

The mandorla is filled with an incised flame-motif and an inner frame of volutes surrounds the Buddha. The incised lines are broken and timid, matching the poor workmanship demonstrated in the execution of the hair, hands and feet.

Despite these shortcomings in technique, the entire statue faithfully follows Northern Wei (430–534)[2] sculpture in iconography and style. Reference should be made to such Wei sculptures as the standing Buddha in the Berenson Collection, dated 529[3]. It is obvious that the monks of the East Temple in Nangnang (P'yŏngyang) used a Northern Wei Buddha of this type as their model. Of the possible dates corresponding to the year *chi-wei* for the statue, 479 is too early for the style and 599 seems too late, making 539 the most probable date.

Both Korean and Japanese scholars have always tended to assume that there must have been a considerable time lag between a Chinese original and its Korean version. Such a time lag, particularly in the case of local schools away from the capital, may have existed, but it need not be regarded as a universal principle to be applied to all cases, for traffic between north-west Korea and north-east China at that time was frequent and speedy. It was certainly possible for a freshly made Chinese Buddhist image to reach Koguryŏ and be used as a model by a Korean craftsman within a very few years.

A gilt bronze Trinity in the Hyung-pil Chun Collection is basically similar to the *yŏn-ga* Buddha. It has an overall height of seven inches and carries a seventeen-character

inscription on the back of the mandorla which includes the cyclic term *kye-mi (kuei-wei)*. Unlike the *yŏn-ga* Buddha, the main Buddha is separate from the mandorla, ★Cat. 91 and the tiny pedestal, shaped like an inverted cone, is inserted into the sunken crown of a tall, hat-like lotus pedestal. The two attendants, however, are not separable from the mandorla. Further differences from the *yŏn-ga* Buddha can be seen in such details as the floral scroll on the mandorla, and the composite lotus petals around the pedestal. Nevertheless, the triangular outline of the main Buddha produced by the fin-like skirt hems, the peculiar arrangement of the drapery in the front, and the smiling face bent forward, are all akin to the *yŏn-ga* image. The composite lotus-pedestal of the *kye-mi* Buddha is more developed, but it is generically similar to the hat-like pedestal of the *yŏn-ga* statue. An obvious advance in workmanship is demonstrated in the fluent lines of the flame designs as well as the masterly execution of the floral scroll round the head. The rigidity, the dynamic linear rhythm radiating from deep-cut folds with steep planes, and the immature crudeness of the sculptural details in the earlier work have now given way to a smooth, fluent handling of the material and improved confidence in execution.

The provenance of this Trinity is unknown and the inscription does not mention the place of casting. Judging from the close adherence, particularly in the facial type, to Chinese sculpture, it seems likely to have come from Koguryŏ[4]. The year *kye-mi (kuei-wei)* again produces several dates, but it is most likely to correspond to 563, which would be some twenty years later than the *yŏn-ga* Buddha[5].

Cat.92   A similar Trinity, but without the lotus pedestal, is in the collection of T.H.Kim, Seoul. It was discovered in 1930 at Kok-san, in north-west Korea, within the former territory of Koguryŏ. Sixty-seven characters in eight columns including the cyclical term *sin-myo (shen-mao)* are

incised on the back of the detachable mandorla. The inscription may be translated as follows:

'In the fourth year of Kyŏng[?], the year of Shen-mao, Priest To[?] and four other donors dedicate this Amitābha Buddha in the hope that our dead parents may be always with the Buddha and our colleagues may meet the Maitreya Buddha. Thus we pray that all may be reborn in Paradise to meet the Buddha and hear his preaching.'

The general features of the Trinity are basically similar to Mr. Chun's *kye-mi* Trinity so far as concerns the general pattern of drapery folds, the boat-shaped mandorla with an inner scroll of honeysuckle design, and the narrow pedestal originally intended to be inserted in a lotus pedestal which has been lost. Nevertheless, there are certain differences in detail, notably the head, which is no longer bent forward as in the *kye-mi* Buddha but held erect. The face is full and round, and the archaic smile has faded away from the fleshy cheeks. The body is slender, enveloped in a langourously falling garment. The linear angularity of the two previous Buddhas is completely gone. Instead, soft folds of drapery end in an inverted *omega*- or M-like form, a type to be observed in Chinese sculptures of the second half of the sixth century.

In mainland China, a new style was evolving about the middle of the sixth century, apparently under the influence of Gupta period India. The face of the Buddha during the latter half of the century becomes round and full, losing the characteristic archaic smile. Single statuettes of Amitābha, the Buddha of the Pure Land, became more and more popular among the people[6]. The heavy flared garment of the previous period gave way to a loosely clinging robe with increasingly schematized drapery, yet with an interesting suggestion of the form of the body underneath.

Our *sin-myo (shen-mao)* Buddha reflects the new trend in all these details and the year *shen-mao* in this case probably corresponds to the year 571. The next *shen-mao*, 631, seems to be too late, if we are to judge by the frequent visits of Korean monks and embassies to the metropolis of China during the latter part of the sixth century[7]. These visits gave plentiful opportunities for importing freshly-made Chinese Buddhist images.

By the mid-sixth century Korean craftsmen had fully acquired the art of religious sculpture and it was now their turn, in 552, to introduce Buddhism and Buddhist iconology to Japan[8]. Japanese sculptures made before about 600 display distinctively Korean features and seem to have been produced either by Korean emigrants or by native artists under Korean supervision.

The new type of Buddha with a mellow, round face like that of the *shen-mao* Trinity is further illustrated by a group of terra-cotta statuettes from a temple site at Cat. 95 Wŏno-ri near P'yŏngyang, the former capital of the Koguryŏ dynasty[9]. These seated Buddhas and standing Bodhisattvas, seven to eight inches in height, now mostly broken, are clay figures of which the front half is shaped by moulds, the rear half of each figure being finished with a sculptor's knife. There are surface traces of the white and red pigment which was applied after the firing. Both Buddhas and Bodhisattvas have a round, boyish face like the *shen-mao* Trinity. The Buddha is seated on a bulging-petal lotus throne which resembles that of the *yŏn-ga* Buddha already described. His hands are clasped horizontally in

Pl. 58 Maitreya. Gilt bronze. H. 3³/₈ in. Three Kingdoms period, ca. second half of 6th century. Tŏksu Palace Museum of Fine Arts, Seoul.

Pl. 59 Maitreya (without head). Granite. From Kyŏngju, south Korea. H. 4 ft. 1¹/₄ in. Old Silla dynasty, ca. second half of 6th century. Kyŏngju Branch of the National Museum of Korea.

front of his body, and the drapery is executed in an archaic style characterized by a simple, symmetrical arrangement. The drapery of the Bodhisattvas, however, is clearly in line with Northern Wei sculptures of the early sixth century, with their X-shaped scarves and the zig-zag lower hems of their closely pleated skirts. The scalloped neck-line is also a replica of a Wei model.

The Buddhas certainly possess earlier features than the Bodhisattvas, but both groups are fundamentally similar in pattern and they are well matched stylistically. The two types must have been made to form Trinities, and there is a uniform style among the Buddhas as among the Bodhisattvas. This would suggest that the two types are contemporary and should not be separated in date. We may date them to a period roughly around the middle of the sixth century[10]. The Koreanization of the facial type by the mid-sixth century is an important phenomenon, and one that hereafter serves to differentiate a Korean Buddha from a Chinese one.

An isolated gilt bronze Bodhisattva in the Tŏksu Palace Museum of Fine Arts, Seoul, manifests the same trend, faithfully copied after a Chinese original. The original place of discovery of this Bodhisattva is not known, but the facial type, as well as the forceful clear-cut planes and lines, seem to belong to the tradition of Koguryŏ sculpture. If we compare this Bodhisattva with one from Paekche, the difference is apparent. Judging from the somewhat schematic treatment of the side-hems and other drapery, the date should be few decades later than the Wŏno-ri clay statuettes.

As has already been discussed, the sculpture of Koguryŏ is marked by a tendency to adhere to the style of the Northern Wei dynasty. Sculptural activity in Koguryŏ seems to have flourished during the sixth century, if we may judge by the number of examples we have today. During the same century, many Buddhist images were made in southern Korea as well as in the north, but the southern images were stylistically almost independent of the northern products, although they, too, stemmed from Chinese sculptures.

A small, four and a half inches high, gilt bronze Bodhisattva in the National Museum of Korea is an outstanding piece of Paekche sculpture representing what may be called the South-western School. This statuette was discovered in 1936 at a temple-site in Kunsu-ri, near Puyŏ, the last capital of Paekche. The front only is cast in relief, and seems to have been detached from an altar piece or a Trinity. The fin-like projection of the hems, the criss-crossing scarves in the front and the scalloped necklet are all familiar features of Chinese sculpture in the sixth century. Compared, however, with contemporary sculptures from north Korea, differences can be noticed in such details as the rounder face and the more subdued and softer fabric of the robe with incised lines to depict the draping. Incised folds and the M-like form of the lower hems are features that appear in Chinese sculpture during the second half of the sixth century. The outstanding characteristic of this Bodhisattva is the face, which is very naïve and human with a quiet peaceful smile. This smile is different from the archaic religious smile we are familiar with in the earlier series of Koguryŏ Buddhist images. Ordinary, yet warm and peaceful, it can be observed on many Paekche images, and I have suggested that it might be called the 'Paekche smile'[11].

116

A small soapstone figure of a seated Buddha from the Pl. 56, 57
same Kunsu-ri site also has this characteristic full round face
with the Paekche smile. The Buddha has a small knob-like
uṣṇīṣa, holds both hands in the *dhyāna mudrā* and is seated
on a solid rectangular throne. The monastic robe is pulled
over both shoulders and its lower hem covers the throne in
a cascade, producing schematic and symmetric folds. The
raised neck-opening, probably carrying on the tradition of
the *yŏn-ga* Buddha, and the schematized drapery over the
throne have an analogy in those of the famous Tori Trinity
in the Hōryūji, Japan, dated 623. The drapery folds of the
upper half of our Kunsu-ri Buddha, however, are much
more naturalistically rendered than those of the Tori Trinity, and the composite folds of the lower half are also less
schematized. Above all, there is none of the idealistic,
abstract approach of the solemn Tori Trinity and our stone
Buddha is fully at ease both physically and emotionally.
He is no longer a Buddha of mystic awe but an ordinary
man with an amiable smile, like a father watching his little
son. A great advance on previous Korean sculptures is to be
noted in this stone figure: it is not a flat frontal piece but
fully rounded sculpture. The profile is completely realized
with a natural posture of the head above the slightly stoop-
ing body. The abandonment of the traditional stylization
of the neck into a truncated cone in this figure adds further
to the natural effect. This Buddha is typical of the sculptures
of south-western Korea in the territory of Paekche around
600.

As has already been mentioned in the Introduction,
Paekche had close contacts with the Liang (502–556) and
subsequent dynasties of southern China. There were even
Buddhist sculptors from Liang living in the Paekche cap-

ital[12]. There can be no doubt that Paekche sculpture reflects
strong influences from southern China, although we have
little knowledge of the sculpture of the Liang dynasty itself.

At about the same period, that is from the late sixth to
the early seventh centuries, a series of the Maitreya Bodhisattva in meditating posture was produced by Koreans in
various provinces. The meditating Maitreya depicting
Śākyamuni at the moment of enlightment under the *bodhi*-
tree was increasingly favoured in China during the second
half of the sixth century. The vogue reached Korea, probably by land through Manchuria, some decades later.

Pl. 59   A headless granite statue in the Kyŏngju Museum
may be an earlier example of the newly introduced
Maitreya. This seated figure, made in the territory of Silla,
has lost both its head and its arms, but the modelling of the
body is not crude, and the vertical parallel drapery folds
are very similar to a white marble Maitreya of the Eastern
Wei dynasty dated 544 in the Museum of Calligraphy,
Tokyo. Our Silla piece is more naturalistic in the rendering
of the torso and in the feeling for soft fabric. Silla, particularly Silla of the unified period, was noted for granite sculpture,
and had already set out on the path towards its full glory
by the second half of the sixth century.

Besides the granite figure, there remains a group of
bronze Maitreyas of various sizes all dating from around
600. Except for one from P'yŏng-yang, they are from
unknown localities, and their provenance can only be
judged by stylistic considerations which is a risky process.

Pl. 60   The first is a bronze Maitreya Bodhisattva, two feet,
seven and a half inches high, preserved in perfect condition except for the broken tip of the *stūpa*-shaped ornament on the diadem. According to the National Museum's

file, it was presented in 1912 to the then Governor General of Chōsen by a Japanese resident, only two years after the Japanese annexation of Korea. However, the facial type and the sculptural technique suggest southern production, away from the Chinese-influenced Koguryŏ area in the north. It wears a diadem fastened by a head-band. Two ornamental *stūpas* on the diadem, symbolizing forthcoming Buddhahood, flank a mountain-like ornament in the centre. The face is rather forbidding because of the square jaw and the broad plane of the cheek under the long, arching eyebrows. The oval vertical groove below the tightly closed lips adds further strength to the severity of the expression. The face is definitely Korean and markedly different from any Chinese figures. The body below the neck is pleasingly shaped and modelled. The arms may be a little thin for the body, but the hands are exceptionally graceful and alive. The torso is attenuated out of proportion, but this distortion seems to contribute to the spiritual quality of the figure. The drapery on the legs and around the throne is indicated by single incised lines. This linear presentation of folds is doubtlessly derived from the northern Ch'i sculptures of China. The narrow vertical folds of the Kyŏngju Museum Maitreya discussed above are changed in this figure to a simpler, somewhat schematized arrangement. As a whole, the statue is stately and tranquil, and together with the thin, vertically falling garment, the general manner is well in line with Chinese sculptures of the last few decades of the sixth century. Compared with Chinese Maitreyas, our figure is much more natural in pose, and as an object of devotion would probably more readily captivate worshippers with its spiritual aura. It can be dated around 600 or slightly earlier.

A bronze Maitreya Bodhisattva in the Tŏksu Palace Pl. 61 Museum of Fine Arts, Seoul, is almost unique in its strongly abstract trend. The origin of this statue is also unknown: it was brought to the Museum by a dealer. The marked departure from Chinese models and the stern face on a much distorted body make it difficult to assign it either to Koguryŏ, which had a tendency to adhere to Chinese standards, or to Paekche, characterized by a naturalism and the Paekche smile. Therefore we have to assign the figure to south-eastern Korea, the triangular territory of Silla secluded from foreign influences, which cultivated a strong regional character. To appreciate the nature of this unique figure, we must compare it with the marble Maitreya dated 544 in the Shodō (Calligraphy) Museum, Tokyo. The difference is clear at once. The Korean figure is much elongated above the throne and the emphasis is now placed on the figure itself, not on the accessories. The deliberate omission of folds of drapery over the legs, creating a clean background for the strands of jewellery, the extremely attenuated torso producing a wide space between the arms, and the simplified schematization of the folds of the skirt, all combine to create an awesome spirituality without the distracting and crowded superficial features of the Chinese images. This extreme abstractionism may possibly have been the accidental outcome of copying a Chinese original through a free-hand sketch brought back by travelling monks. Otherwise the tongue-like projection from beneath the right knee of the Bodhisattva is inexplicable. In a Chinese figure, it would be horizontal drapery falling over the right leg. Even so, the artist was a master who had his own style and technique to create an image which is forceful and characteristic. The firmness and stability of the figure, seated on a cylindrical throne over a monumental lotus base, are especially notable. The combination of the square, octagonal and cylindrical parts of the throne is a pattern later carried on by the stone *stūpas* and lanterns of the Unified Silla period.

*Pl. 59

Cat. 93　　Another bronze Maitreya in the same collection shows a similar abstract trend in its approach. The facial expression is much softer and the whole attitude of the body is naturalistic and supple. That the artist attempted to fit the figure into a triangular outline is indicated by the cone-like throne and the torso continuing to taper upward

*Cat. 94　above it. The drapery that covers the triangular throne

Pl. 60　resembles that of the National Museum Maitreya. But the long, slim arms particularly the right arm with the palm turned inward, are almost identical with those of the Tŏksu Museum Maitreya just mentioned. These three Maitreyas may not be far apart in date and they seem to reflect a common origin in a school of sculpture established in or near the capital of Old Silla.

Pl. 62　　A gilt bronze Maitreya in the National Museum Collection may belong to the same cycle of Silla sculpture, but the Maitreya, with a height of six and a half inches, has details markedly different from the others. Most striking is the deeply-bent head with a plaited lock of hair on each side. The head is not touched by the tips of the fingers but rests on the right palm. Such deeply-bowed Maitreyas existed in China during the sixth century, as is shown by a stone Maitreya in the Museum of Fine Arts, Boston, although the radiant smile of the latter has disappeared completely in the Korean piece. The left hand of our figure does not rest on the ankle of the right foot, but on its sole, which is laid flat, pointing upward. The drapery is not arranged symmetrically, and the fabric looks almost like a thick animal hide. An additional circular base to receive the left foot is attached to the main throne, but the basic form of the throne resembles that of the Maitreya (now headless) in the Kyŏngju Museum. In the Kyŏngju Maitreya, however, a small lotus-bud projects from the circular two-tiered throne. The total lack of lotus petals in the National Museum's bronze figure is most unusual.

The linear stiffness in the rendering of the drapery and the solemn melancholy face exemplify the chief characteristics of the sixth-century sculptures of Old Silla.

A gilt bronze Maitreya in the collection of Mr. T. H. Kim, Seoul, is particularly interesting because its background is known. This statuette, seven inches high, was discovered in 1940 at a temple site at P'yŏngch'ŏn-ri, P'yŏngyang, north Korea. According to the owner's testimony, a separate mandorla was later discovered at the same spot and went into the collection of the P'yŏngyang Museum[13]. The face is full and round with a youthful boyish appearance. The earlobes are long and reach almost to the shoulders, and three horizontal creases appear around the neck for the first time in Korean sculpture. As pointed out by Willetts, such creases are a characteristic of Chinese Buddhist images of the Second Phase, *i.e.*, the latter half of the sixth century[14]. The arms are slender, like those of a young girl, but they are not thin. The right forearm, which must have been lifted toward the right cheek, is broken and lost. Compared with the full, round face and the beautifully proportioned arms, the upper half of the body is thin and attenuated, a tendency common to south Korean Maitreyas of the period. The legs are well proportioned under a rather heavy thick garment, but the artist

was unable to reproduce the correct anatomy of the right foot with its sole turned upward. If we compare this foot with a Chinese original such as the Boston Maitreya, the difference in technique is at once evident. Korean artists either regarded feet as unimportant trifles, or they could not shape them properly. Whatever the reason, this flat foot, resembling nothing more than a broken paddle, is the chief shortcoming of the figure. The horizontally projecting hem immediately beneath the right leg is somewhat out of place, but it is an improvement on the cushion-like shape on the 'abstract' Maitreya in the Tŏksu Palace Pl.61 Museum.

If we compare this P'yŏngyang figure with an early seventh-century bronze Maitreya from Japan in the collection of the Cleveland Museum of Art, the differences are clear. The elaborate workmanship of the Japanese figure, shown in the execution of such details as the drapery and jewellery, is in strong contrast to the simplification of, and even disregard for, details in the Koguryŏ figure. Nevertheless, the Korean Maitreya has considerable naturalness and ease in its posture, as opposed to the ill-proportioned, stiff restraint of the figure in the Cleveland Museum. The difference in the approach to sculpture of the two nations is clearly demonstrated. Japan during the seventh century had established a sculptural style that was distinctly her own, despite earlier strong influences from Korea.

The final piece for our attention from this period is a superb gilt bronze Maitreya in the collection of the Tŏksu Pl.XVIII, XIX Palace Museum. It has a height of three feet one inch, five and a quarter inches higher than the similar figure in the Pl.60 National Museum. The three-lobed flower-like diadem is

Pl. 64 a and b   Bodhisattva (Avalokiteśvara?).   Gilt bronze. H.
4¹⁵/₁₆ in. Three Kingdoms period, ca. first half of 7th century. Tŏksu
Palace Museum of Fine Arts, Seoul.

similar to that of the P'yŏngyang Maitreya just described. The face is round, almost entirely without modelling. The oblique eyes are sharply cut and the eyebrows curve in long clean arcs. The nose is equally clean-cut with a sharp ridge. Under the nose, the upper lip projects a little, but the mouth is as innocent as that of a child, with a gently receding chin. The earlobes now have elongated perforations, a feature to be seen only in Korean Buddhas and early Japanese figures made under Korean influence. The perforation of the earlobes probably reflects the custom, popular in Silla, of wearing large gold earrings; this custom is well attested by the discovery of gold earrings in every excavated tomb of the Old Silla period. The body above the waist is completely naked, save for a simple necklace. The neck is also marked by three horizontal creases. The arms are delicately modelled, and the sensuous forearms and the gesture of the hands are particularly graceful and feminine. Such physical features give the unavoidable impression of a portrait of a young girl, especially when viewed in profile. Notice the slight swelling in the chest, the beautiful curve of the knees, and the animated movement of the toes. The drapery is equally animated in a realistic pattern covering the circular stool. A jade *p'i* disc hangs tied to the end of the belt.

The artist was deeply interested in the beauty of human anatomy, and he elevated this visual beauty to something of a spiritual quality. The almost perfect proportion of the figure, the realistic modelling of the body, the rendering of complicated drapery and, above all, the naturalness of the posture, all suggest that the artist worked from a living model. Such naturalism is basically foreign to Silla sculpture, and there is no north Korean sturdiness in the figure.

This seated Maitreya may thus be related to the South-western School of Korea within the territory of Paekche.

The Korean idea of giving a womanly appearance to Maitreya Bodhisattvas must have evolved out of the Chinese interest in plasticity which arose during the latter half of the sixth century and in turn received a strong influence from Indian sculpture of the Gupta period (320 to 600)[15]. The concept of the benevolence of the Bodhisattva and the feeling of closeness and friendliness towards it in the hearts of Korean Buddhists must also have had their effect in the production of such a graceful statue.

This Maitreya is often compared with a wooden counterpart in the Kōryūji temple in Kyōto, known as the Kōkan Miroku (Maitreya with a high crown). The pair are certainly identical in many features, and the Miroku is made of pine, unlike other wooden sculptures of the Asuka period which are made of camphor wood. The pine-wood Miroku is said to have been given to the founder of the Kōryūji temple by Prince Shōtoku in 603. It was probably an import from Korea or the product of a Korean emigrant[16].

Our bronze Maitreya is also often compared with a wooden seated Maitreya Bodhisattva in the Chūgūji temple, Nara, which is called the Chūgūji Nyoirin Kwannon. The Nyoirin Kwannon, however, shows a marked conventionalization in drapery, and the usual solemn grimness of a Japanese figure. There must have been a time lag between this and any Korean original, if indeed the Nyoirin was a copy.

A small piece, but one of the best produced by Silla artists around that time, is a bronze head of a Bodhisattva Pl. 63 originally from a temple site in Kyŏngju. The serene,

127

Pl. XIX   Detail of Pl. XVIII.

beautiful face with a hint of a smile shows the degree of progress made by Silla sculptors during the last half of the sixth century.

We must now turn to a group of standing Buddhas and Bodhisattvas in bronze and stone preserved from the first half of the seventh century.

A standing bronze Bodhisattva in the collection of the late Mr. H. P. Chun, Seoul, is of particular interest. This statue, little over seven inches high, was reported to have come from a small temple site near Kŏch'ang in south-central Korea on the eastern slope of the Sobaek-san range. These high mountains separated Silla from Paekche, and the Koch'ang area lies on the Silla side. This Bodhisattva, holding a jar-like attribute, cannot be exactly identified. His face is quite unusual. The slit horizontal eyes, straight slim nose between prominent cheekbones and the relatively small, tightly closed thin lips, all contribute to an ugly sullen face. Nevertheless the facial type and expression are highly individualized, as though copied from a living model. It is interesting to note that such an oval face with thin lips and slit eyes, exists even today among south-eastern Koreans. The neck is long and powerful without the creases, and it grows out of the chest without a break. The smooth, cylindrical body is tightly covered by a thin robe and two crossing scarves which reach down to the knee-cap. A strand of jewellery is hung around the neck, almost reaching the knees. The flaring scarves on each side are in the tradition of earlier models, but here they are mere strips of cut metal and have become purely decorative ornaments. The plain cylindrical body wrapped in a tight, foldless robe, the enormous bulky neck and particularly the long, X-shaped strand of jewellery point to

strong influences from Sui sculptures of around 600. This Bodhisattva, then, must be a product of Silla during the early decades of the seventh century.

The strict frontality of the Kŏch'ang Bodhisattva is also to be observed in a tiny (five inches) gilt bronze Bodhisattva Pl. 64 in the Tŏksu Palace Museum. Compared with the big square head, the body is slim and flat, completely hidden ★Cat. 96 beneath thick heavy drapery. The conventionalized folds are arranged in strict symmetry and the beaded edges of the garment further accent the already decorative folds. There is a marked difference from the previous bulky, but simplified figure; yet there are common features, such as the horizontally held hands with a jar, and the loosely crossing scarves around the knee-cap. The projecting side-fins are gone, except the two lower ones, which are shaped as in earlier pieces. The figure belongs to the austere, abstractionist school of Old Silla, and the date must be sometime during the first half of the seventh century, but later than the previous Bodhisattva.

A standing Avalokiteśvara in the National Museum dif- Pl. 65 fers from the previous figure in sculptural style and details, but probably also belongs to the first half of the seventh century. The workmanship is rather crude, but it displays an interest in plasticity, indicated by the rounded arms and the thighs under the loosely falling skirt. The face is full and round with a hint of a smile. This smile and the naturalism of the figure suggest a south-western lineage or tradition. Indeed, the Avalokiteśvara was discovered at a temple site in the southern outskirts of Puyŏ, the last capital of the Paekche dynasty. It would appear to be the product of a minor artist living in the capital who probably worked from a Chinese example of the Sui or early T'ang dynasty.

In 1959, a life-size rock-cut Trinity was discovered at Sǒ-san on the west coast, south of Seoul[17]. It is engraved in relief on a natural rock near a mountain stream. The central figure is a standing Śākyamuni over nine feet high. The Buddha stands on a lotus pedestal consisting of flat, simple petals. The broad face of the Buddha has an open smile, with wide open eyes, and the expression has a strong impact because of the naturalistic rendering. His right hand is in the *abhaya mudrā* and the left hand in the *vara mudrā* with its first two fingers extended. The left hand is in the earlier style of sixth-century sculptures. The garment falls in front in a series of loose arcs and the lower hem ends in a conventionalized inverted *omega*-shape. The drapery folds find analogies in such late sixth-century Chinese figures as an Amitābha in the Royal Ontario Museum of Archaeology, Toronto[18]. The flat linear representation of the body, particularly the feet, in contrast to the superb modelling of the head, is a little strange, and the same can be said of the attendants. This careful rendering of the face combined with a carelessly delineated body seems to be a common characteristic of Buddhist sculpture in southern Korea during the first half of the seventh century.

The attendant to the right is a standing Bodhisattva, three feet, six inches high, who seems to be an Avalokiteśvara. This Bodhisattva takes an obviously feminine form, enhanced by the beautiful smiling face. The horizontally held hands hold a box-like attribute. The skirt is pleated into narrow vertical folds which completely conceal the body beneath. A scarf falls in a loose arc above the skirt, but it is no longer crossed in an X. Here again the complete flatness of the lower body contrasts strongly with the plasticity of the smiling face.

The seated Maitreya on the opposite side has a peach-shaped halo identical with that of the standing Bodhisattva. His face is round and boyish with an amused expression. Nothing remains of his right arm but the fingers seem originally to have touched the right cheek as if to push the whole head upward. The raised face recalls Chinese examples of the mid-sixth century. ★Cat. 97

This Trinity, located in the northern territory of Paekche, shows features both old and new, but the most outstanding characteristic is the strong, local colour. The departure from Chinese example is clearly demonstrated by the facial type and expression of the main Buddha, and the way his feet are depicted. Beyond any doubt, when the artist engraved these relief figures on the natural granite, he had in mind Chinese rock sculptures in cave temples. It is not certain whether he had seen Chinese cave temples himself or merely used sketches of them on paper brought back by Silla monks. In any case, he was a master stone carver and so far as we know, his was the first attempt by a Korean to challenge the natural rock.

Some regard this Trinity as a work of around 600[19], but later elements in the sculpture, such as the drapery, lead me to attribute it to the last years of Paekche, *i.e.* around the mid-seventh century. As already mentioned Paekche had had close contacts with the southern dynasties of China. From the seventh century, however, this contact seems to have decreased because of deteriorating relations with Sui and T'ang. This political situation may have resulted in the irregularity of the sculptural style as well as of the iconography of the later sculpture of Paekche. The late lingering of early features in some seventh-century Paekche sculptures can be thus explained.

Pl.67   Amitābha.   Granite. From Kyŏngju area. H. 5 ft. 3³/₄ in.
Old Silla dynasty, ca. mid-7th century. Kyŏngju Branch of the
National Museum of Korea.

Whatever its date, the Sŏ-san Trinity is, for the present, the earliest known rock-cut Buddhist image on Korean soil, and Paekche can claim the primacy in introducing this new type of rock-cut temple into Korea[20]. The Koreans, however, did not develop the new type of temple and there is nothing that can be termed a true cave temple like those of China. The idea of engraving one or two Buddhist images in relief or by line-incision on natural rocks, however, was wide-spread during the Great Silla period and the ensuing Koryŏ dynasty.

Pl.66   Turning to the east, we have a free-standing Amitābha Trinity probably dating from the last years of the Old Silla period[21]. It consists of an Amitābha, larger than life-size, and two attendants, the Avalokiteśvara and the Mahāsthāmaprāpta, standing in an open site at Pae-ri near Kyŏngju. Although they are free-standing statues, carved in the round, the idea is basically the same as that of the rock-cut Amitābha Trinity of Sŏ-san.

The central Buddha, with a height of nine feet, one inch, is carved out of a single block of granite together with its boat-shaped mandorla. The Buddha has a big round face, too big for the short stocky body. The garment clings tightly to the body, suggesting the legs beneath, and the drapery is represented by simple equidistant raised arcs. The plump round face and the short stocky body are also to be observed in the Bodhisattvas, and all of them clearly reflect influences from Sui sculpture. The grim face of preceding years has given way to a rounder type, apparently stimulated by a fresh wave of influences from the Chinese sculptures of the years around 600.

Pl.67, 68   One Amitābha Trinity, originally from Nam-san and now in the Kyŏngju Museum, has the delightful charm

Pl. 68 Bodhisattvas (Avalokiteśvara, right: Mahāsthāmaprāpta). Granite. Attendants for the Buddha in Pl. 67. H. 3 ft. 2⅝ in. Old Silla dynasty, ca. mid-7th century. Kyŏngju Branch of the National Museum of Korea.

Pl. 69 Buddha. Bronze. From Hoeng-sŏng, central Korea. H. 11⅝ in. Three Kingdoms period, ca. mid-7th century. Tŏksu Palace Museum of Fine Arts, Seoul.

of a set of dolls. The main Buddha is squatting with his knees together in front, and this is the first appearance of the *bhadra āsana* in Korea. It was clearly made after the fashion of T'ang sculpture. The big round face on top of the small body resembles that of the standing Amitābha at Pae-ri. The attendants, Avalokiteśvara and Mahāsthā-maprāpta, are equally short and have kind faces and shy smiles. The facial type is derived from China, but they are certainly some of the most attractive faces that Korean sculptors have ever produced. In all three figures, the garments do not cling very tightly to the body and the drapery is somewhat conventionalized. The rotundity and volume of the body, however, are well perceived and the stiff rigidity of the previous century has gone. These figures must be at least a decade or so later than the Pae-ri Trinity, as can be deduced from such features as the elimination of the long strand of jewellery on the Avalokiteśvara.

Amitābha was now replacing the once popular Maitreya Bodhisattva of southern Korea, both in Paekche and Silla. The same change had occurred in China almost a century earlier[22]. There are no examples for studying the situation in the north, in the territory of Koguryŏ, during the first half of the seventh century. Koguryŏ had been in a constant state of war with the Sui and T'ang dynasties, from the time of her attack on the Liao-hsi area in 598 to her collapse in 668. The political situation must have halted Buddhist traffic between Koguryŏ and north China.

The city of Puyŏ, the third and last capital of Paekche, whose culture was characterized by sensitiveness and open-mindedness towards foreign cultures, fell to Silla in 660, and the whole territory was annexed. This change of government, however, had little influence on art. In the former

Pl. 66

territory of Paekche, the south-western style lingered on, at least for some decades.

Four soapstone Buddhist stelae of the post-Paekche period, still in the south-western style, have recently been discovered in Yŏn-gi, to the north-east of Puyŏ. Three of the four were discovered at the small Piam-sa temple near the town of Yŏn-gi in 1960²³. The Piam-sa stelae are all made of local reddish-brown soapstone and measure one foot, eleven inches; one foot, five inches; and one foot, four inches, in height respectively.

The largest one has the shape of a mandorla with a flat bottom and a rounded top. An Amitābha Trinity with surrounding *lohans* and Guardians is depicted on an elevated lotus throne placed on a terrace. A slantwise staircase with handrails leads one upward to the terrace. The remaining three sides of the stele are left plain except for an inscription incised on its back. Some of the characters cannot be read, but enough of the inscription is deciphered to tell that the Amitābha and Bodhisattvas were dedicated on the fifteenth of the second month in the year *chi-ch'ou*. The exact date of *chi-ch'ou* is not certain, but this piece is similar in material and style to a second stele which is datable to 673, and *chi-ch'ou* may correspond to the year 689. Cat. 98

The second stele is a square block with a short foot to be inserted into a base stone. On the framed frontal plane is an Amitābha Trinity surrounded by *arhats* and Guardians, and behind them is a big mandorla decorated with a rinceau of *apsaras* in adoration. On the sides of the stele are eight music-playing *apsaras* arranged in two tiers, while on the back twenty seated Buddhas are depicted in four tiers. All around the lower frame and in the spaces below the figures is an inscription which includes names and Pl. 70, 71

official titles and a cyclical year name, *kuei-yu*. Unlike the much worn *chi-ch'ou* stele described above, this square piece is in good condition, although some of the characters of the inscription and the face of the main Buddha have been obscured. The drapery of the main Buddha is considerably schematized but the fluent lines and forms of the *apsaras* and the plasticity of the faces of the surrounding images clearly carry on the tradition of seventh-century Paekche sculpture. The official titles held by the donors, however, are not those of Paekche. They belong to the Great Silla dynasty. Thus the stele must be regarded as a product of the former territory of Paekche, made not long after the fall of the south-western kingdom. The year *kuei-yu* may accordingly correspond to 673, because 613 would be too early historically and 733 too late for the style of this sculpture.

The third stele is mushroom-shaped, with a Maitreya Pl. 72 Bodhisattva depicted on the front. A standing Bodhisattva is engraved on each side of the stele and a pagoda on the back. The face of the Maitreya seated under a canopy has again been obscured by the passage of time but the sculptural technique is identical with that of the *kuei-yu* stele, and the image must have been made by the same atelier or artist probably at about the same time.

These three stelae and a fourth piece from Yŏn-gi may represent the last examples of the Paekche style, lingering on into the second half of the seventh century.

As we have seen, there are few sculptures extant today which can reliably be attributed to the Three Kingdoms period and many details of the history of sculpture in that period have yet to be studied. But the general trends can be perceived from what we have so far surveyed:

Koguryŏ, in the north was the first to receive and produce Buddhist images, and had from the beginning a strong tendency to adhere to Chinese models, although an obvious Koreanization or individualization is noticeable during the second half of the sixth century. This tendency to copy China must have been due to her close and direct contacts with northern China. Koguryŏ sculpture is generally characterized by a dynamism created by clean lines and planes. A similar tendency can be observed in other fields of Koguryŏ art.

Paekche in the south-west reflects much influence from the dynasties of southern China, particularly the Liang and the Chen. Buddhist images of Paekche are characterized by a naturalistic, relaxed manner and their most distinctive feature is the full, round, friendly face with what the writer terms the Paekche smile. It was the artisans of Paekche who carried this sculptural style to Japan. They also began making rock-cut images earlier than any of their neighbours. The south-western style created by Paekche artists lingered on for more than half a century after the fall of the kingdom in 660.

Silla started later; Buddhism was not permitted as a religion until the second decade of the sixth century. However, Silla soon caught up with her neighbours and produced many Buddhist images, culminating in the successful casting of the now lost colossal bronze Buddha of Hwangyong-sa in 574.

Silla sculpture shows strong local colour with a marked interest in linear, abstract representation. The Buddhist images are usually solemn and sometimes grim, often with faces of great individuality. Silla people were very conservative and nationalistic, probably due to their geographical seclusion. Influences from China only reached the country through either Koguryŏ or Paekche until, towards the latter part of the sixth century, Silla established direct communications with China by sea. Silla sculptures may sometimes be technically inferior, but they established a type of sculpture distinctly their own.

The sculpture of the Three Kingdoms (from about 500 to 650) as it is preserved today generally shows a rearing towards naturalism, but has a tendency to disregard detail. The artists seem to have been more interested in producing a general impression than in precise workmanship; a similar attitude can be seen in every field of Korean art.

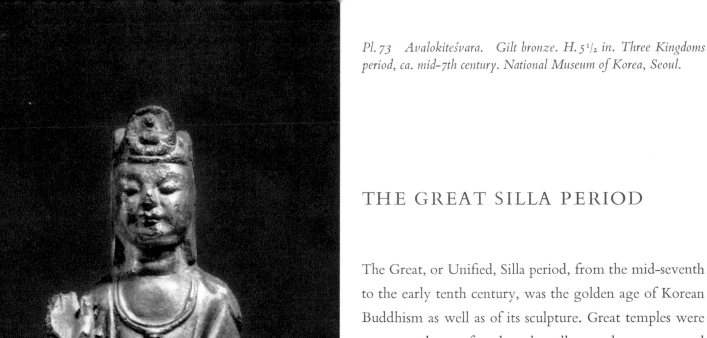

Pl. 73 Avalokiteśvara. Gilt bronze. H. 5¹/₂ in. Three Kingdoms period, ca. mid-7th century. National Museum of Korea, Seoul.

THE GREAT SILLA PERIOD

The Great, or Unified, Silla period, from the mid-seventh to the early tenth century, was the golden age of Korean Buddhism as well as of its sculpture. Great temples were constructed one after the other all over the country and centres or ateliers of Buddhist art multiplied. Pagodas, *stūpas* and other accessories for Buddhist temples were manufactured in large numbers; almost the only material was the abundant granite. Increased familiarity with the working of granite eventually led to a preference for stone rather than metal. Almost every one of the rocky valleys of Nam-san, to the south of Kyŏngju, was turned into an open-air temple by erecting free-standing Buddhas and engraving figures on the rocks.

Some Silla artists, probably inspired directly or indirectly by the cave temples of China, started to carve niched Buddhas in the natural rock. The number of such niches is small and so is the size of each niche. The granite of the Korean mountains is not suitable for large-scale cave temples, and anything like the scale of Lung-men or Yün-kang has never been attempted in Korea.

A seated Buddha carved in relief in a shallow niche in the Valley of Buddhas on Nam-san may be one of the earliest 'cave Buddhas' of the Great Silla period. He is in the *dhyāna mudrā*, seated on a low throne which is covered by the skirts of his robe. His head is bent slightly forward and his facial expression is one of tranquility. He is dressed in a loose robe whose folds are depicted as overlapping scale-like pleats, but the body is clearly felt beneath the fabric.

The static tranquility of the face, the short drapery fall-

Cat. 99

ing over the throne and the manner of the folds, all point to a basic adherence to Sui models, but the soft, gentle contour of the body and face is a new trend initiated from T'ang. This Buddha may be compared with the sculptures of T'o-shan and T'ienlung-shan in the Sui and early T'ang periods.

A much bigger rock-niche was discovered in 1962 at the foot of P'algong-san in Kunwi county, some forty miles to the north-west of Kyŏngju[24]. The niche is cut into a high cliff face overlooking a clear mountain stream and the floor level is some eighteen feet above the water. The niche or cave was originally a natural one and blocks of stone were lifted into it to be carved inside the cave.

Cat. 100 An Amitābha, slightly larger than life-size, is seated on a solid square throne occupying the centre of the small chamber, and is flanked by two standing Bodhisattvas. The mandorla for the Buddha is rather roughly incised on the back wall, and has traces of white pigment. The Buddha has his right hand in the *bhūmisparśa mudrā*, and is stoutly built, with a matchingly stiff facial expression. The eyes are half-closed and there is no hint of a smile on the tightly closed mouth under the monumental flat nose. The neck is short, with a single medial crease, apparently weighed down by the burden of the heavy shaven head with its prominent *uṣṇīṣa*. The solemn monumentality of the face recalls some of the Sui and early T'ang Buddhas, but the drapery folds above the throne are rendered in a very free manner compared with the representation of the face. The drapery covering the front of the square throne follows a tradition which apparently started in sixth-century China, though modifications of the tradition go well into the T'ang period.

The attendants, the Avalokiteśvara and Mahāsthāma-prāpta, are much smaller than the central Buddha, and they are stiffer. The Kwanyin has lost his halo but Mahāsthāma-prāpta or the Shih-chih Bodhisattva preserves a delicate peach-shaped halo. The Bodhisattvas are in the so-called 'thrice-bent', *tribhanga* posture with the hip slightly thrust toward the centre. This Indian pose is seen frequently in T'ang sculptures in the T'ienlung-shan caves. Our Bodhi-sattvas however, are a far cry from the T'ienlung-shan images in sculptural technique, as is shown by the crude and clumsy modelling of the arms and hands and particularly the awkward face and the stiff, shrunken neck. Even the *tribhanga* pose is not thoroughly mastered and many of the details give an unfinished impression.

The Kunwi Trinity is not technically mature and the craftsmanship has yet to be learned. Nevertheless the artist was successful in creating the monumentality of the Amitābha, which is the main impression we receive from Buddhist images of the Sui and early T'ang dynas-ties. The artist, one would guess, was a local master who could not free himself from the tradition of ab-stract sculpture that was still lingering on in regions away from Kyŏngju. The date must have been some time after the mid-seventh century.

A bronze standing Avalokiteśvara in the National Mu-seum may be compared with the Bodhisattvas of the Kun-wi Trinity. They all wear a similar shaped crown, and a double-ring necklace with a jewel pendant. The posture is the same *tribhanga* and the scarf is lifted up on the right forearm so as to cross the body at two levels. Despite the iconographic similarities, the bronze figure is much better executed and is far closer to Chinese originals. The slender

★Pl. 73

Pl. 74 Guardian. Clay, glazed. From Sach'ŏnwang-sa temple
site, Kyŏngju. H. 1 ft. 8⁷/₈ in. Great Silla dynasty, second half of
7th century (around 679). National Museum of Korea, Seoul.

body and simple drapery of the bronze Bodhisattva may place the figure a little earlier stylistically, if not in actual date, than the Kunwi Bodhisattvas.

By the 670s, the dynamic naturalism of early T'ang sculpture was fully dominant in the ateliers of Kyŏngju. The Guardian figure in relief on a glazed tile from the site of Sach'ŏn-wang-sa (Temple of the Four Guardians) in Kyŏngju is an outstanding example of Kyŏngju sculpture from that period. One such Guardian tile was originally installed on each of the four walls of a pagoda at the temple. The whole temple was constructed in 679, and according to *Samguk Yusa*[25], the sculptures were made by the monk-artist Yangji who had also done many figures for other temples.

This Guardian is clad in armour and seated on the backs of two demons. The swelling muscles of the arms and legs of the demons, and the forceful legs of the Guardian glimpsed through the skirt are realistically rendered. The details of the ornaments and the naturalistic representation of the folds and the falling bands are masterly. The best demonstration of the technique is the superb way the depth of the torso is created on the flat panel. The clear details and naturalism of the sculpture as a whole are doubtless a reflection of the seventh-century Guardian figures at Lung-men in China. This Silla sculpture, however, surpasses the former in the technique of modelling the muscles and it avoids the stiffness of the Chinese sculpture.

Starting from such naturalistic yet precise sculptures, Silla artists gradually softened the sharpness to produce a more interior, spiritual quality, culminating in the sculptures of the mid-eighth-century Sŏkkuram cave temple.

Four Guardians made of flat-cast bronze, recovered from a stone pagoda at the site of Kamŭn-sa, are another example of the sharp, clean-cut sculptures of the second half of the seventh century[26]. They were attached to the four *Pl. 74 walls of a bronze *sarīra* (holy relic) case discovered inside the three-storied stone pagoda. The case was placed in a square hole made in the top of the third storey under the roof stone, and the case shared the hole with the bottom of the iron finial mast. Kamŭn-sa was completed in 682 in memory of King Munmu who had died a year before.

All the Guardians are modelled with great care, and every detail demonstrates precise and superb craftsmanship. The Dhṛtāṣṭra has a powerful face with bulging eyes and a self-confident mouth. He stands on the back of a crouching cow or antelope, with his body-weight divided equally between the right leg and the halberd held in his left hand. His body is completely clad in heavy armour which is depicted in minute detail, like the clay Guardian from Pl. 74 Sach'ŏn-wang-sa. Here again, despite the heavy clothing, the form of the body is well suggested.

The Virūḍhaka, the Guardian of the South, holding a Pl. 75 'flame-bead' in his left hand, is done in the same careful fashion. The face, with straight nose, thin lips and characteristic moustache, is foreign to Korea, and undoubtedly Central Asian in character. This does not necessarily mean that Silla artists worked from living Central Asiatic models. The likelihood is that the four figures are faithful replicas of T'ang figurines, copied by a master artist. In any case, it is the type of sculpture produced and preferred in Silla around 670.

Toward the end of the seventh century, the sharpness and cold realism lost much of their vitality and a new

Pl. 76 *Śākyamuni. Gold. From a stone pagoda at Hwangbok-sa temple site, Kyŏngju, south Korea. H. 5 1/2 in. Great Silla dynasty, second half of 7th century, before 692. National Museum of Korea, Seoul.*

Pl. 77 *Amitābha. Gold. From a stone pagoda at Hwangbok-sa temple site, Kyŏngju, south Korea. H. 4 13/16 in. Great Silla dynasty, before 706. National Museum of Korea, Seoul.*

interest in soft plasticity appeared. This later trend is, as we have already seen, the most characteristic feature of Korean art although other factors have intruded from time to time.

A rock-cut Amitābha Trinity in Yŏngju is one of the new naturalistic sculptures of the late seventh century. The central Buddha, some ten feet high, is carved in high relief on a huge granite rock. The head is full and round and the body is well formed, like early T'ang Buddhas. All three figures are clad in heavy robes whose folds are indicated by a few ripple-like rounded ridges in front of the body. The artist is no longer interested in the external precision of form and line, but is concerned with the modelling of the body and the value of a mass. The pose of the attendants is rather stiff, but we feel the almost biological force of their massive bodies. It is at once clear that the artist has eliminated the traditional complex drapery so as to stress the plasticity of his figure.

A group of Buddhist images carved on the four sides of a big granite rock in the outskirts of Kyŏngju is striking for the Gupta-like treatment of the human body. The rock is located at what is known as the site of Kulpul-sa (Temple of the Excavation of the Buddhas). It is recorded in *Samguk Yusa* that King Kyŏngdŏk (r. 742–765) heard an underground voice at the spot while visiting Paeg'yul-sa nearby, and dug up these rock-Buddhas. The engraved rock had apparently been buried under earth or sand as a result of a flood, until it was rediscovered by King Kyŏngdŏk in the mid-eighth century. The king built a temple there to commemorate the discovery.

An Amitābha Trinity, a seated Bhaiṣajyaguru and two images of uncertain identity are carved in relief on the west, east and north walls of the rock respectively. On the south side are a headless standing Buddha and a Bodhisattva. The facial type, the thin tight robes and the plump arms of the Bodhisattva on the south wall suggest the influence of Gupta-sculpture—as has already been suggested by Nakagiri[27]. Whatever the stylistic influences, the sculptor has fully acquired the art of granite carving, showing his virtuosity in the subtle drapery and the soft texture hewn from the rough medium. The anonymous sculptor of the Kulpul-sa rock, which belongs to the last years of the seventh century, is seen here opening up the way to the splendid achievements of the eighth century.

Belonging to the same time, or slightly earlier, are four granite statues of Guardians, civilian and military officials, standing in front of a royal tomb under a mound in Kyŏngju. The earth-covered tomb is called Kwae-nŭng but its real identity is obscure, despite the traditional attribution to King Munmu (d. 681) who unified the peninsula[28]. The bodies of these stone statues are strong and massive, without any suppleness. The artist paid particular attention to the faces, each of which seems to be an individual portrait.

The civilian officer with his arms held before his chest has a square-jawed, flat face with knitted brows and closed eyes, expressing his deep grief for his deceased master. The shape of the eyes is similar to that of contemporary Buddhist images but the expression is a completely different one. The drapery is arranged symmetrically in vertical parallels, but conventionalized, and shows an analogy to that of the zodiac figures installed around the tomb of General Kim Yusin, who died in 673.

The image of the military officer clad in armour is note-

*Pl. xx, Pl. 75, Cat. 97, 101

*Cat. 103

Cat. 105, 106

*Cat. 104

Cat. 105

Cat. 106

146

worthy for the features, which are not Mongoloid but Caucasoid like the bronze Guardians from Kamŭn-sa. The racial characteristics are clear in the big nose, thick curled moustache and deep-set eyes. He too has closed eyes and his facial muscles seem crumpled in sorrow. The artist must have worked from a living model, if he did not copy a pottery or bronze figurine imported from China. The latter seems more likely, though it is possible that there were Iranian soldiers in Silla at that time. The T'ang employed many mercenaries from Central Asia, and these foreign units must surely have been used on the Korean front.

The tomb of Kim Yusin is located in the western outskirts of Kyŏngju. Kim was the commanding general of the Silla army allied with the T'ang. Stone slabs, each representing in relief one of the twelve zodiacal figures, are placed around the bottom of the mound to afford both physical and spiritual protection. A catalogue illustration shows the serpent with a human body. He holds a sword in his right hand and his right hip is thrust forward in the *tribhanga* posture. The body is represented rather flat beneath the garment, and the drapery is more a graphic design than a suggestion of the roundness of the body. The figure as a whole, however, is not frozen or stiff but has a marked degree of flexibility and softness like the Kulpul-sa rock-cut Buddhas. Although these zodiacal figures are done in relief on flat slabs, the technique and style of carving are almost identical with those of the stone Guardians of Kwae-nŭng. These two groups of stone figures may well be the work of the same atelier.

Turning from stone to metal sculpture, we have two interesting figures of gold alloy, one standing and one sitting, discovered in a stone pagoda at Kuhwang-ni, Kyŏngju. The pagoda stands on the site of Hwangbok-sa and the two statuettes were placed within a bronze *sarira* case kept in the pagoda[29].

According to the inscription on the cover of the bronze box, the stone pagoda was built in 692 by King Hyoso (d. 702) in memory of the late King Sinmun (d. 692). Fourteen years later, however, in 706, King Sŏngdŏk put into the pagoda four *sariras*, an 'all gold' statue of Amitābha and a Buddhist *sūtra* (holy text) in memory of King Hyoso and the Queen mother Sinmok, who died in 702.

The inscription, which consists of nail-pitted letters, does not say what was put into the pagoda by King Hyoso at the time of the first offering in 692. We may be sure, however, that the additional Buddha and several objects discovered in the bronze box besides the objects described in the inscription must have been the items put into the pagoda in 692. At the time of the second offering by King Sŏngdŏk in 706, both offerings must have been put together in the newly made bronze box, the inscription apparently ignoring the first offering.

That the newly added Buddha was an Amitābha is indicated by the 706 inscription. Unfortunately the inscription does not mention the *āsana* or posture of the Buddha. Until now, the standing figure has been referred to as the Amitābha[30]. However, the standing Buddha with his right hand in the *abhaya mudrā* and his left hand holding a loop of his gown is not Amitābha but Śākyamuni, as is shown by the *mudrās*, and the seated one with *abhaya* and *vara mudrā*, which may be either a Śākyamuni or an Amitābha, must be the one referred to in the inscription as an Amitābha. Stylistically also, the seated Buddha is certainly later

147

than the standing one, and the identification of the two Buddhas should thus be reversed.

The standing Amitābha, on a lotus pedestal on top of a scalloped plinth, is provided with an elaborate open-work halo. His head is bent slightly forward and his eyes are wide open like those of the rock-cut Sŏ-san Amitābha of the late Paekche period. The loose concentric drapery and the slightly pointed fin-like hems of the skirt also resemble the Sŏ-san Trinity. This is certainly older in style than the seated Buddha, and must be the figure that was installed in 692 by King Hyoso. In view of the expensive material of the image, it must either have been made specially for the occasion, or else it may have been a Buddha personally belonging to King Sinmun (d. 692) to whose memory the Hwangbok-sa pagoda was dedicated. In either case, the image would belong to the middle of the second half of the seventh century.

The seated Amitābha, indicated in the inscription, may also have been King Hyoso's (d. 702) personal guardian Buddha, unless it was cast in 706 by King Sŏngdŏk. The

★Cat. 97

figure consists of three separate parts: the mandorla, the Buddha and the lotus throne. The mandorla is also done in open-work but the design is much simpler than that of the standing Śākyamuni. The face, with a slight hint of a smile, is big in proportion to the sloping shoulders and particularly to the tiny hands. The drapery in front of the body and the falling hems over the throne are in the early T'ang style. The statuette is, as a whole, more Chinese in type than the typical Silla sculpture of that period.

Pl. 78   A standing Buddha, probably a Maitreya, in the collection of Mr. H. P. Chun is unique in its treatment of drapery. The right hand is in the *vara mudrā* instead of the usual *abhaya mudrā*. The left hand is extended forward with the palm up-turned as if in greeting. Something such as a medicine jar or jewel may have been placed on it. The head, with a large *uṣṇīṣa*, the oval face with slit-eyes and the way the forehead is covered by the straight, deep-set hair margin, all have something in common with the seated gold Amitābha from the Hwangbok-sa pagoda described above. The body, however, shows features completely different from the Hwangbok-sa figure. The Buddha wears a skirt tied obliquely at the waistline, but what looks like a gown worn over it is actually a scarf put around the shoulders and falling in a series of scale-like pleats over the legs. A close examination shows further that the Buddha is in the *tribhanga* posture which is associated with Bodhisattvas only. Thus, there is a strange confusion of iconography in the Buddha. The authenticity of the figure is beyond doubt, although the place of discovery is unknown. It seems that the artist placed the head of a Buddha on the body of a Bodhisattva to create something completely new. His ambitious independence is

Pl. 80 Maitreya. Granite. From the site of Kam-san-sa temple, Kyŏngju. H. 6 ft. 1/16 in. Great Silla dynasty, dated 720. National Museum of Korea, Seoul.

Pl. 81 The main Buddha of Sŏkkuram cave temple (from ante-room). Granite. Buddha, H. 10 ft. 8 3/8 in. Throne, H. 5 ft. 2 3/16 in. Great Silla dynasty, mid-8th century. Mt. T'oham, near Kyŏngju.

shown not only in the iconography but also in the carving of the sharp ridged folds over the shoulder, the bulging abdomen below the girdle, and in the unusual facial expression, with a small mouth and long eyes under deep set brows.

In the eighth century, a style belonging distinctively to Great Silla begins to emerge.

A stone Amitābha from the site of Kam-san-sa, Kyŏngju, is one that represents the sculptures of the first half of the eighth century. This Amitābha together with a similar-sized Bodhisattva originally stood at the temple site until they were removed to the National Museum in 1915[31]. According to a long inscription incised on the back of the mandorla, the pair, Amitābha and Maitreya Bodhisattva, were dedicated in 720 by Kim Chisŏng for the happiness of his family. The inscription is interesting in that it identifies the names of the images and the date of production. It is also important in that this is the earliest example of a Buddhist's seeking not rebirth in Paradise but the happiness of living people in the present world. During the previous century, it was the salvation of lost souls in Hades that had been prayed for when dedicating Buddhist figures. The Kam-san-sa inscription testifies to a change of pattern in the Buddhism of Silla around 700. Pl. 79

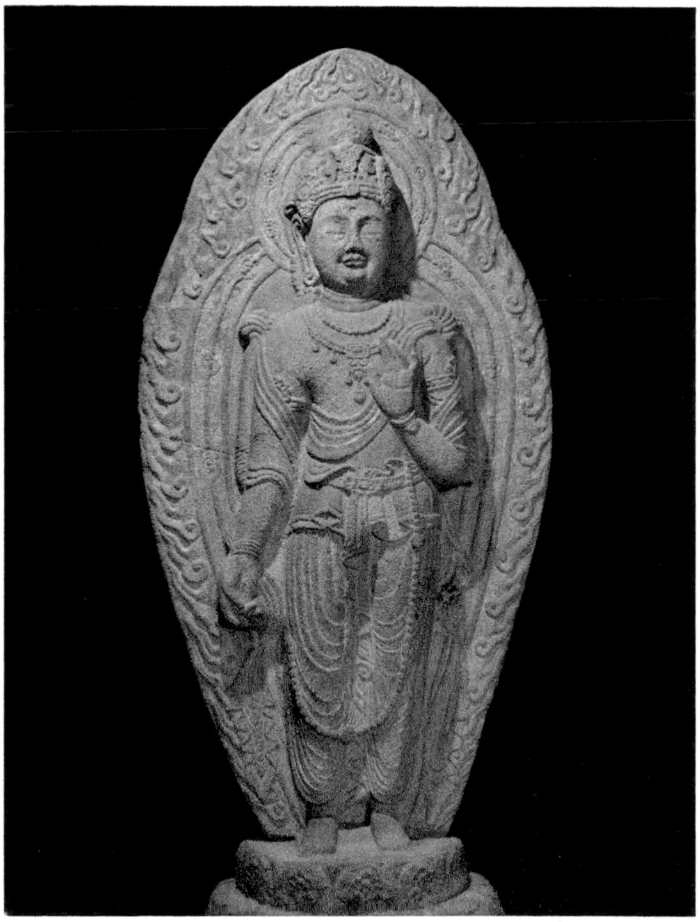

Both statues are carved out of single blocks of granite and have an overall height of six feet. The head of the Amitābha is square and the hair is indicated by tiny flat snail-curls. The face is flat and the almost closed, long, oblique eyes give no suggestion of a smile. The long, pierced earlobes carry on the tradition of the early seventh century. The face is no more of the happily smiling boyish type, but self-contained, static and tranquil. All the features con-

tribute to what can be called the 'eighth century face' of Silla Buddhistic sculpture. The Buddha is clad in a voluminous monastic robe that clings to the body in continuous close parallel folds. The V-shaped neck-opening is rather unusual, but the series of ripple-like folds over the legs and the vertical zig-zag treatment of the side-hems are common features constantly appearing on Silla Buddhist images hereafter.

The Maitreya Bodhisattva displays a similar mood of composed tranquility, despite the flexible *tribhanga* posture and a marked sense of plasticity in the body. Outwardly, however, the attitude of the sculptor is quite different from that shown in the Amitābha. While he tried for spiritual beauty in the Amitābha, in the case of Maitreya, he seems to be more concerned to produce the physical beauty of a shapely feminine body. The taste for rounded, feminine modelling may have been stimulated by T'ang sculpture, though this Maitreya, like the rock-cut figures of Kulpul-sa, reflects a strong influence from Indian sculpture. This is clearly felt in the fleshy oval face, the pronounced plasticity of the arms and chest and particularly in the robe, like a *dhōti* with tucked-up hems.

Such Indian features are even more clearly to be seen in a seated stone Buddha in the campus of Kyŏngbuk National University. Unusually for Silla sculpture, the stone is not granite but bluish sandstone. The Buddha is seated on a high, elaborate lotus throne which is very similar to the lower portion of a *stūpa*. Parivara Guardians are depicted in relief around the pedestal and the lotus petals now carry *ang-hua*, or ornamental volutes projecting upwards from the tip of each petal. The Buddha has lost his left hand, but the remaining portion seems to suggest the *dharmacakra*

(preaching) *mudrā*. The entire body, particularly the interlocked legs, is strongly built and the head is very massive with a big nose and mouth and bulging eyes. The hair is indicated by large snail-curls but the *uṣṇīṣa* is almost unrecognizable from wear. The thin garment pulled over the left shoulder clings tightly to the body and the drapery is fashioned by regularly spaced 'earthworm' waves. The folds follow the Mathurā style of the Gupta period. The massive legs and the fan-shaped end of the garment appearing beneath the legs are features recalling Indian sculptures of the early Pāla period. There is no doubt that this is the work of a person or atelier strongly affected by Indian sculpture. Although few records remain as to the direct relationship between Silla and India, it is established that a number of Silla monks visited India during the early eighth century[32]. The introduction of the Indian style into Silla sculpture during the same century must be a result of such direct communication.

*Pl. 80

Let us examine one more such Silla sculpture showing Indian influence. It is a standing Buddha in the collection of the Kyŏngju Museum. This statue is also made of the bluish sandstone used for the previous Buddha. Both of them seem to have been produced somewhere near Kyŏngju where this stone was available, though we do not know from what locality it was quarried.

*Cat. 104
Cat. 107

*Cat. 108

The Buddha has a big face with fleshy cheeks that taper upwards. His eyelids and nose are damaged but the bulging cheeks are accentuated by the small tight lips. The robe clings to him, creating the archaic V-shape folds on the upper body. The folds are divided into two separate series of loose arcs over the legs like the Kam-san-sa stone Buddhas dated 720. The body itself is rather small in proportion to

Pl. 79, 80

the head, but the volume is clearly sensed beneath the thin fabric and this sensitive plasticity is as exotic as the face itself, which strangely resembles that of the famous Bala Bodhisattva (Buddha) in the Archaeological Museum, Sārnāth[33].

Few such Indian-influenced sculptures are extant today and the particular artist or atelier that emerged suddenly around 700 seems to have died away as abruptly as it came. The basic and dominating pattern of Buddhist images during the first half of the eighth century was the solemn, tranquil type represented by a gilt bronze Bhaiṣajyaguru in the collection of the National Museum. The round face is flanked by extraordinarily large ears and has clear-cut features and almost closed eyes. The *uṣṇīṣa* on the head is prominent and the hair is indicated by small grain-like snail-curls. The body is well built but still small in proportion to the head, and the feet, too small to support the body, are typical of the Silla tradition. The drapery is treated in an archaic fashion, indicated by ripple-like continuous folds from the chest downwards and vertical zig-zag folds on the right side. Every detail shows careful craftsmanship, and the artist was certainly possessed of a masterly technique, but the overall result is a cold portrait, the face smug and the gestures and dress irreproachable. It is 'Romanesque' in spirit: the image is strictly to be worshipped, and not intended to be loved. This cold, self-contained Buddha is a typical example of Silla sculpture around the mid-eighth century, shortly before the creation of the Sŏkkuram cave temple.

In 751, the Prime Minister Kim Taesŏng started to rebuild Pulguk-sa at the foot of T'oham-san, which had first been built in the sixth century. The construction work

Pl. XXI, XXII

was not completed by the time of his death in 774. Separate from the Pulguk-sa complex, an artificial cave temple was also constructed, on top of T'oham-san. It is this cave temple, commonly called Sŏkkuram, that houses probably the best Korean stone sculptures of all time.

The domed temple is constructed with large blocks of granite quarried from the rock cliff immediately behind the structure. In ground plan, it consists of a rectangular ante-room and a circular main chamber connected by a short vestibule[34]. The ceiling of the main chamber is domed but the ante-room was open to the sky. Earlier attempts by Paekche and Silla to excavate real cave temples, such as the Sŏ-san rock-cut Trinity and that of Kunwi, finally found a solution here by erecting a built-up cave covered with an earth mound. Sŏkkuram was certainly influenced by Chinese cave temples, but it was probably at least partially inspired by the tumuli tradition within Korea. In Koguryŏ, in the north, it was now the practice to make burial structures consisting of a domed main chamber and an ante-room. In the case of the Ssang'yŏng-ch'ong (Tomb of the Twin Pillars), near P'yŏngyang, a pair of octagonal pillars are erected in the vestibule that connects the main chamber and the ante-room, exactly in the fashion of Sŏkkuram[35].

Eight Parivara and two Vajra-pāṇi figures, each of them engraved in relief on a stone slab measuring slightly over six and a half feet in height, are lined up symmetrically to form the walls of the ante-room. The Four Guardians are also depicted in relief, two on each side of the vestibule leading toward the main chamber.

The main chamber is occupied at the centre by a monumental figure of Śākyamuni, nearly eleven feet high, seated

★Fig. 3, 4

★Pl. 81

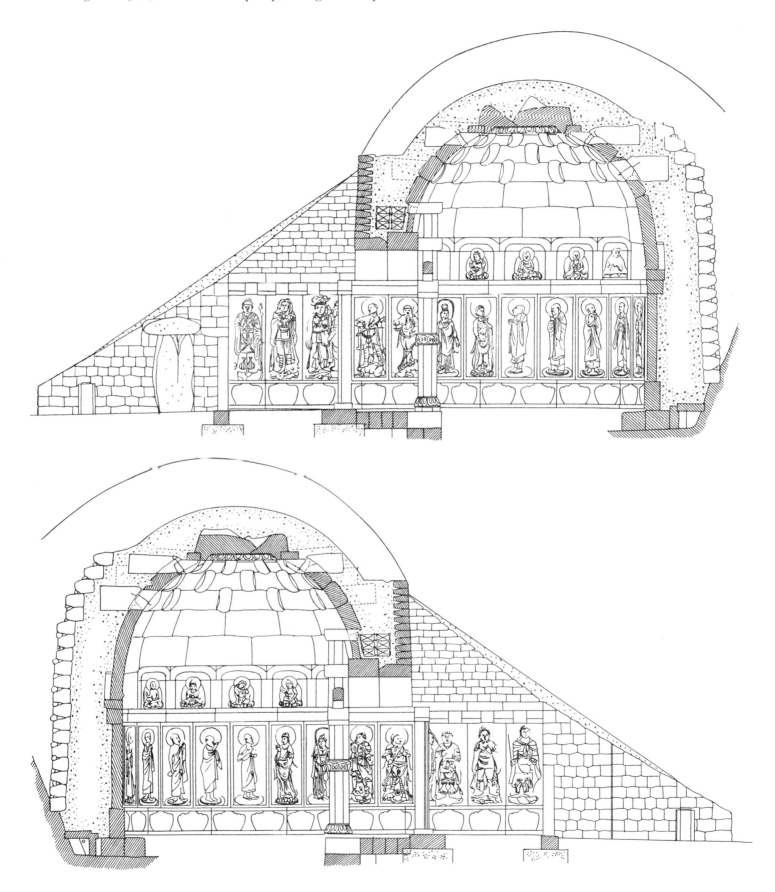

Fig. 3 a and b   Section (north-south) of the Sŏkkuram (before the 1963 repair work). a. The western half; b. The eastern half. H. of the ceiling ca. 26 ft., 3 in. Great Silla dynasty, mid-eighth century.

Fig. 4 a—c Plan and section of the Sŏkkuram (before the 1963 repair work). a. Plan of the ceiling at the niche level; b. section (east-west) of the main chamber; c. plan of the entire cave. Diameter of the main chamber 19 ft., 10⅝ in. Great Silla dynasty, mid-eighth century.

on a five feet two inches high throne. A circular lotus-halo is inserted in the back wall to appear behind the Buddha's head. Around the wall surrounding the main Buddha are three Bodhisattvas (Mañjuśri, Samantabhadra, and the eleven-headed Ekādāsamukha), two *devas* (Brāhma and Sakra-devendra) and the Ten Disciples, all engraved on oblong stone slabs about six and a half feet high. Above the figures are ten deep niches built into the wall. They were each destined to house a seated Bodhisattva, of which two are now missing.

The main Buddha is marked by a perfectly proportioned strong massive body. His face is full and round with a comparatively small nose and a clearly defined mouth which still preserves traces of the original red paint. The eyes are half closed under the long arching eyebrows and there is no hint of a smile.

He is clad in a tight clinging garment whose drapery is simply but naturalistically rendered. His left arm rests on the left thigh in *dhyāna mudrā* while his right hand is placed gently over the right knee with extended fingers in the

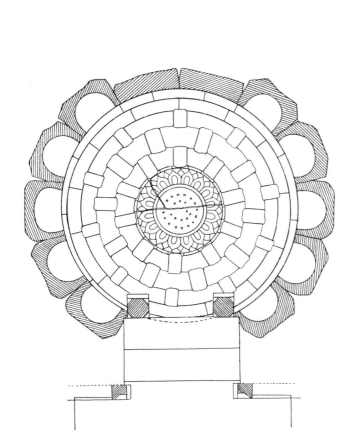

Pl. xxi, xxii

bhūmisparśa or 'earth touching' *mudrā*. The greatness of Buddha, the spiritual power of the Great Hero, the eternal peace of the Enlightened One and the depthless tranquillity of a stone figure are brought into successful fusion in the facial expression, the majestic broad chest and sloping shoulders, the gesture of the hands, and the giant feet with smoothed soles. All these features are well harmonized, but the best part is the face, which is unsurpassed by any contemporary sculpture in the Far East. It is a typical Silla face, independent of any foreign model or type.

★Pl. 82

This Buddha is intended to display a spiritual quality like that of the National Museum's bronze Bhaiṣajyaguru above. The Sŏkkuram Buddha, however, has lost the coldness of the bronze figure and he seems to be almost alive in spite of the cold hard medium. This is a superb example of the idealistic naturalism achieved by the artists of Silla during the mid-eighth century.

Idealistic naturalism is also the style of all the surrounding figures. Best known among them is the eleven-headed Avalokiteśvara who stands directly behind the main

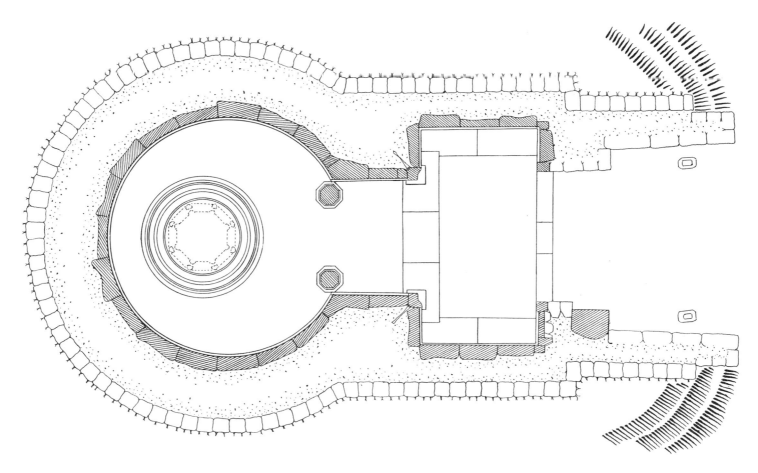

Buddha, dividing the surrounding figures into two symmetrical groups. This image was evidently inspired by such Chinese sculptures as the eleven-headed Avalokiteśvara of Pao-ch'ing-Ssu, Hsian, datable to around 700. Yet, if the two are compared closely, differences in effect and technique are easily noticed. The T'ang image is clearly intended to convey plasticity, although the drapery is highly conventionalized. It has the form of a plump young woman and the face would be like that of any ordinary girl if it were stripped of all the additional heads. The Sŏkkuram Bodhisattva, however, has an idealized face radiating the grace and dignity of an Avalokiteśvara. The garment and scarves are rendered in astonishingly fluent, realistic forms but the flatness of the body beneath the fabric and the overall gracefulness combine to produce a spiritual rather than a physical beauty.

A standing Bodhisattva, which is either a Mañjuśrī or a Samantabhadra, will serve to show the technical standard of the Sŏkkuram artists. The lithe Bodhisattva holds a treasure cup in his right hand; his waist is thrust slightly forward. The figure is no frozen statue carved in stone but seems almost a living organism, stepping from the wall with rustling fabrics. Yet the serene face and the flatness of the lower half of the body transform a beautiful woman into a sacred Bodhisattva of impelling spiritual dignity.

A bronze seated Amitābha and a Vairocana at Pulguk-sa are probably contemporary with the Sŏkkuram sculptures. The Amitābha (five feet, five and a half inches high) has a body as well built and well proportioned as that of the Sŏkkuram Buddha, but is more naturalistic both in posture and modelling. The full round face with a hint of a smile is dominated by curved lines and planes that harmonize well

with the fluent curving lines of the drapery. The S-shaped upper edge of the robe on the chest is particularly characteristic. This Buddha is altogether humane: the main difference from the Sŏkkuram sculptures is in the warmth that surrounds the bronze figure. It is more relaxed, and is probably a reflection of the influence of T'ang sculptors.

The seated Vairocana in the same temple shows exactly Cat. 110 similar details, and beyond doubt the pair were made by the same artist or workshop. The well built but somewhat slender body, the full round face with fleshy ears, the flexed legs with a clear indication of the calf, and the sparsely arranged drapery are identical with the Amitābha, although the facial expression in this Vairocana is stern Pl. xxi, xxii without a smile. Yet compared with the standing Bhaiṣajyaguru of the National Museum, this figure is much warmer and more natural in expression, and the difference from the sculptures of the first half of the eighth century ★Cat. 109 is marked.

A separate head of a Buddha from the Kyŏngju area in Pl. 83 the collection of the National Museum demonstrates mid-eighth-century naturalism in full bloom. It is in granite, and is almost twice the size of a human head. It has a pure and serene smile, fortunately unspoilt by some damage to details and loss of part of the uṣṇīṣa. It is nevertheless a true masterpiece, demonstrating the talent of the Silla artist in dealing with stone. The boyish face with innocent eyes and mouth are reminiscent of late Paekche sculpture, and the naïvety and human feeling of the interpretation seem ★Cat. 111 to return to the Paekche manner. This amiable style can be also observed in the fluent lines and forms of the adoring devas on the famous bronze bell, originally from Pong- Pl. 84 dŏk-sa near Kyŏngju, dated 771.

*Pl. 85

*Cat. 112

Pl. XXII Detail of Pl. XXI.

The few decades immediately after the mid-eighth century were the peak of Silla's fine arts. After that Silla sculpture begins to degenerate. The naturalism demonstrated by the stone head and the bronze figures of Pulguk-sa is somewhat conventionalized and schematized in the well-known standing Bhaiṣajyaguru (five feet, eleven inches high) in the collection of the Kyŏngju Museum. The statue was at Paeg'yul-sa until it was moved to the museum some years ago. For this reason, it is often and better known as the Paeg'yul-sa Bhaiṣajyaguru. The face has become a little flatter and the mood is not so well expressed as in the previous stone head. Despite the shadowy smile it rather recalls the stern faces of Japanese Buddhas.

The Bhaiṣajyaguru wears a full, loosely clinging robe with an equally loose type of drapery. The folds consist of three equi-distant U-shaped arcs separated by a pair of similar arcs broken in the middle. The languid body and garment, the flowing sleeves, the ornamental tendency of the drapery, and the conventionalized facial type without human warmth, all herald the coming of ninth-century sculpture: this Bhaiṣajyaguru stands between mid-eighth-century naturalism and the manneristic conventionalized sculptures of the ninth century.

Some of the characteristics of ninth-century Silla Buddhist sculpture are clearly indicated on a Trinity on Pangŏ-san in south-east Korea. This Trinity, probably a Bhaiṣajyaguru and two attendants, are line-engraved on a mass of rock, except for the faces which are treated in low relief. The Trinity is furnished with an inscribed date corresponding to the year 801. The Buddha's face has no smile and the head is large in comparison with the face itself. This is the advent of the ninth-century style. The Bodhisattvas are small in size but they are of extreme interest because of the facial type, which is quite foreign to Silla and suggests a strong influence from T'ang China, or possibly from Central Asia. The face of the Bodhisattva on our right is particularly reminiscent of the central Asiatic type.

⋆Cat. 112

A bronze seated Buddha on a high lotus pedestal in the collection of the Tŏksu Palace Museum is almost a replica of a T'ang original. The small round spherical face is of the same type as those on the limestone stelae of Pao-ch'ing-Ssu, in China, of about 700[36]. The *uṣṇīṣa* is not clearly separated from the head, and the hair is indicated by large snail-curls. The body is well proportioned and well felt beneath the robe. The drapery in front of the body is depicted by a series of concentric arcs framed within folded U-shape hems. The pattern is obviously ornamental, like the details of the lotus throne. This tendency continued to develop until it reached the schematic play of folds in the gilt bronze Bhaiṣajyaguru in the National Museum.

⋆Pl. 86

⋆Cat. 114

A seven and a half inches high bronze Śākyamuni in the collection of the National Museum may be cited as a typical example of ninth-century Silla Buddhas. The T'ang-type fleshy face with a prominent *uṣṇīṣa* is rather solemn, almost grim, in spite of the small handsome mouth. The body is rather feebly built compared with the voluminous head, and the monastic robe falls languidly in loose rippling arcs above the vertical plate-like skirt. The twisted neck-opening is in the classic Gandhāra style, but this is a typical piece of late Silla sculpture, of the first half of the ninth century.

⋆Cat. 113

What should probably be identified as a standing Bhaiṣajyaguru, in the Tŏksu Palace Museum, displays a similar
trend although the drapery is somewhat livelier. The head
is again marked by an prominent *uṣnīṣa* and head-like
snail-curls. The face is rounder than the previous one but
it is also a typically T'ang face with horizontal eyes and a
pretty mouth. The arrangement of drapery in the front is
different from that of the previous figure in that the folds
over the legs are now divided into two separate series and
express more animation. Action is further indicated by the
left foot, which is set slightly forward. This attitude may
reflect the gay sculptures of T'ienlung-shan in China, but
the manner of rendering each of the folds and the way the

vertical folds are depicted on the left arm are almost identical with those of the previous figure. Even the texture of   ★Pl. 87
the material is identical, and notwithstanding the slight
difference in the overall effect of the drapery, this Bhaiṣajyaguru Buddha must also date from the first half of the   Cat. 113
ninth century, not far separated from the National Museum Śākyamuni. `

A gilt bronze Bhaiṣajyaguru in the National Museum is   Cat. 114
an extreme example of the conventionalized images of the
mid-ninth century. The head is monstrously large and the
plate-like ears are enormous. The face is round but rather
flat, with eyes and mouth converging toward the central
apex. The face has changed to a new type. The body,
particularly the lower half, is thin and feebly built under
the heavily schematized folds. The drapery, nevertheless,
is derived from that of the toe-lifting Buddha just mentioned, especially in the characteristic folds of the triangular
space between the legs. This Bhaiṣajyaguru, with a height
of one and a half feet, seems to be the ultimate expression
of the Silla style of Buddha in bronze.

The popularity of the free-standing Bhaiṣajyaguru during the first half of the ninth century may have been due
to a series of disasters: frequent bad harvests and uprisings
of bandits in which many lost their lives[37], and drove the
people to seek help from the Buddha of Medicine.

During the second half of the ninth century, Vairoçana
took the place of Bhaiṣajyaguru and instead of expensive
bronze ore, iron became the favourite material for large
sized Buddhas.

A seated Vairoçana at Porim-sa in south-west Korea is   Cat. 115
the earliest dated iron Buddha of the late Silla period. The
eight feet, three inches high Buddha is fortunately provided

with the inscribed date of 858. Probably cast by a local artist, it displays a naturalistic, yet completely new style of drapery that tends to focus attention on the edges of the garment.

The facial expression has been much changed by the later addition of painted eyebrows and moustache and the pupils of the eyes. The flat ridge of the nose, thick lips, large ugly ears, all make the face into a cool, emotionless mask, remote from the Pulguk-sa Buddhas of a century before. The head is big and the prominent *uṣṇīṣa* covered with tiny curls is not clearly separated from the head, thus, making the whole head egg-shaped. This oval head with a flatter *uṣṇīṣa* is one of the characteristics of the late ninth-century sculpture. Another new feature of the figure is the half-moon shaped tonsure on the head which appears here for the first time. The shaved spot in this case, however, together with the crowding tiny curls and the button-like ornament on top of the *uṣṇīṣa*, seems to be a later remodelling in plaster. This tonsure is regarded as a characteristic of Buddhist images of the Liao (916–1125) and Chin (1115 to 1234) dynasties[38], but they are likely to have occurred already in the late ninth century.

In 865, another iron Vairoçana was cast in the northern province of Silla at Top'ian-sa in Ch'ŏrwon. According to the inscription on the back of the Buddha this seated figure on a composite lotus throne is the result of the labour of 1,500 donors.

The oval head is basically akin to the Buddha of Porim-sa temple in that the *uṣṇīṣa* is not separated from the head. Of particular interest is the drapery which consists of rows of overlapping scale-like pleats. Such drapery lingers on in Korea as late as the early fifteenth century.

*Cat. 116

Pl. 86 Buddha. Gilt bronze. H. 8³/₁₆ in. Great Silla dynasty, ca. 9th century. Tŏksu Palace Museum of Fine Arts, Seoul.
Pl. 87 Buddha. Bronze. H. 10³/₄ in. Great Silla dynasty, ca. 8th century. Tŏksu Palace Museum of Fine Arts, Seoul.
Pl. 88 Buddha. Gilt bronze. From the Pusŏk-sa temple, south Korea. H. 1 ft. 2¹¹/₁₆ in. Great Silla dynasty, ca. 8th century. National Museum of Korea, Seoul.

A colossal seated iron Śākyamuni in the Tŏksu Palace   Cat. 117
Museum is a revival of the mid-eighth-century style although such details as the sharpness and rigidity of the face, the twisted earlobes and the small tonsure on the head clearly suggest the approach of the Koryŏ period. This statue, from Kwangju in the southern outskirts of Seoul, has a posture and anatomy akin to those of the Sŏkkuram Buddha. However, it can be assigned to the early decades of the tenth century—either late Silla or early Koryŏ[39]. It is a transitional style combining features of both dynasties.

THE KORYŎ AND YI PERIODS

Koryŏ arose in central Korea in 918 with its capital at Kaesŏng, some forty-five miles north of Seoul. Silla survived until 935, but with her surrender and the transfer of the members of the former royal family to the new capital, the centre of artistic activities also moved northward. The ateliers and artists transferred from Kyŏngju worked hard to build new temples in central Korea. Probably because the artists were the same, iron was still the favourite medium of early Koryŏ sculptors. The sculptural style did not change abruptly or drastically during this early period, as is demonstrated by the Kwangju iron Buddha of typical transitional style.

Pl. 89   An iron head of a Buddha in the collection of the National Museum displays features similar to the Kwangju iron Buddha. The flat *uṣṇīṣa*, the dense forest of snail-curls, the small tonsure, the sharply cut nose, the small pretty mouth and the horizontal eyes, are features that also characterize the Kwangju figure. The face is, however, warmer and kinder than that of the Kwangju image. The cheek around the mouth is particularly well modelled and there is a sincere attempt at a naturalistic approach. This revival of naturalism dominates early Koryŏ sculpture, although the rigid abstract tendency also survives.

Cat. 118   An iron Buddha in the National Museum shows early Koryŏ characteristics. The face is marked by clean-cut eyebrows and long horizontal eyes, a short nose and idealized mouth. The smile is warm and pleasant, and the modelling of the cheeks and the sloping chin is clearly in the tradition of the iron head mentioned above. The mass of the body is well indicated beneath the thin folded

garment, but there is an undeniable attenuation in the torso and the forearms. Such attenuation is not found among iron Buddhas of the late Silla period. The Koryŏ figure, nevertheless, is very relaxed and at ease compared to ninth-century Silla Buddhist images. The naturalism combined with the idealistic face with its exaggeratedly long eyes distinguishes this Śākyamuni as an early Koryŏ figure. The entire figure consists of seven parts cast separately and welded together. Horizontal and vertical welding marks can be seen along the neck-line and abdomen and on the sides of the body.

Cat. 119   The early Koryŏ naturalism observed in this iron Buddha is intensified in a bronze Buddha in the Tŏksu Palace Museum. Like the seated Buddha mentioned above, the fore-

*Cat. 122   head of this Tŏksu Palace Museum figure is extended sideways because of the retreating side-locks. The face is well built though the eyelids seem excessively swollen. Yet the quiet peaceful smile is superbly expressed by the tightly closed small mouth.

Cat. 120   A similar plump facial type is to be seen on the stone Worshipping Bodhisattva at Kangnŭng and on another at Wŏlchŏng-sa. These Bodhisattvas are akin not only in posture but also in the plump oval face and the cylindrical head-dress.

Cat. 117   The rigidity already suggested by the Kwangju Buddha
Cat. 121   can also be seen in a seated Śākyamuni(?) at Pusŏk-sa. This
Fig. 5   Buddha is the only clay Buddha dating from the period. It is coated with a thick layer of lacquer applied on a hemp base and then gilded. The mandorla, with an outer frame of sweeping flame design, is made of carved wood. The

*Cat. 117   Buddha as a whole carries on the tradition of Silla sculpture typified in the prominent uṣṇīṣa, solemn, voluptuous

face and well proportioned body wrapped around with a closely folded robe. The mudrā is the same as in the main Buddha of Sŏkkuram. This type of seated Buddha with the bhūmisparśa mudrā was apparently in vogue during the early Koryŏ dynasty, replacing the Vairoçana Buddhas of the late Silla period.

The similarity in iconography, however, is not paralleled in the sculptural details. The difference is noticeable in the limp right arm with its flat hand and the meaningless plate-like feet placed on the thighs. The body is sensed under the drapery, but the folds submerge it and the figure as a whole is devoid of the grand monumentality of Silla sculptures. This Buddha is probably a post tenth-century product copied from an earlier model.

A seated iron Buddha at Taewŏn-sa in Ch'ungju, south central Korea, is unique in the rigid conventionalization of the drapery. According to a tradition of the temple, the image was cast in 1145, and this seems to be an appropriate date.

The uṣṇīṣa, prominent but not clearly separated from the head, is in the tradition of the iron Buddhas of the late Silla period. The tonsure is now enlarged but the ears are markedly reduced. The face is not full, but rather bony, and the large, half-closed eyes, with their corners pointed down, make the entire face, with its M-shaped mouth, awe-inspiring and unfriendly, rather like that of a Japanese kabuki player. The Buddha is clad in a robe pulled over both shoulders, which scarcely suggests the body beneath. The folds are sharp-edged ridges arranged in perfect symmetry. This schematic drapery can be traced back to the iron Buddha from Kwangju of the early tenth century.

The Ch'ungju Buddha marks the final phase of the

rigid and abstract school of early Koryŏ that developed from late Silla sculptures side by side with the new dominant naturalist school. From this point on, the academic school loses its rigidity and slowly develops into early Yi sculpture.

During the Koryŏ dynasty, the worship of *arhats* or *lohans* became an important ceremony frequently sponsored by the kings. Many temples today have a special hall for small figurines of seated *lohans*, but these figurines are relatively late in date and few original Koryŏ remain today.

A clay head of a *lohan* at Tongguk University, Seoul, must serve as an example of a Koryŏ clay *lohan*. This severed head came from the site of a lost temple in southwest Korea. It is clean-shaven and the ears, which were applied to the sides, have fallen off. The realistic rendering of facial details such as the bulging cheek and thick lower lip, projecting almost like a tongue, are very striking. The eye-cavities are perfectly spherical, probably shaped by the use of a wooden ball which was then burned away during the firing. The eyelids of the left eye have been broken but those of the right eye are almost intact, and show the degree of realism sought by the artist. The nose is not prominent but it has a peculiar, pointed tip which was certainly modelled by pinching it between the fingers. This is a unique feature. It reminds one of the early *nō*-masks of Japan. The clay head is not merely an idealized face but appears to be the portrait or death mask of a particular person, probably made by a foreign resident or a naturalized emigrant, possibly from Central Asia.

This exotic clay *arhat* is joined by a group of wooden dramatic masks from Hahoe in south-east Korea. These masks are made of willow wood. They have been kept in the village of Hahoe for centuries. The villagers can trace the history of the masks back to the sixteenth century. Close investigation however, leads beyond the tradition to a possible dating of the late Koryŏ dynasty because the sculptural style is utterly different from that of the Yi period.

The deep-set eyes are arranged asymmetrically so that they appear alive under the play of changing light and shade. The nose is extraordinarily long and aquiline: a type Cat. 131 that never occurs in the Korean race. This is again a reflection of foreign sculpture such as we have seen in the clay *Cat. 123 *lohan*. This new type of sculpture must have entered Korea from outside during the Koryŏ period. The lineage of Japanese *nō*-mask sculpture, which is believed to have originated in China, might be established with these Korean masks as the link.

From the late thirteenth century onwards, numerous artists from the Yüan dynasty settled in Kaesŏng, the capital of Koryŏ. Their influence on Korean sculpture was immediately felt. One such Mongol type sculpture of that Cat. 124 time is shown here. It is a gilt bronze Avalokiteśvara seated on a typical Mongolian throne of bent lotus petals. The figure is easily differentiated from the usual Koryŏ figures by the excessive use of jewellery, the relaxed posture, and the face with oblique Mongolian eyes.

Late Koryŏ artists lost the great Silla tradition of working on large-scale stone Buddhas. However they mastered the skill of casting small figures of bronze and iron, mostly in the Yüan or early Ming style. Several bronze figures of the late Koryŏ period, about 1300, clad in thick heavy robes, seem to reflect influences from contemporary Chi- *Pl. 90, Cat. nese sculpture. 130, 131, 132

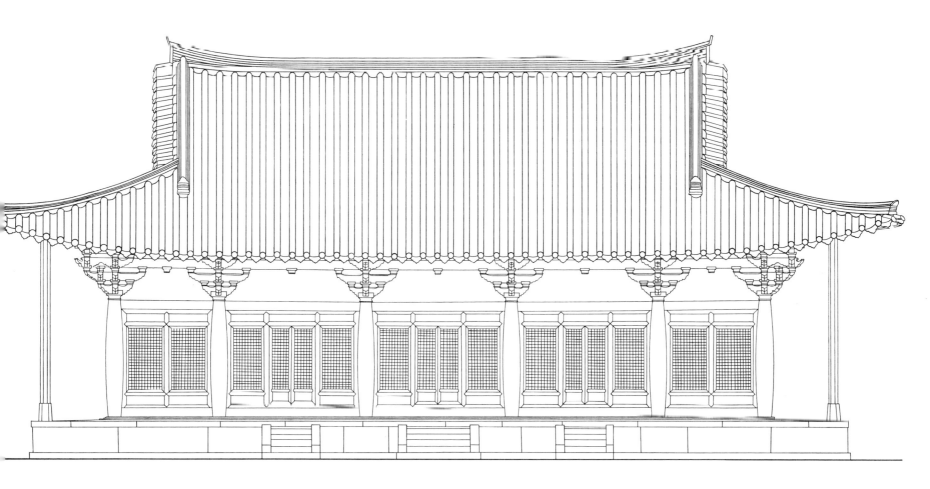

Cat. 125   A seated gilt bronze Buddha in the National Museum is a typical example of such late Koryŏ images. The flat face with sleepy eyes and projecting lips has the type of face that characterizes the Buddhas of the Yi dynasty (1392 to

★Cat. 126   1910). The leather-like robe with simple conventionalized drapery also continues far into the Yi period. The square flat face without the slightest hint of spiritual beauty is vastly different from the classic sculpture of the Great Silla period. Buddhism itself has changed and degenerated, and the monk-artists are now lacking in the artistic inspiration that springs from pure religious zeal.

A bronze Kṣitigarbha at Sŏnun-sa in south-west Korea would be a typical Yi sculpture were it not for the absence of stiffness in the drapery folds and in the face. The simple treatment of the drapery on the legs, particularly in the single arc that sweeps upward from the knee-cap, is a characteristic technique of that period. It is strictly in the fashion of early Ming sculpture.

During the Yi period, the degeneration of sculptural technique which had already begun during the Koryŏ period, continued without interruption, until a Buddhist figure became a mere block of wood, bronze or other material, on which meaningless features of human anatomy and drapery were impressed. During the first half of the Yi dynasty—that is, up to the sixteenth century—Buddhas followed the pattern set by late Koryŏ sculpture, but were sometimes enlivened by the naïvety characteristic of the Yi period.

A seated bronze Buddha in the collection of the Tŏksu Palace Museum is an early Yi sculpture with a quiet, emotionless face and a fluent but schematic arrangement of drapery patently in the tradition of late Koryŏ sculptures. This figure, however, has an air which reflects the rationalistic tendency of early Yi thought.

*Cat. 127

The final piece for our discussion is a seated Buddha in the famous Haein-sa, south-east Korea, made in 1769. The face is square and flat and there is nothing of spirituality in it. The *uṣṇīṣa* is almost flattened and the shaved spot shines like a crescent moon. The drapery is rendered in clean lines and forms but is not meant to be naturalistic. The artist had no aspiration beyond reproducing Buddhistic iconography as faithfully as possible according to the manual. The situation was the same throughout the Far East.

*Cat. 128

PART IV

GOLD, BRONZE AND

LACQUER WORKS

PREHISTORIC PERIOD

Nothing of artistic value has been preserved from the Neolithic period. It is only after the Early Iron Age which started around the third century B.C. and continued until the third century A.D., that works of art in bronze and iron emerge.

Pl.91   Many bronze daggers and halberds, sometimes associated with twin-knobbed mirrors, have been discovered from simple burial pits. The halberds do not differ much from Chinese types, but the daggers show distinctive features such as a high central ridge, a narrow blade and a separately cast detachable hilt. They are evidently of non-Chinese origin and they have not been found anywhere in the Huang-ho (Yellow River) basin of northern China. Their birth place cannot be definitely decided, but a recent discovery of similar daggers with even earlier features, in Ch'aoyang province outside the Great Wall in north-eastern China, threw some light on the problem of their
*Pl.91 lineage and the culture to which they belong[1].

The twin-knobbed mirrors also differ significantly from Chinese mirrors. In typical cases the edge of the mirror is semi-circular in section, unlike the 'raised platform' edge or sharp pointed edge of Chinese mirrors. The knob on a Chinese mirror is always a single one placed in the centre, but on the Korean mirror, there are two knobs set away from the centre. The decoration of the mirror also differs from the Chinese type in that it consists of linear geometric designs. Like the bronze daggers, such mirrors are to be found only in Korea and Korean-influenced western Japan. It is significant that a prototype of the two-knobbed mirror was discovered at the above-mentioned site in Ch'aoyang

together with various bronze objects which are clearly of Siberian origin but which show the admixture of some Chinese elements. In the light of the Ch'aoyang finds, we may assume that the dagger, halberd, mirror and other related bronze articles represent a culture originating outside China; it was the culture of a people whom the Chinese called by the generic name of Tung-hu or Eastern Barbarians. They lived in what are known today as the Jehol and Liaoning provinces and in the lower reaches of the Yalu extending into north-western Korea. The Wei-mo of northern Korea, already described on p. 10 also belonged culturally and ethnically to the Tung-hu.

Sandstone moulds for bronze daggers and mirrors have been discovered in many places in Korea and it is clear that such tools were cast locally. In most cases, the bronzes are brittle and covered with a beautiful black patina. The great quantity of tin in the bronze is doubtless due to the strong influence of Chinese metallurgy at that period.

Outstanding among these early Korean bronzes are the two bronze buckles of animal shape discovered in 1918 at a remote village near Yŏngch'ŏn, south-eastern Korea. In August of that year, while cutting through the foot of a small hill at a site a mile or so from Yŏngch'ŏn station, a band of labourers discovered a rich hoard of bronze tools and ornaments, consisting of fifteen mirrors, more than a hundred rivet-shaped mountings for leather straps, and other pieces including the two belt buckles[2]. Three of the mirrors are Chinese-made, belonging to the Former Han dynasty (206 B.C. – A.D. 208) while the rest are local copies of poorer quality.

The horse-buckle has an overall length of six inches from the trimmed tail to the tip of the projecting hook on the breast. The short tail and neck are cast in the round but the body is flat with the reverse side concave. The horse is forcefully represented in the bulging dynamic torso, massive strong legs and contracted neck with erect mane. The small but sharp face suggests a strong feeling of movement which is accentuated by the horizontally raised tail. This dynamic impression is further enhanced by the addition of two ornamental bands around the shoulder and torso decorated with a strictly geometric linear design.

The tiger also is cast on one side only, like the horse, and has similar ornamental bands arranged around the torso and shoulder, but it is much poorer in the quality of the modelling, especially in the clumsy legs and awkwardly modelled hip. Its face is completely devoid of detail except for the wide open mouth and ring-like eyes. The sides of the head are also decorated with a geometric linear design. It is interesting to compare a similar bronze tiger of the Han dynasty discovered in Inner Mongolia[3]. Although the Chinese tiger is not a belt-buckle and the body is much more naturalistically rendered, the posture and the head with its wide open mouth are almost identical with our Yŏngch'ŏn piece. Together with the Han mirrors mentioned above, the animal-buckles from Yŏngch'ŏn were undoubtedly inspired by Han period pieces which were in turn derived from earlier Ordos bronzes[4].

Besides these animal buckles from Yŏngch'ŏn, there are also isolated finds of pole-caps, rattles and other bronze ornaments reportedly from the lower reaches of the Naktong River. They are clearly int he tradition of Scythian art of the Steppes and again we recognize in early Korean bronzes strong Siberian elements allied with undeniable Chinese influence.

THE THREE KINGDOMS PERIOD

The fall of the Lo-lang colony in north Korea stimulated the spread of the highly developed Lo-lang art into the local native communities. Bronze and iron were well known to the Koreans by that time, but the introduction of gold- and silver-mining seems to have coincided with the fall of the Chinese colony. The rich gold deposits within the territory of Silla in south-eastern Korea became a source of wealth for the rapidly rising kingdom, and Silla craftsmen who had been trained by Lo-lang technicians soon began to produce their own gold ornaments. Kings and aristocrats of the kingdom were sumptuously decked with gold and jewellery, and the ruling classes of Silla seem to have demonstrated their power in the glitter of precious ornaments.

GOLD CROWNS

Most impressive of all were the gold crowns, which display more spiritual force than artistic beauty. They are made of cut sheet-gold and none of them seem to be solid enough for practical use.

Three gold crowns have been excavated in the royal cemeteries at Kyŏngju, all dating from the Old Silla dynasty. Best known among them is the elaborate one from the Gold Crown Tomb, so christened after the discovery of the crown in 1921[5]. Pl.XXIII

On 24 September of that year, a policeman noticed several children searching for glass beads in a pile of earth thrown out from a nearby construction site in the southern

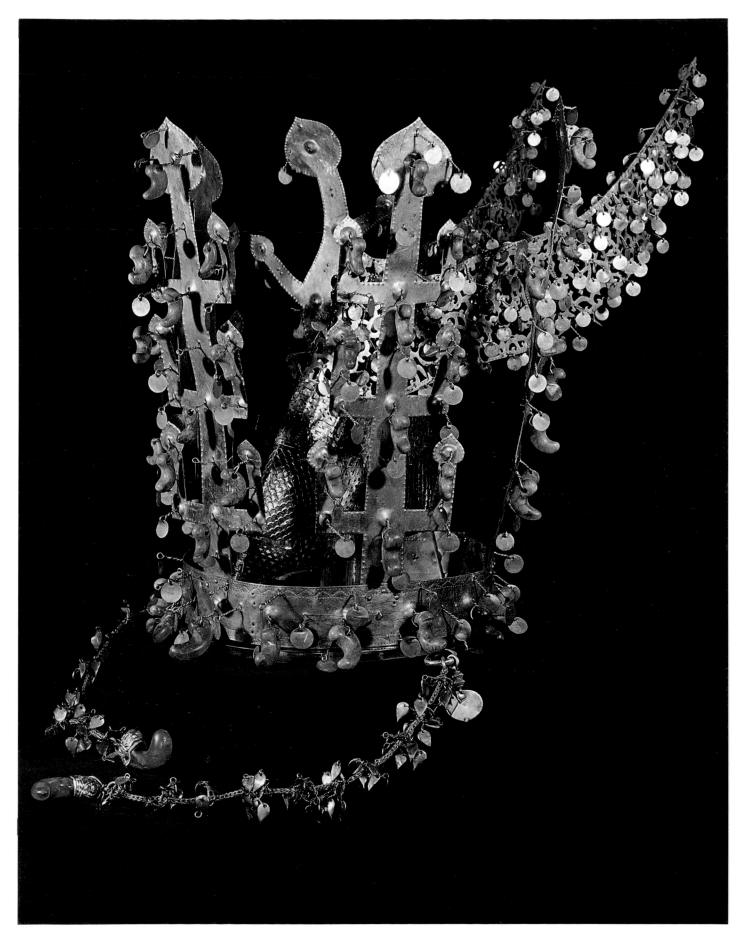

part of the town of Kyŏngju. He saw to his surprise that pieces of gold were showing in the ground. It was the ruined site of a once huge tumulus which had been gradually levelled off with the passage of time. The body interred there had long since disappeared, but had originally been buried with a hoard of jewellery. The small glass beads alone numbered more than 20,000, apart from other precious gems and gold ornaments. The body wore a gold crown, a gold belt with rows of pendants, and was laid out in a box-like wooden funeral chamber which had also long since perished and disappeared. Undoubtedly a great king, he was surrounded by all kinds of burial gifts, and even his toes were decorated with gold rings. The quantity and quality of the funeral gifts is unsurpassed in any other Silla tomb. Judging from the style of these gifts and the other personal ornaments, he lived about the beginning of the sixth century, A.D. Buddhism had not yet officially been accepted as an authorized state religion, but had been infiltrating into Silla for some time. This situation is hinted at by the lotus designs on the locally made lacquer wares discovered in the tomb.

The gold crown worn by the king consists of an outer circlet with five uprights and an inner cap with horn-like branches. It is made of cut sheet-gold like the other gold crowns of the period. The outer circlet has three frontal uprights in highly conventionalized tree-shapes, flanked by two antler-shaped uprights. The outer edges of the circlet and of the uprights are decorated with punched dots, and numerous spangles and jade *magatama* (comma-shaped ornaments) are attached to them by means of twisted wire. Finally there are two long pendants suspended from the circlet like earrings. The separate inner piece is a pointed cap with T-shape designs in open work and the two horn-like branches rising from it. These horns are also decorated with spangles fastened on with wire. The significance of the horns is still controversial, but they seem to be a gold version of bird feathers.

To ancient Koreans feathers were the symbol of a mysterious power of flight in the spiritual world. The Chinese *San-kuo-chih* (History of the Three Kingdoms) describes the custom of the southern Koreans who used feathers as a funeral gift to speed the flight of the dead spirit (Vol. 30). In north Korea the Koguryŏ also valued feathers highly, particularly the tail feathers of the cock, probably because of the universal belief that cocks disperse darkness and evil spirits. In the mural paintings of Koguryŏ tombs the warriors have their head-dresses decorated with cocks' tail-feathers. Their nickname of 'cock-worshippers' reached as far as India[6]. In view of this background, there is a strong possibility that the 'horns' of a Silla crown were really meant for feathers.

As for the outer circlet, the religious significance of the tree and antler-forms are easily understood since the worship of these two objects was almost universal among ancient peoples in the Palaeolithic age. When we think of the wide range of such a cult, particularly among the peoples of the Eurasian Steppe, their appearance on a Silla crown is not surprising. Attention should be paid to a Roman-made diadem discovered from a Sarmatian kurgan in Novocherkassk on the north-eastern shore of the Black Sea[7]. In this diadem, miniature stags and trees are arranged on the upper edge of the circlet. The highly stylized form of the Silla crown must have been derived from some such original diadem of the steppe.

*Fig. 6

Fig. 6 Drawing of the outer circlet of a gold crown from the Gold Crown Tomb. H. 11³/₄ in. Old Silla dynasty, ca. 6th century.

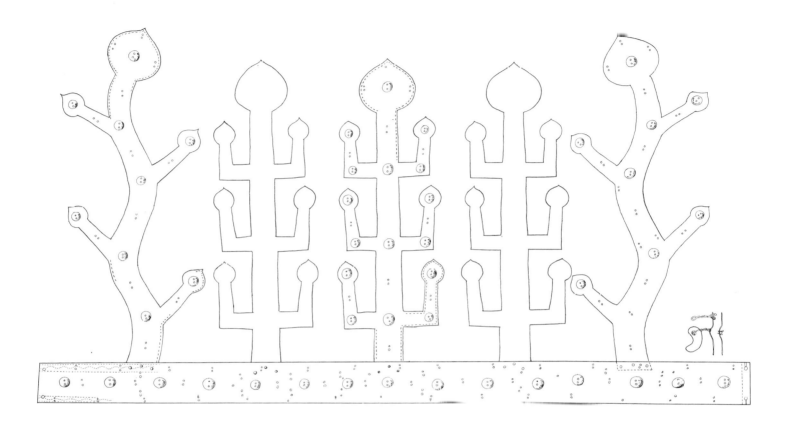

*Pl.93 As has already been pointed out by Hentze, the Silla crown displays a strongly Shamanistic character, and the striking similarity in basic idea to Shaman diadems of the Yenissei region of Siberia must be emphasized[8].

Under these circumstances, we may assume that the crowns were worn by kings of the Old Silla dynasty for special occasions, such as coronations or major religious ceremonies, in which the king himself acted as the head priest. The crown in question is so weak in construction *Cat.133 that there is also a possibility that the crown was merely a funerary object copied after a more solid one used by the king while he was alive. In either case, the crown is unique both in form and quality, and is an interesting indication of the basic pattern of Silla's aboriginal culture.

The jade *magatama* are of the type commonly found in the tumuli of Kofun period Japan (fourth to sixth centuries A.D.). The white jadeite with blue or greenish mottling is not found in a natural state in modern Korea, but the abundance of the stone as finished *magatama* in Silla tombs and isolated discoveries of proto-type *magatama* from earlier sites suggest that rich deposits of raw jadeite once occurred somewhere in the Kyŏngsang Triangle[9].

Another gold crown has been excavated from a tomb in Kyŏngju which has since been called the Lucky Phoenix Tomb from the discovery of a crown with a phoenix-like finial. The circlet made of cut sheet-gold with three branched frontal uprights, two rear antlers and suspended

double pendants is identical with that described above. This crown, however, has no inner cap but instead has a domed frame made of two arching bands crossing at right angles each with both ends riveted to the outer circlet. It was doubtless worn without an inner cap, and is a simplified form of the complex gold crown discussed above. Three phoenix-like birds in cut-out silhouette are seated on the edge of the flame-like finial on top of the crown. The identity of the birds is, however, not certain and it is possible that they may be intended to represent the imaginary three-legged crow which symbolizes the sun in Chinese myths. On a Koguryŏ gilt-bronze cap, to be described later, the sun-crow is represented in open work in the centre of two side-panels that form the pointed cap.

Besides the gold crowns, several gilt bronze crowns of exactly the same form and size have been preserved, although certain details have been simplified and there is less decoration. These bronze crowns, however, all came from peripheral areas such as Taegu and Yang-san, well away from Kyŏngju.

There are two examples of a quite different form, which may be regarded as the proto-type of Silla crowns. One came from a jar-coffin in the Naju district, which was in the territory of the Paekche dynasty[10], and the other from Silla's Ŭisŏng area some forty-five miles to the north of Kyŏngju[11]. The head-dress discovered from the Silla tomb in Ŭisŏng has three feather-like uprights, hatched up the sides with scissor-cuts and twisted to give a tassel-like effect. The upper end of each upright is made into a finial with a kidney-shaped opening in the centre, giving the effect of a peacock feather. If they are really meant for feathers, the Ŭisŏng head-dress must be related to the helmets of Koguryŏ as well as the inner cap of the Silla gold crown.

Cat. 135

★ Cat. 134

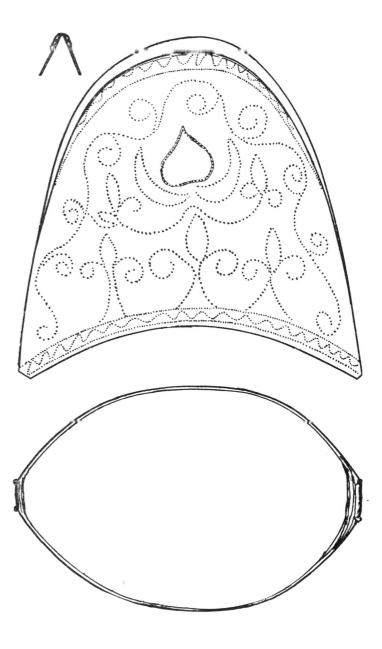

Cat. 137   The gilt bronze crown from Naju quoted above, like the gold crown from Kyŏngju, consists of an outer circlet with three uprights and a separate inner cap made of thin

Fig. 7,8   bronze sheet. The outer circlet, decorated with tiny round spangles, is of particular interest. The three uprights are all identical in form, a very complicated yet highly stylized tree-shape adorned with a flower-like finial at the top. The shape is unlike the gold crowns from Silla, but the type was not confined to south-western Korea, because the Naju type crown or diadem with complicated tree-shape uprights is worn by a warrior depicted in a Koguryŏ tomb painting near P'yŏngyang[12].

In relation to these head-gears with tree-shaped uprights, we notice a similar diadem on a Buddhist Guardian of the sixth century at T'ienlung-shan, China. As was pointed out long ago by Hamada, such a plant-like upright, probably originally part of a diadem, has been discovered in Alexandropol, south Russia[13].

All these facts suggest that there was a type of diadem with less conventionalized tree-shaped uprights that spread widely across the Eurasian continent. This type of diadem was used by the Koguryŏ as well as by the Paekche, but in Silla the tree-shaped uprights were transformed into the highly conventionalized shape which we see today in the gold crowns of the Old Silla dynasty. This evolution of the diadem from the prototype must have been achieved by the people of Silla themselves.

No diadems or crowns with tree-shaped uprights are preserved from Koguryŏ although, as is mentioned above, such a diadem is depicted in mural paintings of that period.

Cat. 134, Fig. 9   A pointed cap made of gilt bronze discovered from a tomb in P'yŏngyang in 1941 is one of the two remaining head-

dresses from Koguryŏ[14]. It is a rare piece but suffices to demonstrate the technical achievement of Koguryŏ art. It is made of two side-panels joined together by rivets at the centre. Each panel is a piece of open-work depicting two dragons and a phoenix around a central medallion of the sun-crow. This motif is doubtless a royal emblem, demonstrating the power and lineage of the Koguryŏ kings, and there is little doubt that the cap was worn by a Koguryŏ king who lived about the sixth century. The creatures are represented in sweeping forceful lines and the whole design is full of animation. It is somewhat crowded, but there is no confusion in the execution and the entire composition is perfectly set into the beaded frame. Wings of *tamamushi* beetle (*Chrysochroa fulgidissima*) plastered on birch skin are used as the back plate for the metal piece, and furnish a lustrous bluish or green background with reddish striations.

Tamamushi wings as a background for open metal-work were widely used at the time as, for example, on the famous Tamamushi shrine now kept in Hōryūji, Japan. The wings were even used on some stirrups found in the Gold Crown Tomb of Silla.

GOLD EARRINGS

The objects most frequently encountered during excavations of Silla tombs are gold earrings. Indeed, they are the trademark of tombs of the Old Silla period.

A typical example consists of a main ring that goes through the earlobe and a pendant from which is suspended a heart-shaped finial. There are two varieties in the main ring; a thick hollow ring and a wire-like thin solid ring. Stylistically the solid ring type is an earlier form than the hollow thick type, but both occur together in the same tomb and they do not reflect differences in date or the sex of the bearers: a woman's tomb in Pomunni, Kyŏngju produced a pair of the thick-ring type and the great king of the Gold Crown Tomb also wore the same type.

We show here a typical example of the solid-ring type Pl. xxiv discovered from a tomb in Kyŏngju. A cube-shaped pendant with designs in filigree and granulation is suspended from the main ring, and a pointed finial, shaped like a pen nib with two spangles, is hung from the tip.

Filigree and granulation was a technique familiar to the Lo-lang Chinese, as is best shown in the famous gold buckle from the Sŏgamni Tomb 9 near P'yŏng-yang[15]. This technique apparently spread southward together with the basic pattern of the earring after the fall of the Lo-lang colony in the early fourth century. The Chinese wore glass earrings called *er-tang* consisting of a perforated tubular piece to go through the earlobe, one or two spherical beads and a leaf-shaped finial pendant all held by a thread hung from the main tubular glass pieces. The basic idea and structure of the Chinese *er-tang* are identical with those of the gold earrings of Silla and Koguryŏ. Several gilt bronze earrings from Koguryŏ tombs are all of the thin solid-ring type with a simple pendant and pen-pointed finial, that closely corresponds to Lo-lang's glass *er-tang*.

It is apparent then that Silla's gold earrings were evolved from the glass *er-tang* of the Lo-lang Chinese, but the evolution from glass to gold seems to have taken place in north Korea during the fourth century. The discovery of a thick-ring earring in a Chinese tomb in P'yŏngyang dated 353 A.D. [16], and of gilt bronze earrings from Koguryŏ tombs in north Korea supports this theory.

A pair of earrings from a tomb in Pomunni, Kyŏngju, is the best and most elaborate piece of the thick hollow-ring type. The thick ring is richly decorated with a kind of trefoil design set within hexagons depicted in filigree. The spherical medial-pendant is made of small gold rings fused together to make an open-work sphere and adorned with numerous leaf-shaped spangles. Such a ring-built medial pendant is typical of thick-ring earrings. In the thin and solid ring type, the medial pendant is always a

ᴜᴜᴜll solid piece of gold, often with set stones, but without spangles attached.

*Cat. 138   The thick ring of the Pomunni piece has a slit-like opening for the earlobe to pass through, but the slit is so narrow and tight that it is questionable whether it was ever used.

Gold and gilt bronze bracelets have also frequently been discovered in Silla tombs. In most cases, a Silla bracelet is a simple solid ring with tiny notches around the outer edge which suggest its possible derivation from prehistoric

bracelets made of ridged shells such as *Pecton nobilis* or *Arca radiata.*

There are, however, much more elaborate examples such as the one shown here. This pair of bracelets was discovered in a tomb in Hwang-ori, Kyŏngju, together with a fragment of an originally splendid pocket knife. The bracelets are made of solid bronze, and two dragon-like creatures with long hooked beaks are twisted around the narrow space in an animated posture. There is plasticity in the shallow engraving, but the real merit of the bracelets

lies in the masterful setting of the design into the narrow circular space. They are certainly the work of a master craftsman of the time, probably about the sixth century, apogee of the Old Silla dynasty.

GOLD GIRDLE

We show here a gold girdle from the Gold Crown Tomb. Pl. 92 The girdle is over six feet long and consists of thirty-nine

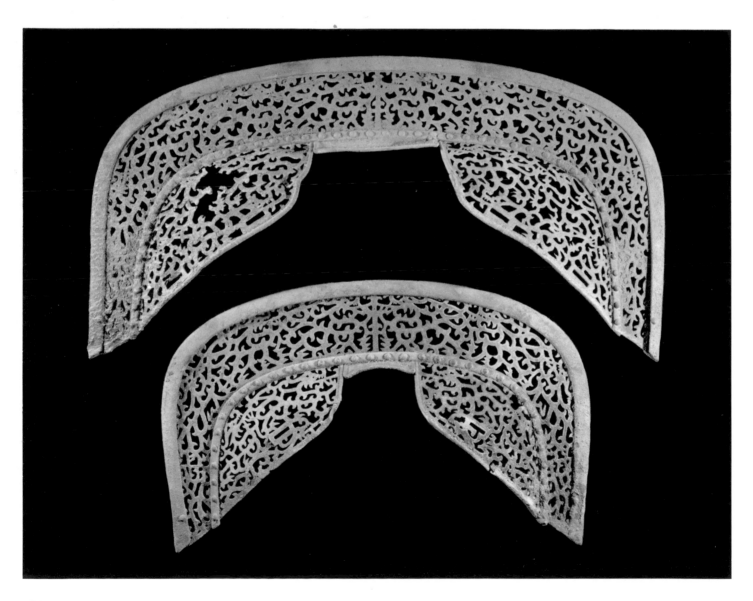

plaques, a long buckle and a flat thong. Originally, the plaques were riveted to a leather or cloth backing but this material has now completely decayed. Each plaque or link (called *k'ua* in Chinese), as well as the heart-shaped pendant hinged to the plaque, has a complicated floral design in open-work apparently derived from the so-called *kuai-yün-wen* or 'Fantastic Cloud Pattern'. This design, which is a vine-like cloud with a bird-head projecting from each curve, was a very popular one that appeared in almost every scene. The *kuai-yün* was somewhat modified during later periods, but the pattern continued to be used by Chinese and other Far Eastern artisans. Until the recent discovery from a fifth-century tomb near Nanking, in south China, however, it was not known that belt plaques with an exactly identical *kuai-yün* design were used in China during the Six Dynasties[17]. The discovery of the same type of belt plaque in a Paekche tomb[18], to the west of Silla, makes the lineage of the Silla metal girdle clear. It came from China and reached Silla by way of Paekche.

The gold girdle from the Gold Crown Tomb was accompanied by seventeen pendants originally suspended from the girdle. Unfortunately, however, the original order of the pendants and method of fastening them to the girdle is not known, for the treasure was hastily collected by amateurs.

Each of the pendants, except for three woven chains, comprises six to ten ovoid gold plaques, slightly concave on one side, hinged to each other by small interstitial plates. The ovoid plaques with two ears on the longer sides exactly recall the so-called *er-p'ei* or 'eared wine-cup' of the Han dynasty. It is possible that the ovoid plaques are an ornamental imitation of real bronze or lacquer *er-p'ei*. The

adoption of the cup-shape in the girdle pendants may have originated in the suspension of a real cup by the nomads of the steppe. It is a well known fact that in the Han period the Hsiungnu nomads of Mongolia used many Chinese utensils of the Han dynasty[19].

The end-finials of these pendants include gently flaring flat tablets, flat tassel-like pieces with spangles, fishes both naturalistic and highly conventionalized, egg-plant-shaped containers of blue glass, octagonal tubes, *magatama*-jade and a hexagon with the *kuai-yün* design in open-work. The *Chapter on Chariots and Uniform* in the *T'ang-shu* (Annals of the T'ang dynasty) lists the 'Seven objects' or girdle pendants to be worn by government officials as follows: 1) sword, 2) knife, 3) whetstone, 4) *ch'i-pi*, 5) *chen-chüeh*(?), 6) needle case, 7) flint bag. In the Annals the seven objects are called saddle accessories and they seem to be a kind of traveller's kit. However, they were to be suspended from the girdle, and the same Annals list the *yü-tai* as an additional yet compulsory girdle pendant.

The *yü-tai* or 'fish case' is a fish tally *(yü-fu)* in a container. The two fish-shaped finials in our girdle are no doubt *yü-fu*. According to the *Chapter on Uniform* of the *Sung-shih* (Annals of the Sung dynasty), the fish tally or *yü-fu* was a T'ang dynasty invention which displaced the earlier *hu-fu* (tiger tally), a kind of credential or warrant for military personnel. The same source further explains that the *yü-fu* of the T'ang dynasty were made of gold and silver, and were suspended from the girdle to distinguish official ranks. It also states that during the Sung dynasty *yü-fu* were worn only as a decoration[20].

According to these official Chinese sources, it is clear that the *yü-fu* or fish tally was an emblem of rank during the T'ang dynasty. A serious discrepancy arises, however, from the fact that the *yü-fu* from the Gold Crown Tomb is datable to the sixth century and is certainly earlier than the T'ang period which started in 618. The only explanation of this is that the historians of the Sung dynasty were ignorant of the existence of pre-T'ang *yü-fu* or else simply ignored the practice of wearing them. Judging from the general trend of cultural communications between China and Korea, the *yü-fu* of Silla was doubtless introduced from pre-T'ang China, and the custom of wearing such girdles by the people of Silla is related to the ancient custom of the pre-T'ang Chinese, who in turn must have learned it from northern nomads of the steppe region at a time as early as the Chou period.

The Chinese classic *Li Chi* (Book of Rites) states that a son, when serving his parents, suspends from his belt, among various other things, a whetstone. Indeed, a girdle pendant suspending a real whetstone discovered from a Silla tomb is in the former Sugihara Collection[21]. The elongated rectangular finials, six in number, of the Gold Crown Tomb girdle also represent whetstones, and are another sign that the girdle pendants of the Old Silla period are linked to the time-honoured custom of mainland Asia.

The egg-plant-like glass case held in wire net may be either a medicine container or tinder holder like that listed in the *T'ang-shu*.

Besides two *magatama* of gold and jade, there are two pieces of unknown significance: a tassel-like piece with spangles, and a hexagonal piece in open-work. Apart from these additional unidentifiable objects, the whetstone, *yü-fu* and the needlecase-like box on our girdle all seem to match the description in the *T'ang-shu*.

ORNAMENTED SHOES

Cat. 139 In the catalogue we show the sole of a gilt bronze shoe discovered from Tomb 3 at Nodongni, Kyŏngju. Several such ornamental shoes have been unearthed from Silla tombs, but this one is the best from a technical as well as an aesthetic point of view. The entire space framed by *Pl. 94 double rows of embossed bead design is divided between an inner area and a surrounding band filled with the G-shaped flames so popular in Buddhist haloes of the Northern Wei period in China. The inner space is divided by three rows of hexagons of which the two marginal ones are half concealed by the flame scroll. A squatting demon viewed frontally and a pair of birds with their heads turned back to face each other, alternately occupy each hexagon of the central row. The two marginal rows are filled with peacocks, *kalabinka* with human heads and a beast with a wing-like projection of the shoulder.

These designs are cast in moulds and the sharp details prove the excellent workmanship. The designs show a foreign idea in the Sassanian double-birds motif, but the main source is Buddhism, indicated by the flame pat-
*Cat. 140 tern, the *kalabinka* and, especially, the floral design which is certainly a lotus flower. Many tiny holes on the sole show that it was originally riveted to some inner material such as wood or leather. The bronze sole and the top part of the shoe are sewn together by means of wire. The top of the shoe is decorated with spangles.

We are not sure if such ornamental shoes were actually worn at that time. Most probably these are replicas of real shoes, specially made for funerary use. Indeed, there are many similar Silla shoes with delicate designs on the sole,

even with spangles attached to the sole by wire which prove that they were never intended to be worn.

SADDLES

Most of the Silla tombs yield various pieces of harness, and among them is a saddle with iron stirrups and other bronze fittings. Two ornamental bronze fittings for the front and rear bows of a saddle, illegally dug out of a tomb near Koryŏng, serve well to indicate the original beauty of a well-wrought Silla saddle. The wooden bridge has gone but the bronze fittings for the bows are in perfect condition, which is rare in discoveries from Silla tombs. They are made of cast and gilded bronze and the whole surface is decorated with the complicated *kuai-yün* design done in open work.

CHIAO-TOU

A splendid piece of bronze from the Gold Crown Tomb is a kettle-ewer of the type called *chiao-tou* in Chinese. The spherical body of the kettle is supported by three long curved legs and it has a short spout in the form of a dragon's head and a flat cover decorated with lotus petals. A long flat handle with a dragon's head at each end is attached to the body. The inner dragon bites the rim around the kettle and the outer dragon spits out the floral finial. Such a kettle-ewer is a developed form of simpler Han dynasty examples and was commonly used in ancient China, as is shown by the famous painting 'Admonitions to Court

Ladies' by Ku K'ai-chih of the fourth century. We are not certain whether this particular *chiao-tou* was made in China or in Korea. The late Dr. Hamada, who originally reported on the Gold Crown Tomb, thought it was Chinese-made because of the fine workmanship[22]. The vessel, however, displays the same sturdiness and craftsmanship as is shown in other bronze objects discovered from the Gold Crown Tomb and other Silla tombs, and there is no reason to label all these Silla bronzes as Chinese products.

THE GREAT SILLA PERIOD

The barbaric taste for pure gold that characterized the aristocrats of Old Silla subsided with the advent of the Great Silla period, and from now on we have more objects in bronze, mostly related to Buddhism. Silver seems to have been a favourite material for personal ornaments and utensils, but they have long since perished. There are several splendid lacquer pieces bearing the name of Silla in the famous Shōsō-in Treasure House in Japan. We do not know whether the name 'Silla' is meant for the place of production or for the type of vessel. It is regrettable that these materials are not available for close examination and study, particularly for foreign students.

A drastic change in the burial custom during the seventh century, from tumuli to simple urns, has resulted in the almost total lack of materials for the study of the minor arts of the Great Silla period. Thus we have to turn to Buddhist art for information on the type of art prevalent during the Great Silla period.

SARĪRA CASE (HOLY RELIC CASE)

As has already been briefly mentioned in the chapter on sculpture, the bronze *sarīra* case from the western pagoda of the Kamŭn-sa temple site is one of the best examples of the craftsmanship of the period.   Pl. 95

The *sarīra* shrine was encased in a square box with a low pyramidal cover. Each panel of the box is framed by a narrow scroll of lotus and leaf design, and each main inner

Pl. xx, Pl. 75,
Cat. 141

space is occupied by a separately cast relief figure of one of the Four Guardians. The figures are pasted on the panels with lacquer-like adhesive. Each Guardian is flanked by two demon-mask knobs also pasted to the panel. Finally a lotus bud is arranged at each of the four corners of the panel. The triangular panels that form the pyramidal cover are each decorated with a peacock standing on a lotus leaf base. The birds are also fixed to the panels by the same method as the Guardians. A lozenge-shaped knob is mounted on a decorative floral cushion on the top of the cover. The case has an overall height of one foot, and is covered with a bluish green patina, but there are traces of gilding still partially visible on the surface.

★Cat. 148
Cat. 142

The *sarīra* shrine within the outer bronze case is a superb piece. It shows the most exquisite care by the artist or artists although the overall structure is somewhat over-decorated and over-sophisticated. The shrine is a table shaped square platform on which a miniature glass bottle containing the *sarīra* is placed under a rich canopy supported by four articulated corner poles. The platform is richly decorated with lotus petals and the bead-and-arabesque design, and the Eight Parivaras, in the round, are set into window-like recesses in the four sides of the stand. In the centre of the raised upper platform is a crystal ball covered with flames of bronze, resting on top of the tiny bottle-shaped crystal container for the *sarīra*. A peacock projects from each of the four corners of the double-tiered ceiling, and chain-pendants with bells and tassels are suspended from the demon masks arranged on the ceiling. Every detail of the shrine is executed with utmost delicacy and the piece is a *chef d'œuvre* of the Great Silla period.

BRONZE BELLS

Large bronze bells were painstakingly cast during this period, and several are preserved today in perfect condition. The date of casting of four of them is known, two now in Japan and two in Korea. The Japanese obtained many Korean bells either as loot during the Hideyoshi Invasion of the sixteenth century or as gifts from the Yi government who yielded to persistent requests during times of peace. Silla products and other Korean bells were highly esteemed by the Japanese for their superb taste. Although they derived the original form and structure from Chinese bells, the Koreans developed a unique type of their own, which is quite different from the forms of China and Japan.

A Korean bell differs from a Chinese bell in that it has a hollow cylindrical tube on the *wu*, or the crown of the bell. The tube is not a handle because there is the usual dragon knob beside the tube. Some suggest that the tube plays a subtle part in the sound of the bell, because the hollow tube goes through the crown letting the vibrating air inside the bell run through the tube. The idea is ingenious but nobody has ever proved it scientifically, and, to the ears of an amateur, the sound of a bell with the tube completely blocked does not differ from one with it open.

The complicated knob of a Korean bell seems to be a combined form of the usual dragon-knob of the *chung* bells and the cylindrical handle of the *t'o* bells of ancient China. The *chung* is a bell to be hung and a *t'o* is a bell to be held in the hand by the cylindrical projecting handle on top of the bell. Why the Koreans should combine the two types, almost a millenium later, is not known.

The surface decoration of a Korean bell also differs greatly from that of a Japanese or Chinese bell. In a Korean bell the upper and the lower rims of the body are each surrounded by a horizontal band usually filled with honeysuckle or *pao-hsiang-hua (udumbara,* a flower*)* design. Four equidistant square blocks encasing nine *ju* studs in three rows are arranged around the shoulder immediately below the upper ornamental band or scroll *(sangdae)*. The square blocks, called *yugwak* in Korean, with nine studs are one of the traditional features of ancient Chinese bells.

On the broad sides of the trunk are a pair of lotus medallions placed on opposite sides of the bell, and a similarly arranged pair of flying *devas*. The lotus medallions always serve as the point for striking the bell when ringing it. In Chinese and Chinese-influenced Japanese bells, the body is decorated with a linear rope design that binds up the entire bell crosswise, and there is nothing to correspond to the flying *devas* or ornamental scrolls. The differences are thus strikingly obvious.

Korean bells, however, show some changes in detail after about the tenth century, *i.e.* at the beginning of the Koryŏ period (918–1392). After the tenth century a band of upward-pointing lotus petals appears immediately above the upper ornamental scroll, and often the four *yugwak* are separated from the upper scroll in a 'floating' position. The flying *devas* are frequently replaced by awkward linear representations of Bodhisattvas or Buddhas. The size of the bells also diminished and large bells were seldom cast.

The earliest dated Buddhist bell from Silla now in existence is the one at Sangwŏn-sa in the mountainous Odae area in central Korea. This bronze bell was cast in 725 with funds donated by Hyudori, the wife of a local aristocrat.

The bell has a diameter of just under three feet at the bottom and stands slightly over five and a half feet high. Two heavenly musicians playing a harp and a *shêng* flute, are depicted in relief on either side of the body of the bell. The fluttering scarves of the flying *devas* are realistically rendered as are the *devas* themselves and the graceful lines beautifully match the trailing tone of the note. The darker shade of the square area around the flying *devas* is due to repeated careless ink-rubbing. The structural details, their size and form, are in perfect harmony with each other and all the details are gracefully fitted into the gently sloping outline of the bell. Notice the clear-cut design of honeysuckle around the lotus medallion at the striking point.

About a half century later than the Sangwŏn-sa bell, a much bigger bronze bell was cast in Kyŏngju after many years of hard effort. It is the so-called Pongdŏk-sa bell now Pl. 96 in the Kyŏngju Museum. This grand bell has a height of ten feet, one inch (almost twice the height of an average Korean), and a diameter of six feet, eight inches.

According to a long inscription on the surface of the Fig. 10 bell, its casting was started by King Kyŏngdŏk (d. 765) in Fig. 11 memory of his deceased father King Sŏngdŏk (d. 736), but the casting was not completed by the time Kyŏngdŏk himself died, and the task was left to his son Hyegong who completed it in 771. *Samguk Yusa* tells of the difficulties of the master bell founder who spent years in repeated failure ★ Cat. 148 and finally succeeded only after throwing his little daughter into the molten bronze as a human sacrifice. This legend of human sacrifice is an illustration of the difficulty of cast- ★ Cat. 143 ing such a colossal bell. There are traces of numerous piece-moulds on the surface and ten pouring holes on the crown. The thickness of the wall and the size of the bell must have

Pl.95 *Sarīra shrine. Bronze. From the western stone pagoda at the site of the Kamŭn-sa temple. H. 6 5/16 in. Great Silla dynasty, 682 or slightly earlier. National Museum of Korea, Seoul.*

Pl.96 *Buddhist bell. Bronze. H. 11 ft. 8 9/16 in., D. 7 ft. 4 5/8 in. Great Silla dynasty, 771. Kyŏngju Branch of the National Museum of Korea.*

caused tremendous problems in the casting, but they were successfully solved. The bell produces a mysterious deep sound that vibrates with religious emotion. The lingering tone is thought to suggest the cry of '*emille*' ('Mother'), the sad helpless cry of the little girl thrown into the molten bronze. Because of this grim legend the bell is often called the *emille* bell.

Fig. 10 *Ink-rubbing of the inscription on the Pongdŏk-sa bell. H.
2ft., 7½ in. Great Silla dynasty, 771.*

Fig. 11 *Ink-rubbing of a deva offering an incense burner, depicted
in relief on the Pongdŏk-sa bell. H. 3 ft., 6½ in. Great Silla dynasty, 771.*

THE KORYŎ PERIOD

During the Koryŏ period there was much progress in
fields of art such as ceramics and lacquer, but other minor
arts lost much of the elegance and animation of the Silla
period.

Bronze temple bells, mostly of small size, continued to
be made. The practice of bell-casting must have been a
major burden on the people, since the monks and government agencies ordered compulsory donation of used bronze
ware for casting new bells. There is indeed a legend of the
Koryŏ period about a monster called Pulgasari (literally
meaning Buddhist Temple Dweller) who lived on bronze
and iron and even ate sewing needles. The monster's only
merit was his ability to chase away any devils. In his final
rage, he ran around the streets of the capital city and melted
away whatever metal his red-hot body encountered. This
legend surely reflects the heavy burden of bronze donation
inflicted upon the people by the government-backed
temples.

Today, more than a dozen large Koryŏ bells are preserved besides numerous small ones[23]. The majority of these
large bells is now in Japan and the earliest of them, a bell
dated 956, kept at Naha in the Ryūkyūs, was destroyed
during World War II.

Pl. 97   Inside Korea, the best Koryŏ bell is one dated 1010, now
in the collection of the Tŏksu Palace Museum of Fine Arts,
Seoul. According to an inscription on the body, the bell
was cast for Ch'ŏnhŭng-sa on Sŏnggŏ-san, south of Seoul.
Five and a half feet high with a diameter of three and a
quarter feet, it faithfully follows the classic Silla style in

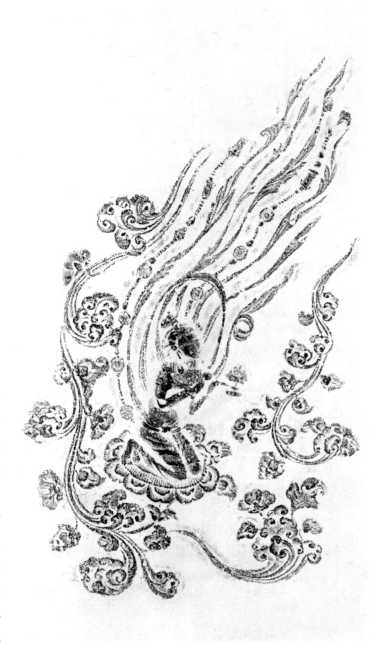

195

Pl. 97 Buddhist bell. Bronze. H. 5 ft. 6¹⁵/₁₆ in., D. 3³/₈ in. Koryŏ dynasty, 1010. Tŏksu Palace Museum of Fine Arts, Seoul.

every detail and no Koryŏ features are apparent. Its immediate model must have been a typical Silla bell such as the Sangwŏn-sa piece. It has the cylinder-dragon complex on the crown, the upper and lower ornamental bands filled with the *udumbara* design. The nine studs within the four square blocks are not of the flat medallion type but projecting buds like those on the Sangwŏn-sa bell. The two lotus medallions at the striking points and two flying angels in relief around the trunk also accord with classical Silla tradition.

Cat. 144   One of the most typical Koryŏ-style bells, however, is the one at the temple of Naeso-sa in south-western Korea. This bell, cast in 1222, was at Ch'ŏngnim-sa, until it was moved to its present location in 1853. It stands three and

★Cat. 145 a quarter feet high with a diameter of two and three quarter inches. It has the usual tube-dragon complex on the crown, but the cylindrical tube has now four spherical ornaments arranged on top of the upper edge. As Tsuboi has already pointed out, this is a feature that first appeared in the early thirteenth century[24]. The outer edge of the crown is marked by a band of lotus petals that project obliquely out of the upper ornamental scroll. This is also a new feature introduced by Koryŏ bell-smiths. Other features of the bell are still in the tradition of Silla, but a major change may be discerned in the adoption of a Trinity under a flying canopy in place of the otherwise classical flying *devas*. The figures in low relief are much inferior in quality to those on the eighth-century Silla bells. The lotus medallion at the striking point looks almost like a sunflower and the change from earlier elegant examples

Pl. 98 is sadly apparent. Many small Koryŏ bells, however, followed the pattern and quality of this Naeso-sa bell.

INCENSE BURNERS

The degeneration of bell-casting during the Koryŏ period seems strange in view of a series of beautifully finished bronze incense-burners still treasured in many temples. These censers, called *hyang-wan* or *hyangno* in Korea, have the shape of a pedestal cup, with designs in inlay. The original inscriptions on these bronze censers call the inlay technique *hamŭn* (silver-bearing) or *ipssa* (thread inserting). The technique of metal inlay must have been derived from a similar method in lacquer work, which, as will be explained later, originated in the *p'ing-t'o* technique of T'ang-dynasty China. Inlay in ceramics seems to have been evolved from metal inlay technique.

The earliest dated and probably the finest existing Koryŏ bronze incense-burner is the one at P'yo-ch'ung-sa, near Miryang, south-east Korea. This bronze censer is eleven inches high and the entire surface is covered with beautiful, glossy, dark patination. The dark patina seems to have been deliberately produced at the time of manufacture, probably by a heating and polishing process. The dark colour can also be obtained by chemical treatment with arsenic sulphide or salt, but Korean bronze of the Koryŏ period is more truly brass than bronze because of its high zinc content and this alloy responds well to the former process.

KUNDIKA

A bronze *kundika*, standing one foot three inches high, is an exact replica of pottery ware, even to the design executed in beautiful silver inlay. This Buddhist ritual vessel originated in India and was widely used both in China and Korea, particularly during the Koryŏ period. In Koryŏ, the vessel was a favourite utensil among the upper classes and was manufactured in both bronze and pottery. *Kundika* were originally for offering holy water to the Buddha, but Koryŏ monks and aristocrats found them excellent as wine-servers or containers for honey water.

The *kundika* reproduced here is the best of several known examples, although it now suffers from a serious degree of bronze disease (causing a powdery surface and falling out of the inlaid silver wire). The vessel is a vase-like long-necked bottle with a covered spout on one side and a long erect spout joined to the flaring lip of the neck in the other position. Silver is used for the fitting around the joint as well as for the ring-foot of the bottle.

The designs done in inlaid silver over the body comprise veined leaves around the upper spout, vertically placed cloud designs on the neck, a band of bow-like patterns around the shoulder and the bottom, and a main scene of an autumn landscape. The landscape, of willow trees, reeds, boats, ducks, geese and fishermen, actually portrays scenes of hunting and fishing, a theme both improper and impossible for a Buddhist vessel. Despite this scene, however, the presentation is peaceful and amiable like a picture from a fairy tale. The artist shrewdly depicts flocks of geese and ducks frightened away by hunters and fishermen. The agitated birds seem almost literally to flap their wings in the autumn breeze. Realistic reeds and willow trees are beautifully harmonized with the half-conventionalized patch of land. The overall effect of the decoration, the manner of presentation as well as the elements of the design, clearly

display the style of classic celadon wares of the Koryŏ period, suggesting a date around the eleventh to the twelfth century.

BRONZE MIRRORS

Tombs of ancient Koreans up to the end of the Silla dynasty are characterized by their almost complete lack of bronze mirrors. We do not know whether this phenomenon indicates the scarcity of mirrors in Korean society or simply that it was not the custom to bury mirrors in funeral chambers. The Koryŏ period is marked by a sudden increase of bronze mirrors discovered in tombs. All the bronze mirrors so frequently encountered in antique dealers' booths on the streets of Seoul belong to this period.

Koryŏ mirrors in general are poorly made, with less tin in the bronze than those of China. They are copied after the mirrors of contemporary neighbours such as Sung, Liao, Juchen, Yüan and Japan. There are of course many imported mirrors among those found in Koryŏ tombs and it is often very difficult to distinguish domestic from imported products. Sung mirrors are known for the revival of ancient styles of the Han and pre-Han periods and there also appeared among Koryŏ mirrors exact replicas of ancient Chinese mirrors at least as far as the decoration is concerned. These later revivals are, however, easily differentiated from the original pieces by the softer material of the bronze, which has less tin in it, and the much reduced sharpness of the sculptural details in the decoration. Ancient Chinese mirrors are made of a harder, nickel bronze that usually develops a dark glossy patina.

Two favourite designs for Koryŏ mirrors were the dragon and the phoenix. In the giant mirror with a diameter of nine and a half inches reproduced here, two dragons in pursuit of bell-shaped jade ornaments are depicted in relief around a central medallion with a typical Koryŏ-type lotus flower with pointed narrow petals and veins. The whole scene is surrounded by a band of stylized cloud pattern, which is strikingly similar to those appearing on the neck of the *kundika* discussed above.

Cat. 146

Cat. 147 Another illustration shows a sixteen-lobed mirror with a phoenix design. The outer margin is separated from the inner part by double lines and is filled with the so-called *udumbara* flowers. Two phoenix among vines occupy the main space of the mirror around the central quatrefoil medallion.

LACQUER WORK

Lacquer work in ancient Korea must have spread from the Chinese colony of Lo-lang and fragments of lacquer wares have often been discovered from Old Silla tombs. Sometimes they are painted with geometric designs in red, green and white. In the case of the Gold Crown Tomb, the wooden coffin was painted all over in black lacquer and the wooden dishes were painted red inside and black outside, in the fashion of Han dynasty lacquer wares.

★Cat. 149 During the Unified Silla period, lacquer work must have progressed a great deal, to judge from the T'ang lacquer wares preserved in the Shōsō-in Treasure House in Japan. We have, however, no original product of the Silla period preserved in Korea. The few lacquer objects in the Shōsō-in mentioned above which bear the name of Silla are likely to be so named for their place of production, or merely according to the type of instrument or vessel.

The Koryŏ dynasty is noted, together with celadon ware, for the progress of lacquer work, particularly in the technique of decoration using mother-of-pearl or tortoise-shell and copper wire. According to the *Koryŏsa* (History of Koryŏ) a special government agency was set up in 1272 under the orders of the Empress of Kublai Khan[25] to manufacture lacquer cases for a set of the *tripitaka*.

The shell decoration known as *najŏn* has its origin in the *p'ing-t'o* method of lacquer work of the T'ang dynasty. In the *p'ing-t'o* method, thin pieces of gold, silver or shell, cut according to the design, are pasted over the surface of a vessel and a coat of lacquer is applied over the entire surface. After the coating is completed the excess layer above the cut decoration is removed, to reveal the design set in the lacquer background, thus producing an effect of inlay. This *najŏn* technique was extensively practised also during the Yi dynasty; indeed the *najŏn* lacquer industry was a speciality of the period, and the tradition is carried on to the present day.

There are more than a dozen Koryŏ lacquer works preserved today, but most of them are in Japan. As pointed out by Mr. Yoshino the scarcity of old work in Korea may be due to the dry climate which might easily destroy lacquer ware[26].

Among the few examples of Koryŏ lacquer works in Korea, a covered box in the collection of the Tŏksu Palace Museum of Fine Arts is the most important and significant piece. This box, probably intended for carrying cosmetics, stands only four and a half inches high and the longer side is eleven and a half inches long. It is damaged considerably, both inside and out, and has lost its original cover. Nevertheless, it preserves enough of its original shape and decoration to permit restoration of the clean-cut *najŏn* design.

The box has a wooden core covered with lacquer-coated hemp cloth. A thick layer of black lacquer is applied above the frame in which pieces of shell are sunk to produce the decorative pattern. The inside of the box is left plain without decoration but the outside is decorated with willow and other trees produced by the *najŏn* technique, using white mother-of-pearl and the abalone shell, and partly painted in gold. There are also flying birds in the sky and a few ducks floating on the water around the trees. The scenes are then framed with bands of X-shapes and floral patterns. The retouching of the design with gold is a technique also to be observed on Koryŏ celadon wares around the thirteenth century[27]. The practice of placing painting-like landscapes against wide spaces is the trend of the classic Koryŏ celadons of the twelfth to early thirteenth centuries. The date of the lacquer box may thus be roughly established.

The second piece for our discussion is a small circular box said to be a rosary container now in the Ōkura Shūkokan Museum in Japan. It is a covered flat case with a diameter of four and three quarter inches and is in perfect condition, preserving all the details of the decoration. It is made of wood covered with lacquered hemp. The top of the cover is divided into a central space and a narrow marginal rim by a band of beads arranged within parallel lines, of which the twisted outer one is made of copper and the inner straight one is of tin. The marginal rim is also framed by a single twisted copper wire. In the centre is a Sanskrit character, a symbol of the Buddha, also surrounded by beaded bands. The Sanskrit letter is then further surrounded by an eight-lobed medallion filled with vine-and-flower design. The rest of the central space is filled by the same vine-and-flower design except for four independent medallions depicting a pink-like flower. The stems of the vines and floral scrolls within the inner space are made of single tin wire. Mother-of-pearl is used for most of the decoration, such as the leaves and petals, but tortoiseshell is used for some petals and most of the central core of each flower. The underside of the tortoiseshell is painted either red or yellow like stained glass. Such painted tortoiseshell is called in Chinese *fu-hung* (covered red) or *fu-ts'ai* (covered colour) and was produced in quantity during the T'ang dynasty, as is demonstrated in the Shōsō-in Treasure; but it did not originate during the T'ang period, for its history goes back as early as the Han dynasty[28].

The whole design of the cover appears to have been copied from a bronze mirror. This is clearly indicated by the division of the space, the central knob and the four characteristic *ju* studs that come down from classic mirrors of the Han dynasty. As has been already pointed out, the revival of classical mirrors was in great vogue during the Sung dynasty, and the fashion reached the Korean peninsula.

Finally, in the collection of the Tokyo National Museum there is a *sūtra* (Holy Text) box believed to be a product, dated to the 1270s, of the special government agency of Koryŏ mentioned above. This *sūtra* box is made of pine wood covered both inside and out with hemp cloth. The entire surface of the box is covered with conventionalized wild camomile flowers arranged in crossing lines. The frames of the four sides of the box are outlined with the

Pl. 98 *Kundika bottle. Bronze with silver inlay. H. 1 ft. 2³/₄ in. Koryŏ dynasty, ca. 11th/13th century. National Museum of Korea, Seoul.*

familiar X-shapes and bead patterns divided by three twisted copper wires. The sloping sideplanes of the cover, however, are decorated with the usual vine-and-flower design. The flowers are all done with cut shells but the flower-centres are again of tortoiseshell painted in red. The cover is attached to the box by two hinges. A lock and two ring-handles are placed on the front and sides respectively. Seven shell-inlaid Chinese characters reading the *avatamska sūtra* at the centre of the cover indicate that this is probably one of the lacquer boxes manufactured by the government agency, *chŏnham togam* (Office of Lacquer *sūtra* Boxes), set up in 1272. The adoption of isolated flowers instead of a crowded vine-and-flower design follows the manner of celadon with inlaid design not that of celadon with painted design. When we remember the oil bottle in the collection of the Tŏksu Palace Museum of Fine Arts which is decorated exactly in the manner of painted celadon, the close relationship between the lacquer and pottery of the Koryŏ dynasty is sufficiently clear.

THE YI PERIOD

The Yi dynasty was marked by a considerable deterioration in the minor arts except in the field of ceramics. The art, however, was distinctively Korean in both form and character. Indeed, Yi artisans had a mode of expression and a dynamism unique to the dynasty. The spontaneous artistry of the Yi, however, showed a steady degeneration after the turn of the seventeenth century, and the tradition seems to be completely dying out among Koreans of the post-Yi period.

BRONZE

Buddhist temple bells are the only major bronze works of the period. Yi bells are basically in the succession of Silla bells, but there are certain changes that clearly differentiate a Yi bell from one of Silla or Koryŏ.

The traditional form as well as the changes in detail are best shown on a sixteenth-century bell belonging to Kap-sa near Kongju, western central Korea. The shape of the bell with its gentle contours seems at first sight to be the familiar Korean form. There are the upper and lower deco-

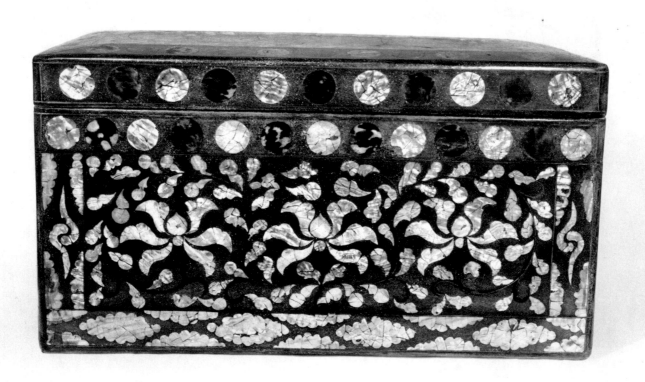

rative scrolls, four square blocks with nine *ju* studs, two Buddhist figures and lotus medallions at the striking points. These features are what we have seen on bells of the Silla and Koryŏ periods.

But there are clear differences from earlier examples. Firstly, the dragon knob on top is not a single-headed dragon firmly grasping the crown of the bell with his four legs but a rainbow-like double-headed one with the breast attached to the crown. The knob has apparently taken the form of the Chinese knob that entered Korea during the last years of the Koryŏ dynasty. An equally

significant change is the disappearance of the characteristic cylindrical tube that had always stood beside the dragon in Silla and Koryŏ bells. The obliquely projecting lotus band, around the crown in Koryŏ times, is now folded downward and the lotus petals have become a horizontal scroll in relief above the upper band of Sanskrit letters. These lotus petals have taken the place of the traditional upper band filled with the vine-and-flower design.

At the bottom, the lower scroll keeps the traditional design of *udumbara* flowers, which is very well executed for a Yi piece, but the band is now shifted upward and

there is a new vacant space below it. Between the upper and lower bands are four linear representations of Buddhist figures and small lotus medallions floating on cloud cushions. This bell was cast in 1590 and stands four feet, eleven inches. It is the finest example of Yi Buddhist bells of the pre-Imjin period, *i.e.* the fifteenth and the sixteenth centuries.

After the sixteenth century, Yi bells show a sharp decline in quality and craftsmanship, and the tradition of Korean bells both in form and quality was almost forgotten.

LACQUER WORK

Lacquer pieces of the early Yi period preserved today are as scarce as those of the previous Koryŏ period. A covered box in the collection of the Tŏksu Palace Museum of Fine Arts is one such rare piece (Pl. 99).

The entire surface of the box is decorated with *udumbara* flowers all done in shell inlay. The design occupies the entire space as in Koryŏ lacquer work, but the vines crawl freely and expressively, leaving ample space for the background. Leaves and flowers are much more fleshy than the narrow wire-like Koryŏ motifs, and the whole design emphasizes the spacious feeling of the framed plane. If we compare this pattern with some of the inlaid designs on *punch'ŏng* pottery, we can clearly see the establishment of a new period both politically and artistically. The Yi period and its art have arrived. The use of tortoiseshell with *fu-hung* and metal wire for framing now ceased.

The lacquer industry never died despite the hard blow dealt by the Hideyoshi Invasion of the sixteenth century,

but the character of the work shows changes in style after the invasion. During the ensuing three centuries Yi artists ceased to produce space-filling designs like the piece just discussed and preferred a single unit design. It was a return to Koryŏ taste. Instead of creeping vines, a plant or tree or a spray of flowers is depicted in the centre of the given space, sometimes with auspicious animals as the deer or crane. The 'Four Gentlemen' *(szu-chün-tzu)*, *i.e.* pine, bamboo, orchid and chrysanthemum, are repeatedly used. The plum tree is another popular motif, probably the best loved by the Yi people.

Pl. 100   Another illustration shows a late Yi lacquer piece decorated with bamboo and pine. The composition is neat and decorative but the earlier carefree manner has now changed to a somewhat awkward primitivism, although the feeling is of the same unsophisticated mood that flows through all Yi art.

Upon close examination the workmanship of the shell inlay shows marked carelessness. The angularity of the design results from careless cutting of the shell. The joints of the cut shells are clearly visible because of the slipshod attitude of the artist. This spontaneity helped to give dynamism and force to the design, but its carelessness gradually led to the total loss of the real spirit of Yi art which vanished before the fall of the kingdom. The strong artistic impulse of the early Yi period was unable to keep its momentum for half a millenium.

The best raw lacquer today comes from north Korea, but there are many centres of the lacquer industry in south Korea which use south Korean materials. Modern lacquer workers use native pine wood as a base because pine is best suited for lacquer application. The wooden vessel is well polished with paper before the application of raw lacquer. After a lapse of seven to ten hours for drying, any holes or indented parts of the vessel are caulked with a filler made of sawdust, boiled rice and raw lacquer. Hemp or cotton cloth is then pasted over the vessel with a glue made of raw lacquer (55%) and boiled rice (45%). After another coating of filler to make the surface even, pieces of shell are pasted on with fish glue and pressed with a hot iron. Layers of lacquer and glue are then coated all over until they conceal the surface of the shells. It is then polished with whetstone and gingko wood charcoal in turn until the surface of the shell is exposed to reveal the design. Finishings of finer lacquer are applied at intervals between the charcoal polishings. Finally, the vessel is polished with tooth powder and soya bean oil to obtain a glossy surface[29].

HWAGAK WORK

In relation to the inlaid lacquer work of the Yi dynasty, a unique handicraft called *hwagak* (coloured horn) should be mentioned, however briefly. *Hwagak* is indeed the prettiest thing the Yi people produced. The naïve yet colourful designs of *hwagak* show us a view of the world as seen by the Yi people: they accepted the world as it was, enjoyed it however difficult it might be, and departed from it by wholeheartedly indulging in it. At the same time it reveals the deep roots of Korean art, yet admits the foreign elements which linger on in it.

Hwagak means thin sheets of ox horn painted on one side with multicoloured designs. The painted side of the horn is then pasted on to the surface of some object, such as a box, comb, spool, or side-panels for a pillow, to produce a stained-glass effect and a decoration that never fades or rubs away.

Hwagak was no doubt derived from the *fu-hung* or *fu-ts'ai* technique of the T'ang dynasty. The only difference is that ox horn is used instead of tortoiseshell, and whole scenes are depicted instead of small elements of design. The peak of the industry was passed by the end of the Yi dynasty, but the tradition still lingers on today. According to modern accounts, the process of making *hwagak* is as follows[30].

The lower part of a young ox's horn is the most suitable material for *hwagak*. The horn is boiled or dried in the sun to remove the inner soft core. The inner wall of the horn is slowly scooped out with a concave iron gouge until it is about an eighth of an inch thick. The horn is then cut open and pressed flat by hot ironing. The sheet is polished with sand paper, Dutch rush or charcoal. Decoration is done on the polished side using mineral pigments imported from China. The pigments are mixed with a kind of fish glue and heated over a slow fire. In painting the designs, the pigment must be applied evenly lest the under side of the horn-sheet becomes uneven. Black outlines are first drawn, then the spaces are filled with colour. The colours are used independently and never mixed. The horn is then pasted on to the surface of a wooden vessel with more fish-glue.

There is a typical late Yi dynasty *hwagak* piece in the collection of the Tŏksu Palace Museum of Fine Arts. The pair of deer occupying the central panels, the fanciful rocks and clouds, and, above all, the scheme of primary colours with prominent red and yellow remind us of its derivation from the lacquer *fu-hung* technique of the T'ang dynasty, so well displayed in the Shōsō-in Treasure.

The *hwagak* of the Yi dynasty may seem at first to be an invention of the Yi, but, in fact, it must have evolved out of the lacquer working of the Unified Silla dynasty. As an undercurrent, it somehow survived somewhere in the Korean peninsula to appear again at the end of the Yi dynasty.

*Pl. 101

CATALOGUE

Cat. 1

Jar. Dark grey earthenware. H.6⁷/₈ in., D., at base, 4⁷/₁₆ in. Koguryŏ dynasty, 5th/6th century. National Museum of Korea, Seoul.

This is a very hard pottery and can be easily distinguished from Silla pottery in colour and shape.

Cat. 2

Jar with cover. Black earthenware. Found near P'yŏngyang. H. 8³/₈ in., D., at base, 5¹¹/₁₆ in. Koguryŏ dynasty, 5th/7th century. National Museum of Korca, Seoul.

Though the cover is the original one, it is grey in colour, probably due to having been fired at a lower temperature than the jar.

Cat. 3

Pedestal cup with cover. Grey stoneware. Found at Koryŏng-gun, Kyŏngsang Pukdo. H. 5¹/₄ in., D. 6⁷/₁₆ in. Kaya States, 5th/6th century. National Museum of Korea, Seoul.

This flattened cup is typical of the pedestal cups with covers from the Kaya group.

Cat. 4

Long necked jar with cover. Grey stoneware. H. 1 ft. 6⁷/₈ in. Old Silla dynasty, 5th/6th century. Tŏksu Palace Museum of Fine Arts, Seoul.

Cat. 5

Cup. Grey stoneware. H. 1 ft. 8¹/₂ in., D., at base, 3⁷/₈ in. Old Silla dynasty, 5th/6th century. Kyŏngju Branch of the National Museum of Korea.

The cup is formed by the rim of this vessel, crowning a perforated round body and stand. There is a small ball in the body serving to produce a bell-like sound.

Cat. 6

Pottery stand. Grey stoneware. H. 1 ft. 10⁵/₈ in., D., at base, 1 ft. ¹/₈ in. Old Silla dynasty or Kaya States, 5th/6th century. Coll. Roger Chambard, Seoul.

In recent years, many pottery stands have been found in Kaya areas. They have exactly the same shape as those from the Kyŏngju area.

Cat. 7

Pottery stand. Grey stoneware. H. 1 ft. 8¹/₂ in. Old Silla dynasty or Kaya States, 5th/6th century. Kyŏngju Branch of the National Museum of Korea.

Cat. 8

Stand for horn-shaped cups. Grey stoneware, partly covered with natural glaze. H. 9¹/₁₆ in., D., at base, 6⁷/₈ in. Kaya States, 5th/6th century. Coll. Yŏn Namgung, Seoul.

A similar stand is in the Ogura Collection, Japan.

Cf. Kyoichi Arimitsu, 'Siragiyaki no hensen' (Evolution of Silla Pottery), Fig. 79, *Sekai Toji Zenshu*, Vol. XIII, Tokyo 1955.

Cat. 9

Ink slab. Grey stoneware. H. 6 in., D. 8¹/₂ in. Paekche dynasty, 5th/6th century. National Museum of Korea, Seoul.
This ink slab originated from Paekche. Similar finds may be expected in the Kyŏngju area. It has very interesting feet.

Cat. 10

Jar with applied deer figurines. Grey stoneware. H. 6⁵/₁₆ in. Old Silla dynasty, 5th/6th century. Tŏksu Palace Museum of Fine Arts, Seoul.

Cat. 11

Human figurines. Grey stoneware. H. 9¹⁵/₁₆ in. Old Silla dynasty, 5th/6th century. Kyŏngju Branch of the National Museum of Korea.

Cat. 12

Vessel in the form of a warrior on horseback. Grey stoneware. Excavated from the Gold Bell Tomb, Kyŏngju. H. 8³/₄ in., L. 10³/₈ in. Old Silla dynasty, 5th/6th century. National Museum of Korea, Seoul.

Cat. 13
Human figure on horseback. Grey stoneware. H. 5¹¹/₁₆ in., W. 5¹/₈ in. Old Silla dynasty, 5th/6th century. Kyŏngju Branch of the National Museum of Korea.
This is an another example of a mounted horseman. There are similar specimens in Japanese collections.

Cat. 14
Animal figure. Grey stoneware. H. 6⁷/₈ in., L. 8¹/₄ in. Old Silla dynasty, 5th/6th century. Kyŏngju Branch of the National Museum of Korea.

Cat. 15
Vessel in the shape of a duck. Grey stoneware. H. 6¹/₂ in. Kaya States, 5th/6th century. National Museum of Korea, Seoul.

Cat. 16
Clay house. Grey stoneware. H. 1 ft. 5⁵/₁₆ in., W. 1 ft. 6¹/₄ in. Great Silla dynasty, 7th/8th century. National Museum of Korea, Seoul.
This is one of the model houses most recently acquired by the National Museum. It gives a clue to many aspects of ancient Korean architecture.

Cat. 17
Cup with stand, in the form of a straw sandal. Grey stoneware.
H. 5 in., D., at base, 3 1/8 in. Old Silla dynasty, 5th/6th century.
Kyŏngju Branch of the National Museum of Korea.
There is every indication that this jar was used as an urn after
the introduction of Buddhism, since it has a decoration in the
form of a pagoda on the cover.

Cat. 18
Jar with cover. Grey stoneware with stamped designs. H. 8 in.
Great Silla dynasty, 7th/8th century. Tŏksu Palace Museum of
Fine Arts, Seoul.

Cat. 19
Covered jar. Grey stoneware, incised decoration. H. 10⁵/₈ in.,
D. 8 1/8 in. Great Silla dynasty, 7th century. National Museum
of Korea, Seoul.

Cat. 20
Urn. Grey stoneware covered with an olive-green ash-glaze.
H. 7³/₈ in., D., at base, 3 1/2 in. Great Silla dynasty, 7th century.
National Museum of Korea, Seoul.

Cat. 21
Tile with medallion of phoenix in relief. Grey earthenware. Excavated in Puyŏ. H. 11½ in., W. 11½ in., Depth 1¾ in. Paekche dynasty, 7th century. National Museum of Korea, Seoul. The tiles Cat. 22 and 23 all belong to the same group as Pl. 22 and 23.

Cat. 22
Tile with lotus flower in relief. Grey earthenware. Excavated in Puyŏ. H. 11¼ in., W. 11⅛ in., Depth 1¾ in. Paekche dynasty. 7th century. National Museum of Korea, Seoul.

Cat. 23
Tile with spiral clouds and lotus flower in relief. Grey earthenware. Excavated in Puyŏ. H. 11½ in., W. 11½ in., Depth 1¾ in. Paekche dynasty, 7th century. National Museum of Korea, Seoul.

Cat. 24
Tile with floral medallions in relief. Grey earthenware. Found at the site of the Imhae-jŏn Palace, Kyŏngju. H. 1 ft. 2½ in., W. 1 ft. 5¾ in., Depth 3½ in. Great Silla dynasty, 7th century. National Museum of Korea, Seoul.
This tile is reported to have been found at the same place as Pl. 24.

Cat. 25
Roof tile. Grey earthenware. H. 4¹/₈ in., W. 6⁷/₁₆ in. Great
Silla dynasty, 7th/8th century. National Museum of Korea,
Seoul.

Cat. 26
Roof tile with demon mask.   Grey earthenware. H. 5⁷/₈ in. Great
Silla dynasty, 7th/8th century. National Museum of Korea,
Seoul.

Cat. 27
Bottle.   Black stoneware. H. 1 ft. 4¹/₁₆ in., D., at base, 3³/₄ in.
Koryŏ dynasty, 11th/12th century. Coll. Roger Chambard,
Seoul.
Partly covered with natural glaze. The unglazed stonewares of
the Koryŏ dynasty have the peculiarity of being very light in
weight.

Cat. 28
Food jar.   Bottom of the jar Pl. 1. Celadon glaze without
decoration, with inscriptions of cyclical date 993 A.D. D. 4³/₄ in.
Koryŏ dynasty, 10th century. Ehwa University Museum,
Seoul.
The inscription consists of eighteen Chinese characters. It reads:
'Made in the fourth year of Ch'un-hua the year Kuei-szu (993,)
for use in the First Room of the Shrine of King T'aejo, by the
potter of Choe Kil-hoe'.

Cat. 29

Wine pot with cover. Celadon glaze without decoration. H. I ft. ⁵/₈ in. Koryŏ dynasty, 11th/12th century. National Museum of Korea, Seoul.

There are very few wine pots of this size. The surface is partly discoloured and has become yellowish.

Cat. 30

Water pourer or sprinkler. Celadon glaze, incised decoration. H. I ft. I¹/₂ in., D., at base, 3⁹/₁₆ in. Koryŏ dynasty, 12th century. Tŏksu Palace Museum of Fine Arts, Seoul.

The shape poses a problem as to the vessel's use. It is probably a type of vessel used in Buddhist ceremonies. The vase has incised decoration and the upper neck has a decorative ring. Typical Korean ornaments such as geese, reeds, willow trees and mandarin ducks are to be seen on the body.

Cat. 31

Head of a Buddha. Celadon glaze. H. 2¹⁵/₁₆ in. Koryŏ dynasty, 12th century. National Museum of Korea, Seoul.

This is a rare object.

Cat. 32

Drinking bowl. Celadon glaze, incised decoration. H. 2¹/₈ in., D. 4⁵/₈ in. Koryŏ dynasty, 11th century. National Museum of Korea, Seoul.

The exterior has no decoration, but the interior is decorated with thirty-two lotus petals and a pod.

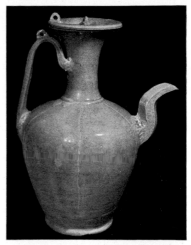

Cat. 33
Wine pot with cover. Celadon glaze, incised decoration. H.
10⅛ in. Koryŏ dynasty, 11th century. National Museum of
Korea, Seoul.
The glaze is not refined and this pot was probably made before
Koryŏ celadon achieved its later perfection.

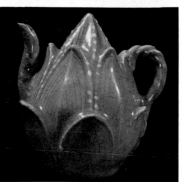

Cat. 34
Writer's water-dropper. Celadon glaze, incised and white slip
decoration. H. 4 in., D., at base, 1¹³⁄₁₆ in. Koryŏ dynasty, 12th
century. National Museum of Korea, Seoul.
A fine example of a water-dropper for a scholar's desk. It is
shaped like a lotus-bud to which are added a spout and a
handle resembling a twisted vine.

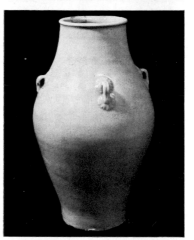

Cat. 35
Vase. Celadon glaze, modelled and incised decoration. H.
9½ in., D., at base, 3¹⁄₁₆ in. Koryŏ dynasty, 11th/12th century.
National Museum of Korea, Seoul.
Four handles are placed about the body and form the only
decoration on this vase.

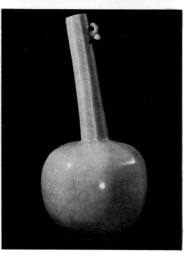

Cat. 36
Wine bottle. Celadon glaze, incised decoration. H. 1 ft. ¹⁵⁄₁₆
in., D., at base, 3¹³⁄₁₆ in. Koryŏ dynasty, 11th/12th century.
National Museum of Korea, Seoul.
The lower part of the body is slightly faceted to form an octa-
gon. Each of the eight sides has an incised spray of peony flowers. The tall neck is also octagonal.

Cat. 37
Vase. Celadon glaze, incised decoration. H. 1 ft. ¹³/₁₆ in., D., at base, 5¹/₈ in. Koryŏ dynasty, 11th/12th century. National Museum of Korea, Seoul.
A fine example of a *maebyŏng (mei-p'ing* in Chinese). It has a large incised pattern of lotus blossoms.

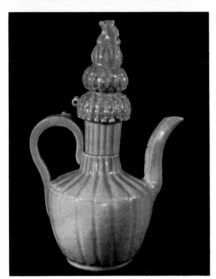

Cat. 38
Wine pot and cover. Celadon glaze, modelled, undecorated. H. 7³/₁₆ in., D., at base, 3³/₈ in. Koryŏ dynasty, 11th/12th century. National Museum of Korea, Seoul.
The body has the ten-lobed melon form and the handle is shaped like a twisted vine.

Cat. 39
Wine pot. Celadon glaze, modelled and incised decoration. H. 1 ft.¹/₁₆ in., D., at base, 3³/₈ in. Koryŏ dynasty, end of 11th/early 12th century. National Museum of Korea, Seoul.

Cat. 40
Roof tile. Flat type. Celadon glaze with moulded decoration. Excavated in Tangjŏnni, Kangjin in 1964, together with semi-cylindrical roof tile Cat. 41. L. 7⁷/₈ in., H. 1¹¹/₁₆ in. Koryŏ dynasty, mid-12th century. National Museum of Korea, Seoul.
This is the first flat roof tile to be found intact. The previously found fragment of a flat roof tile in the collection of the National Museum of Korea was made from the same mould.

CERAMIC ART

Cat. 41

Roof tile. Semi-cylindrical type, broken. Celadon glaze with moulded decoration. Excavated in Tangjŏnni, Kangjin in 1964, together with the roof tile Cat. 40. H. 2 3/16 in., D. 3 3/16 in. Koryŏ dynasty, mid-12th century. National Museum of Korea, Seoul.

There were two different sizes of roof tiles of semi-cylindrical form but all with the same tree peony designs. This one is yellowish green in colour.

Cat. 42

Wine pot. Celadon glaze, modelled and incised decoration. H. 9 3/16 in., D., at base, 4 1/16 in. Koryŏ dynasty, end of 11th/early 12th century. National Museum of Korea, Seoul.

This wine pot is shaped like a carp-dragon called *ŏryong* in Korean. The dragon's mouth forms the spout and its tail lifts up to form a lid. All other features are executed by modelling and incised lines.

Cat. 43

Wine waste container. Celadon glaze, incised and inlaid decoration. H. 4 in., D. 8 3/4 in. Koryŏ dynasty, 12th/13th century. Tŏksu Palace Museum of Fine Arts, Seoul.

Probably a spitoon, or spitoon and wine waste container.

Cat. 44

Bowl. Celadon glaze, incised and inlaid decoration. H. 2 3/8 in., D. 6 5/8 in. Koryŏ dynasty, 12th century. National Museum of Korea, Seoul.

This is the piece illustrated as Pl. 39. Whereas the interior is decorated with reverse inlay in white, the exterior has the usual inlay technique.

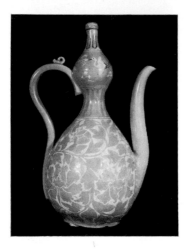

Cat. 45
Food jar with cover. Celadon glaze, inlaid decoration, crane and cloud designs. H. 9⁵/₈ in., D., at base, 4¹¹/₁₆ in. Koryŏ dynasty, 12th century. National Museum of Korea, Seoul.

Cat. 46
Wine pot and stopper. Celadon glaze, inlaid decoration, partly reverse inlay, and raised dots in white slip. H. 1 ft. 1¹/₈ in., D., at base, 3⁷/₁₆ in. Koryŏ dynasty, 12th/13th century. National Museum of Korea, Seoul.
This pot is made with a special technique, the so-called reverse inlay. The background and some of the details, not the design itself, are inlaid. In this case the surrounding arabesques of peony flowers and leaves have been inlaid with white slip to create a contrasting effect.

Cat. 47
Vase. Celadon glaze, incised and inlaid decoration. H. 1 ft. 1¹⁵/₁₆ in., D., at base, 6 in. Koryŏ dynasty, 12th/13th century. National Museum of Korea, Seoul.
Four sprays of peony flowers and leaves are incised into the body and a simulated cloth cover on the shoulder is decorated with chrysanthemum in white.

Cat. 48
Rectangular open-work toilet case with cover, tray and cosmetic boxes nested inside. Celadon glaze, inlaid decoration. H. 4⁷/₈ in., L. 5⁹/₁₆ in., W. 8¹³/₁₆ in. Koryŏ dynasty, late 12th century. National Museum of Korea, Seoul.
This toilet case was excavated from a tomb at Changhŭng, Chŏlla Namdo. The open-work is hexagonal, in 'tortoise-shell' style, except along the bevelled edges of the cover, where *ju-i* sceptre-head and lattice patterns have been used. The lower part of the box is partitioned into two sections and contains in one of them four crescent-shaped boxes fitted round a circular box in the centre (the illustration shows them, incorrectly, within the tray). A rectangular bronze mirror, a needle case and an inlaid celadon oil bottle were found in another section.

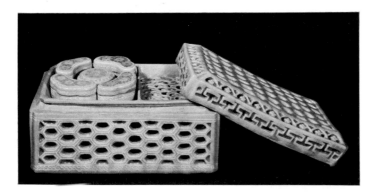

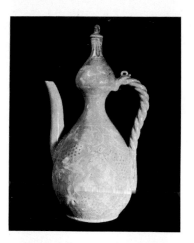

Cat. 49

Wine pot and cover. Celadon glaze, inlaid decoration. H. 1 ft.
1 1/2 in., D , at base, 3 9/16 in. Koryŏ dynasty, early 14th century.
Coll. Pyŏng-dŏ Min, Seoul.
A small boy swings on a vine with clusters of grapes which
crosses over the body. Though not clearly recognizable in the
illustration, the paste of the pot is coarse and the glaze is not
quite as refined as the products of the previous century.

Cat. 50

Vase. Celadon glaze, inlaid decoration, lotus and willow
designs. H. 11 in., D. 7 1/8 in. Koryŏ dynasty, 14th century.
National Museum of Korea, Seoul.
This is the typical form of *maebyŏng* vase as often seen toward
the end of Koryŏ dynasty. A fine example of the period.

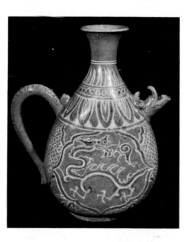

Cat. 51

Wine pot. Celadon glaze, inlaid decoration, lotus and dragon
designs. H. 9 9/16 in. Koryŏ dynasty, 14th century. National
Museum of Korea, Seoul.
A very interestingly shaped wine pot, yet the designs and colours clearly show the degeneration of the 14th century.

Cat. 52

Wine bottle. Celadon glaze, painted in underglaze iron. H.
1 ft. 7/16 in., D., at base, 4 5/16 in. Koryŏ dynasty, 12th/13th
century. National Museum of Korea, Seoul.
The celadon glaze has turned a buff colour in firing.

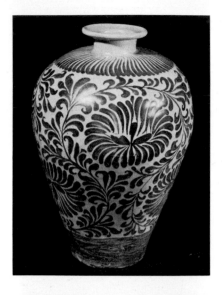

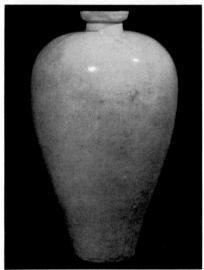

Cat. 53
Vase. Celadon glaze, painted in underglaze iron. H. 10¹³/₁₆ in., D., at base, 3⁵/₈ in. Koryŏ dynasty, 13th/14th century. National Museum of Korea, Seoul.
Six chrysanthemums are placed amidst the leaf pattern round the body.

Cat. 54
Vase. White Koryŏ ware without decoration. H. 10⁷/₈ in. Koryŏ dynasty, 12th century. Tŏksu Palace Museum of Fine Arts, Seoul.

Cat. 55
Bowl. White Koryŏ ware with inscriptions of Chinese characters including cyclical date 1391 A.D. H. 7³/₄ in., D., at mouth, 7⁷/₈ in. Koryŏ dynasty, 14th century. National Museum of Korea, Seoul.

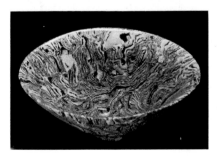

Cat. 56
Drinking bowl. Marbled ware with black and greyish white clay. H. 2¹⁵/₁₆ in., D. 4³/₈ in. Koryŏ dynasty, 12th century. Coll. Yŏn Namgung, Seoul.

Cat. 57

Food jar. Punch'ŏng ware, inlaid decoration. H. 1 ft 8¼ in., D., at mouth, 11⁹/₁₆ in. Yi dynasty, 15th century. Tŏksu Palace Museum of Fine Arts, Seoul.
The bands above and below are incised and filled with white slip; the central part is stamped and filled with white slip.

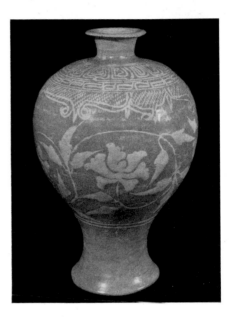

Cat. 58

Vase. Punch'ŏng ware, inlaid decoration. H. 10³/₈ in., D., at base, 3⁷/₈ in. Yi dynasty, 15th century. National Museum of Korea, Seoul.
This piece greatly resembles the vase Cat. 50, and clearly shows that *punch'ŏng* is a continuation of Koryŏ inlaid ware.

Cat. 59

Drinking bowl. Punch'ŏng ware, celadon glaze, stamped decoration filled with white slip. H. 3⁷/₁₆ in., D. 7³/₄ in. Yi dynasty, late 14th/early 15th century. National Museum of Korea, Seoul.
A typical example with stamped patterns over which white slip has been brushed.

Cat. 60

Bowl. Punch'ŏng ware, painted in underglaze iron. H. 5¹/₈ in., D., at mouth, 5¹³/₁₆ in. Yi dynasty, 16th century. Tŏksu Palace Museum of Fine Arts, Seoul.
Brush-strokes over the body are clearly discernible.

Cat. 61

Covered rice bowl. *Punch'ŏng* ware, the exterior: celadon glaze, painted in white slip; the interior: *punch'ŏng* ware, inlaid decoration. H. 4¹³/₁₆ in., D., at base, 1¹⁵/₁₆ in. Yi dynasty, 15th/16th century. National Museum of Korea, Seoul.
An overall pattern of peony leaf and blossoms, painted in white slip into the incisions and depressions under the celadon glaze.

Cat. 62

Wine bottle. *Punch'ŏng* ware, incised and decorated with white slip applied with a broad brush. H. 1 ft. ¹³/₁₆ in., D., at base, 3¹/₄ in. Yi dynasty, 15th/16th century. National Museum of Korea, Seoul.

Cat. 63

Food jar. *Punch'ŏng* ware, incised decoration. H. 1 ft. 4¹⁵/₁₆ in., D., at base, 7 in. Yi dynasty, 15th century. National Museum of Korea, Seoul.

Cat. 64

Wine bottle. *Punch'ŏng* ware, decorated with white slip applied with a broad brush and painted in underglaze iron. From a kiln located at Keryong-san. H. 11³/₄ in., D., at base, 3 in. Yi dynasty, 15th/16th century. Tŏksu Palace Museum of Fine Arts, Seoul.
This is a very similar bottle to Pl. 47 from the Hong-keun Yi Collection.

Cat. 65
Wine bottle. Punch'ŏng ware, painted in underglaze iron.
Probably made at Keryong-san kiln. H. 11 1/4 in., D. 6 5/8 in.
Yi dynasty, 15th century. Coll. Hyung-pil Chun, Seoul.

Cat. 66
Jar with cover. Punch'ŏng ware, lotus and grass decoration
in underglaze iron. H. 10 11/16 in., D., at base, 4 7/8 in. Yi dynasty, 15th/16th century. National Museum of Korea, Seoul.

Cat. 67
Bowls, for ceremonial use. White porcelain without decoration.
Left: H. 3 1/8 in., D., at base, 3 1/2 in. Right: H. 3 in., D., at
base, 3 5/16 in. Yi dynasty, 17th century. National Museum of
Korea, Seoul.
The shape is derived from ancient Chinese ritual bronzes.

Cat. 68
Vase. White porcelain with peony design, pierced work.
H. 10 1/2 in., D., at base, 6 1/2 in. Yi dynasty, 18th century.
National Museum of Korea, Seoul.

Cat. 69
Bowl. White porcelain without decoration. H. 6¹/₂ in., D., at base, 6⁵/₁₆ in. Yi dynasty, 18th/19th century. National Museum of Korea, Seoul.

Cat. 70
Wine cup and stand. White porcelain without decoration. H. 5¹/₂ in., D., at base, 4¹³/₁₆ in. Yi dynasty, 19th century. National Museum of Korea, Seoul.

Cat. 71
Water pitcher and cover. Bluish white porcelain without decoration. H. 7¹¹/₁₆ in., D., at base, 3⁵/₈ in. Yi dynasty, 19th century. Coll. Yŏn Namgung, Seoul.

Cat. 72
Water droppers. White porcelain. Right below: H. 1¹/₁₆ in. Yi dynasty, 19th century. National Museum of Korea, Seoul.

Cat. 73
Water droppers. White porcelain, underglaze blue. H., from left to right, 1 3/16 in., 3 1/2 in., 2 9/16 in., 1 7/16 in. Yi dynasty, 18th century. National Museum of Korea, Seoul.

Cat. 74
Brush stand. White porcelain, underglaze blue. H. 5 7/8 in., D., at base, 3 11/16 in. Yi dynasty, 18th century. National Museum of Korea, Seoul.

Cat. 75
Food jar. White porcelain with underglaze blue decoration. H. 1 ft. 2 3/16 in., D., at base, 5 11/16 in. Yi dynasty, 18th century. Coll. Yŏn Namgung, Seoul.

Cat. 76
Flower pot. Light bluish white porcelain with underglaze blue decoration. H. 5 7/8 in., D., at base, 6 11/16 in. Yi dynasty, 19th century. Coll. Yŏn Namgung, Seoul.

Cat. 77
Bowl. White porcelain, painted in underglaze blue. H. 5⁹/₁₆ in.,
D., at base, 4⁵/₈ in. Yi dynasty, 19th century. National Museum of Korea, Seoul.
The design is a stylized Chinese character meaning 'longevity'.

Cat. 78
Bowl. White porcelain, painted in underglaze blue, pomegranate designs. H. 6⁵/₁₆ in., D., at base, 6³/₄ in. Yi dynasty, 19th century. National Museum of Korea, Seoul.

Cat. 79
Vase. White porcelain, painted in underglaze blue, landscape designs. H. 1 ft. 10¹⁵/₁₆ in., D., at base, 6¹³/₁₆ in. Yi dynasty, 18th/19th century. National Museum of Korea, Seoul.
This vase is outstanding by reason of its large size. The painting seems to have been executed by a professional painter commissioned by the government.

Cat. 80
Covered rice bowl. White porcelain, painted in underglaze blue, *posang-hwa* designs. H. 9 in., D., at base, 6¹/₄ in. Yi dynasty, 19th century. National Museum of Korea, Seoul.
A representative rice bowl, no doubt used at court.

Cat. 81
Wine bottle. White porcelain, painted in underglaze blue, lotus designs. H. 1 ft. ½ in., D., at base, 5 in. Yi dynasty, 18th century. Coll. Wŏn-jŏn Kim, Seoul.

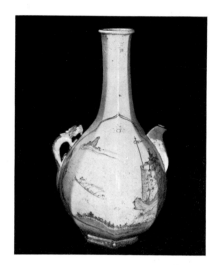

Cat. 82
Wine bottle. White porcelain, painted in underglaze blue, landscape and squirrel designs. H. 1 ft. 5¹¹/₁₆ in., D., at base, 5⁷/₁₆ in Yi dynasty, 18th century. Coll. Pyŏng-do Min, Seoul.

Cat. 83
Food jar. White porcelain, painted in underglaze blue, ten longevities designs. H. 1 ft. 6½ in., D., at mouth, 6⅛ in. Yi dynasty, 19th century. Coll. Tong-su Kim, Seoul.

Cat. 84
Bottle. White porcelain, modelled, incised and underglaze blue decoration. H. 6⅞ in., L. 1 ft. ¹³/₁₆ in. Yi dynasty, 19th century. National Museum of Korea, Seoul.
It has a tortoise shape, and was probably used as as wine bottle.

Cat. 85
Food jar. White porcelain, inlaid decoration, grass designs. H. 4³/₄ in., D., at base, 3 in. Yi dynasty, 15th century. National Museum of Korea, Seoul.
This is one of the earliest white porcelains decorated with iron pigment. See Pl. 53.

Cat. 86
Food jar. Cream coloured porcelain, painted in underglaze iron, dragon designs. H. 1 ft. 1³/₈ in., D. 11¹/₈ in. Yi dynasty, 17th/18th century. Tŏksu Palace Museum of Fine Arts, Seoul.

Cat. 87
Food jar. White porcelain, painted in underglaze blue and copper, phoenix designs. H. 11 in., D., at mouth, 4⁷/₁₆ in. Yi dynasty, 19th century. National Museum of Korea, Seoul.
An interesting example painted in underglaze blue and copper.

Cat. 88
Food jar. White porcelain, painted in underglaze copper, lotus designs. H. 11¹/₂ in., D. 9⁷/₁₆ in. Yi dynasty, 18th century. Tŏksu Palace Museum of Fine Arts, Seoul.

Cat. 89
Food jar. White porcelain, painted in underglaze copper, phoenix designs. H. 11 ¹¹/₁₆ in., D. 9³/₁₆ in. Yi dynasty, 19th century. Tŏksu Palace Museum of Fine Arts, Seoul.

Cat. 90
Seated Śākyamuni. Gilt bronze. Provenance unknown. H. 3⁹/₁₆ in. Three Kingdoms period, ca. early 6th century. Coll. Yŏn Namgung, Seoul.
The halo and square base are lost but bright gilding remains. An early Korean Buddhist image strictly in the northern Wei style.

Cat. 91
Trinity. Gilt bronze. Provenance unknown. H. 6⁷/₈ in. Three Kingdoms period, 563?. Coll. Hyung-pil Chun, Seoul.
The statue has an inscription including the year *kuei-wei*.

Cat. 92
Trinity. Gilt bronze. From Kok-san, north-west Korea. H. 6¹/₈ in. Koguryŏ dynasty, 571? Coll. T. H. Kim, Seoul.
The statue has an inscription including the year *shen-mao*.

231

Cat. 93
Seated Maitreya.   Gilt bronze. Provenance unknown. H. 8 1/4 in.
Three Kingdoms period, ca. 600. Tŏksu Palace Museum of Fine
Arts, Seoul.

Cat. 94
Seated Maitreya.   Gilt bronze. From P'yŏngyang, north Korea.
H. 6 7/8 in. Koguryŏ dynasty, second half of the 6th century.
Coll. T. H. Kim, Seoul.
Much of the original gilding is gone and the left forearm is
broken off and lost.

Cat. 95
Standing Bodhisattva.   Clay. From a temple site near P'yŏngyang, north Korea. H. 7 1/16 in. Koguryŏ dynasty, ca. mid-6th
century. National Museum of Korea, Seoul.
The head and body were recovered separately. Traces of
reddish pigment preserved.

Cat. 96
Standing Bodhisattva.   Gilt bronze. H. 7 3/8 in. Old Silla dynasty,
first half of the 7th century. Coll. Hyung-pil Chun, Seoul.

232

Cat. 97
Śākyamuni Trinity. Granite. Main Buddha, H. 9 ft. 2¹/₄ in.
Seated Maitreya, H. 5 ft. 5³/₈ in. Standing Avalokiteśvara, H.
5 ft. 6¹⁵/₁₆ in. Paekche dynasty, ca. first half of the 7th century.
Sŏ-san, west-central Korea.

Cat. 98
Buddhist Stele. Brownish soapstone. H. 1 ft. 10⁵/₈ in. Great
Silla dynasty, 689? National Museum of Korea, Seoul.
Seated Amitābha and attendants on an elevated lotus seat above
a platform depicted by railings and staircases. With inscription
including the year *chi-ch'ou.*

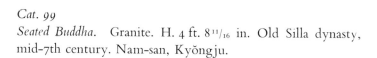

Cat. 99
Seated Buddha. Granite. H. 4 ft. 8¹¹/₁₆ in. Old Silla dynasty,
mid-7th century. Nam-san, Kyŏngju.

Cat. 100
Amitābha Trinity. Granite. Main Buddha, H. 9 ft. 5³/₈ in.
Shih-chih (Mahāsthāmaprāpta), H. 6 ft. 3⁵/₈ in. Kwan-yin
(Avalokiteśvara), H. 5 ft. 10⁷/₈ in. Great Silla dynasty, second half
of the 7th century. Mt. P'algong, Kunwi, south-east Korea.
The mandorla for the main Buddha is incised on the back wall
and painted with white pigment.

Cat. 101
Standing Vaiśravaṇa. Bronze, originally gilded. From a bronze *sarīra* case within the western stone pagoda at the site of Ka-mǔn-sa, near Kyŏngju. H. 8½ in. Great Silla dynasty, second half of the 7th century, before 682. National Museum of Korea, Seoul.
To-wen-t'ien (Much Hearing *deva*), the Guardian of the North, is cast flat and attached to the outer wall of the *sarīra* case by means of a lacquer-adhesive.

Cat. 102
Two musicians. Bronze. From the same *sarīra* case mentioned above. H. 1½ in. each. National Museum of Korea, Seoul.

Cat. 103
Amitābha Trinity. Granite. Main Buddha, H. 10 ft. 6 in. Great Silla dynasty, second half of the 7th century. Yŏngju, south-east Korea.

Cat. 104
Standing Buddha and Bodhisattva. Granite. Buddha, H. 4 ft. 5½ in. Bodhisattva, H. 4 ft. 9¹/₁₆ in. Great Silla dynasty, late 7th century. On the site of Kulpul-sa, Kyŏngju, south-east Korea.

Cat. 105
Guardian. Granite. H. 8 ft. 9⅛ in. Great Silla dynasty, ca.
second half of the 7th century. Kwae-nŭng Tomb, Kyŏngju.
One of a pair of civilian officers in stone from the front of the
mounded tomb of an unidentified king of Silla.

Cat. 106
Guardian. Granite. H. 8 ft. 5³⁄₁₆ in. Great Silla dynasty, second half of the 7th century. Kwae-nŭng Tomb, Kyŏngju.
One of a pair of military officers in stone from the front of the
mounded tomb of an unidentified king of Silla.

Cat. 107
Standing Buddha. Sandstone. H. 4 ft. 1³⁄₁₆ in. Great Silla dynasty, around 700. Kyŏngju Branch of the National Museum
of Korea.

Cat. 108
Seated Śākyamuni. Sandstone. Provenance unknown. H. of
Buddha: 2 ft. 11⁷⁄₁₆ in. Great Silla dynasty, ca. 8th/9th century.
Kyŏngbuk National University, Taegu, south-east Korea.
Style very similar to the previous standing Buddha in Kyŏngju
Museum. The throne is decorated with Guardian figures in
relief. The *mudrā* must have been the *dharmacakra*, but the left
hand is broken and lost.

Cat. 109
Standing Manjuśrī. Granite. H. 6 ft. 6³/₄ in. Great Silla dynasty, mid-8th century. Sŏkkuram cave temple, south-east Korea.

Cat. 110 (left)
Seated Vairoçana. Gilt bronze. H. 5 ft. 9¹¹/₁₆ in. Great Silla dynasty, mid-8th century. Pulguk-sa, Kyŏngju.
The eyeballs and moustache are modern additions. A thick layer of white pigment over the entire body, also a modern addition, has recently been scraped off to reveal the original sculpture.

Cat. 111 (right)
Seated Amitābha. Gilt bronze. H. 5 ft. 5³/₈ in. Great Silla dynasty, mid-8th century. Pulguk-sa, Kyŏngju.

Cat. 112
Amitābha Trinity. Granite Main Buddha, H. 9 ft. 11³/₁₆ in. Great Silla dynasty, dated 801. Mt. Pang-ŏ, south-east Korea.

Cat. 113
Standing Śākyamuni. Bronze. H. 7⁷/₈ in. Great Silla dynasty, ca. 9th century. National Museum of Korea, Seoul.

Cat. 114
Standing Bhaiṣajyaguru. Gilt bronze. Provenance unknown. H. 1 ft. 4⁵/₁₆ in. Great Silla dynasty, ca. 9th century. National Museum of Korea, Seoul.

Cat. 115
Seated Vairoçana. Iron. H. 8 ft. 2¹³/₁₆ in. Great Silla dynasty, dated 858. Porim-sa, south-west Korea.
The gilding and painting are of a much later period. The crescentic shaven spot on the head is also a later addition.

Cat. 116
Seated Vairoçana. Iron. H. 2 ft. 11¹³/₁₆ in. (without throne). Great Silla dynasty, dated 865. Top'ian-sa, central Korea.
The face and body are covered with white pigment.

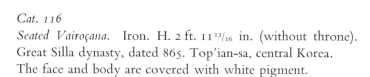

Cat. 117
Seated Śākyamuni. Iron. From a temple site south of Seoul.
H. 9 ft. 5³/₈ in. Koryŏ dynasty, ca. 10th century. Tŏksu Palace
Museum of Fine Arts, Seoul.
The fingers of both hands are recent plaster restorations.

Cat. 118
Seated Buddha. Iron. Provenance unknown. H. 3 ft. ¹/₄ in.
Koryŏ dynasty, ca. 10th/11th century. National Museum of
Korea, Seoul.

Cat. 119
Seated Buddha. Bronze. Provenance unknown. H. 2 ft. 8¹/₄ in.
Koryŏ dynasty, ca. 10th/11th century. Tŏksu Palace Museum
of Fine Arts, Seoul.

Cat. 120
Seated Bodhisattva. Granite. H. 5 ft. 5 in. Koryŏ dynasty, ca.
10th/11th century. Kangnŭng, central Korea.
The Bodhisattva kneels facing a three-storied stone pagoda
(not shown). The octagonal capstone on top of the cylindrical
hat does not belong to the figure. It seems to have come from a
lost stone lantern.

Cat. 121

Seated Buddha. Clay, wood and lacquer. H. 9 ft. 1 7/16 in. (without the mandorla), Koryŏ dynasty, ca. 10th/11th century. Pusŏk-sa, south-east Korea.

This gilded Buddha has a clay core coated with a thick layer of lacquer. The mandorla is made of wood.

Cat. 122

Seated Buddha. Iron. H. 3 ft. 3 3/8 in. Koryŏ dynasty, ca. 12th century. Taewŏn-sa, Ch'ungju, central Korea.

This Buddha is characterized by the strictly symmetrical and schematic drapery folds. The shape of the eye and the M-like mouth recall Japanese Buddhist images. The hands are lost.

Cat. 123

Head of Lohan. Clay. From a temple site in south-west Korea. L. 4 5/16 in. Koryŏ dynasty, ca. 12th/13th century. Tongguk University Museum, Seoul.

Cat. 124

Seated Avalokiteśvara. Gilt bronze. Provenance unknown. H. 5 3/8 in. Koryŏ dynasty, ca. 13th/14th century. National Museum of Korea, Seoul.

A Bodhisattva in the *lalit-āsana* on a lotus throne. The facial type as well as the lotus petals indicate influences from Mongolian Buddhist images.

Cat. 125
Seated Buddha. Gilt bronze. Provenance unknown. H. 2 ft. 6³/₁₆ in. Koryŏ dynasty, ca. 13th/14th century. National Museum of Korea, Seoul.

Cat. 126
Seated Kṣitigarbha. Gilt bronze. H. 3 ft. 2³/₁₆ in. Late Koryŏ or early Yi dynasty, ca. 14th/15th century. Sŏnun-sa, Koch'ang, south-west Korea.

Cat. 127
Seated Buddha. Gilt bronze. H. 9¹³/₁₆ in. Early Yi dynasty, ca. 15th/16th century. Tŏksu Palace Museum of Fine Arts, Seoul.

Cat. 128
Seated Vairoçana. Gingko wood, lacquered and gilded. H. 7 ft. 8¹/₈ in. Yi dynasty, dated 1769. Haein-sa, south-east Korea.

240

Cat. 129
Mask (Old Man)   Wood. From Hahoe, south-east Korea.
L. 9⅝ in. Koryŏ dynasty, ca. 12th/14th century.
This is one of a set of eleven wooden theatrical masks preserved
in the village of Hahoe, south-eastern Korea. They are the
oldest of their kind extant. The threads are modern.

Cat. 130
Mask of Old Man (Butcher).   Wood. L. 9½ in. Koryŏ dynasty,
ca. 12th/14th century.
The mask of a laughing man with a separately made lower jaw.
Four tiny holes immediately below the lower lip are for attach-
ing a beard. Note the realistic modelling of the upper lip. Faint
red colour, except the hair and eyebrows in black.

Cat. 131
Mask of Old Man (Scholar).   Wood. L. 8⅜ in. Koryŏ dynasty,
ca. 12th/14th century.
An old man mask with a separately made jaw. Tiny holes
around the mouth to attach beard and moustache. Wrinkles
and eyebrows indicated by grooved lines. Face faint red, head
and eyebrows black.

Cat. 132
Mask (Woman).   Wood. L. 11¾ in. Koryŏ dynasty, ca. 12th/
14th century.
A young woman with prominent cheekbones and thin lips.
Traces of white pigment remain on the face. Eyebrows and
hair are black. Three red spots, one on the forehead and two
on the cheeks, well preserved.

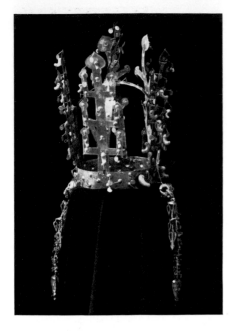

Cat. 133
Crown. Gold. From Sŏbong-ch'ong (Lucky Phoenix Tomb), Kyŏngju. H. 1 ft. ¹/₈ in., D. 7¹/₄ in. Old Silla dynasty, ca. 6th century. National Museum of Korea, Seoul.
Made of cut sheet-gold, decorated with gold spangles and comma-shaped jades. On top of the inner cap of arching bands is a twig-like ornament with three phoenix-shaped birds also made of sheet-gold.

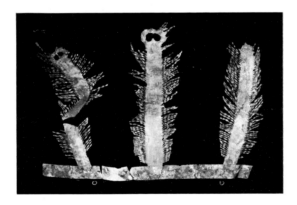

Cat. 134
Crown. Gilt bronze (frame), birch bark pasted with wings of beetle *(Chrysochroa fulgidissima Schoenherr)*. From a tomb near P'yŏngyang. H. 5³/₁₆ in. Koguryŏ dynasty, ca. first half of 7th century. P'yŏngyang Museum, north Korea.

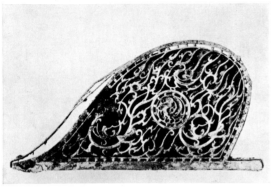

Cat. 135
Diadem. Gilt bronze. From a tomb in Ŭisŏng, south-east Korea. H. 1 ft. 1³/₄ in., D. 5⁷/₈ in. Old Silla dynasty, ca. 6th century. National Museum of Korea, Seoul.
A horizontal band and three feather-like uprights, probably a simplified form of a sacred tree. Two small rings attached to the band are for suspending pendants.

Cat. 136
Diadem. Gilt bronze. H. 5⁷/₈ in. Koguryŏ dynasty, ca. 6th/ 7th century. Private Collection, Japan.
The design in open-work seems to be some kind of floral pattern, but the central part is lost.

Cat. 137
Crown. Gilt bronze. H. 10 in., D. 6¹¹/₁₆ in. Paekche dynasty, ca. 5th/6th century, National Museum of Korea, Seoul.
The crown consists of an outer circlet with three tree-shaped upright ornaments and an inner cap all made of gilded sheet-bronze.

Cat. 138
Bracelet. Gilt bronze. From a tomb in Kyŏngju. D. 3¹/₈ in. Old Silla dynasty, ca. 6th century. National Museum of Korea, Seoul.

Cat. 139
Sole of shoe. Gilt bronze. From a tomb in Kyŏngju. L. 1 ft. 1 in. Old Silla dynasty, ca. 6th century. National Museum of Korea, Seoul.
This is the bottom of a shoe with designs cast in relief. An outer band of flame-design is separated by a garland from the inner part filled with hexagons. The hexagons are decorated with demons, kalabinkas, fancy birds and animals. The sole is nailed to an inner board attached to the instep.

Cat. 140
Chiao-tou. Bronze. From the Gold Crown Tomb, Kyŏngju. H. 6¹/₄ in., L. 1 ft. ¹³/₁₆ in. Old Silla dynasty, ca. 6th century. National Museum of Korea, Seoul.
The vessel is actually a portable kettle with three legs, a spout and a long handle. It must have been used as a ewer for wine or herb concoctions to be heated directly on the fire. The spout and both ends of the handle are in the shape of dragon heads. On the cover are lotus petals in relief.

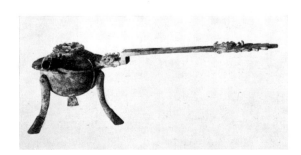

Cat. 141
Sarīra case (drawing). Gilt bronze. From the Western Stone Pagoda at the site of Kamŭn-sa, near Kyŏngju. H. 1 ft. ³/₁₆ in. Great Silla dynasty, 682 or slightly earlier. National Museum of Korea, Seoul.

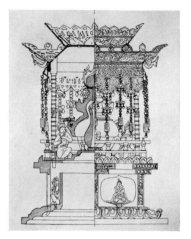

Cat. 142
Sarīra shrine (drawing). Gilt bronze. From the Western Stone Pagoda at the site of Kamŭn-sa, near Kyŏngju. H. 7⁷/₈ in. Great Silla dynasty, 682 or slightly earlier. National Museum of Korea, Seoul.

Cat. 143
Buddhist bell. Bronze. H. 5 ft. 6¹⁵/₁₆ in., D. 2 ft. 11⁷/₈ in. Great Silla dynasty, dated 725. Sangwŏn-sa, central Korea.
The darker colour around the flying musicians is due to careless ink-rubbings.

Cat. 144
Buddhist bell. Bronze. H. 3 ft. 4⁹/₁₆ in., D. 2 ft. 2³/₈ in. Koryŏ dynasty, dated 1222. Naeso-sa, south-east Korea.
The flying angel of Silla bells has now changed to a seated Buddha under a flying canopy. Four *tang-cha* are arranged around the body.

Cat. 145
Incense burner. Bronze, inlaid with silver. H. 10¹³/₁₆ in., D. of the rim, 10¹/₄ in. Koryŏ dynasty, dated 1177. P'yoch'ung-sa, south-east Korea.
A typical example, and the earliest dated, of the Koryŏ incense burners used in Buddhist temples. Sanskrit letters symbolizing Buddhas are arranged around the main body in silver inlay, and below the lotus band, around the pedestal, is a winding dragon and clouds design.

Cat. 146
Mirrors. Bronze. D. 9⁹/₁₆ in., 9¹/₁₆ in. Koryŏ dynasty, ca. 11th/13th century. National Museum of Korea, Seoul.

Cat. 147
Mirror. Bronze. D. 9¹³/₁₆ in. Koryŏ dynasty, ca. 11th/13th century. National Museum of Korea, Seoul.

Cat. 148
Bell. Bronze. Originally from a temple in Seoul area. H. 11¹³/₁₆ in., D. 7¹/₂ in. Koryŏ dynasty, ca. 13th/14th century. Tŏksu Palace Museum of Fine Arts, Seoul.
The canopy-like ornament to the left of the standing Bodhi-sattva, framing the incised inscription, is a new feature of Koryŏ bells. The ornamental band below is also wavy instead of in the usual floral pattern.

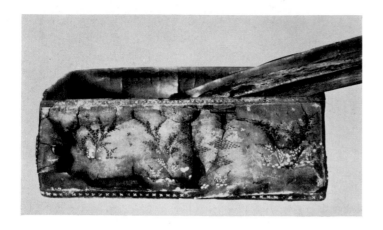

Cat. 149
Lacquer box. Wood, hemp and lacquer. L. 11³/₈ in., W. 7¹/₂ in., H. 4⁵/₁₆ in. Koryŏ dynasty, ca. 12th/13th century. Tŏksu Palace Museum of Fine Arts, Seoul.
Badly damaged, with many pieces of inlaid shells missing.

Cat. 150
Writing box. Lacquered wood with shell inlay. H. 6¹/₄ in., W. 1 ft. 3⁷/₈ in. Yi dynasty, ca. 18th/19th century. Tŏksu Palace Museum of Fine Arts, Seoul.
A box for the ink-stone and other writing materials. The freely executed design is morning-glory.

Cat. 151
Mirror box. Lacquered wood with shell inlay. H. 5⁵/₈ in. Yi dynasty, early 20th century. Coll. Pyŏng-do Min, Seoul.
The mirror on top can be folded in under the two-piece cover. The drawer is for a cosmetic set.

Cat. 152
Women's boxes. Lacquered wood with shell inlay. H. 11¹³/₁₆ in. Yi dynasty, early 20th century. Coll. Pyŏng-do Min, Seoul.
Small boxes with drawers to keep valuables. The animals are always in pairs, a familiar tradition that goes back to T'ang dynasty China, which in turn learned it from the Arabs.

For the sake of clarity the reproductions of a number of pieces are greater than actual size: Plates 13, 30, 45, 54–58, 62, 63, 65, 73, 75–77.

Photographs by:

Hans Hinz, Basel: Pl. II–XVI, XVIII, XIX, XXI, XXII, XXIV; Pl. 34, 39, 44, 47; Cat. 30, 44, 52, 65.

Kyong-mo Lee, Seoul: Cat. 40, 41, 43, 49, 81, 82, 86, 92–94, 97, 99–101, 103, 105, 106, 108, 109, 112–116, 118–126, 128, 133–147, 149, 151, 152.

Mikihiro Taeda, Tokyo: Pl. I, XVII, XX, XXIII; Pl. 1–33, 35–38, 40–43, 45, 46, 48–101.

APPENDIX

AUTHORS' NOTES

PART I
INTRODUCTION

1. A full report of the Unggi site is not available except that news of the discovery appeared on *Kogominsok* (Archaeology and Ethnology), P'yŏngyang 1963, Nr. 2. — The Kongju site, which was originally discovered by an American named Mr. Mohr, was excavated by Yŏnsei University in Nov. 1964.

2. For the comb-pattern pottery, see: Ryōsaku Fujita: *Kushimemonyō-doki no Bumpu ni tsuite* (On the Distribution of Comb-pattern Pottery) in his *Chōsen Kōkogaku Kenkyū* (Archaeological Studies on Korea), Kyōto 1948, pp. 140–168. — Kyoichi Arimitsu: *Chōsen Kushimemon-doki no Kenkyū* (Studies on the Comb-pattern Pottery of Korea), Kyōto 1962. — Won-Yong Kim: 'Some Aspects of the Comb-pattern Pottery of Prehistoric Korea', in: *Arctic Anthropology*, Vol. I, No. I, Madison 1962, pp. 42–50.

3. Won-Yong Kim: 'Dolmens in Korea', in: *Journal of Sciences & Humanities*, No. 16, Seoul 1962, pp. 1–11.

4. The best survey of the Lo-lang relics is: *Chōsen Kobunka Sōkan* (Illustrated Album of Ancient Korean Culture), Vols. II, III, edited by R. Fujita and S. Umehara, Kyōto 1948, 1959.

5. Or Khūrdādhbih, the royal postmaster at Sāmarrā who compiled the first Arabic Itinerary in the ninth century.

6. For a recent English account of *hwarang* see: Richard Rutt: 'The Flower Boys of Silla (Hwarang)', in: *Transaction of the Korea Branch of the Royal Asiatic Society*, Vol. XXXVIII, Seoul 1961.

7. The latest and best study of the Korean Alphabet is: Sang-beck Lee: 'Hangŭl ŭi Kiwŏn' (The Origin of the Korean Alphabet Hangŭl), in: *Publication of the National Museum of Korea*, Series A, Vol. III, Seoul 1957.

8. Among the many Korean potters who were taken or who went to Japan, Yi, who was called by the Japanese Ri Sambei, was the best known. He is commemorated by a stone stele standing at Arita, in Japan. He is said to have come from the Kŭmgang area of central Korea and to have gone voluntarily to Japan in 1598 because of his collaboration with the Japanese army during the war as a guide. In 1616 he discovered a rich mine of clay suitable for porcelain in Arita, and started to produce the famous Arita yaki or Imari-yaki pottery which was the first porcelain ware to be made in Japan. The main source for his personal history is the *Kanegae Monjo* (Kanegae Document) which was submitted by Sambei to his Lord Nabeshima after he opened the Arita kiln. *Kanegae* is the Japanese-style pronounciation of Kŭmgang, and Sambei apparently used it as his Japanese surname. — Cf. Kazuzō Mizumachi: 'Hizen-jiki no Sōgyō Jidai' (The Beginning Period of Hizen Porcelain) (I), Yūzankaku ed., in: *Tōki Kōza*, Vol. XI, Tokyo 1936, pp. 1–90.

9. *Tonghak* (Eastern Learning) was the name of a new religion opposed to *Sŏhak* (Western Learning, *i.e.* Christianity). It was started by Ch'oe Che-u (1824–64) who fused elements of Buddhism, Taoism and Confucianism in a 'New Way'.

PART II
CERAMIC ART

1. See: Won-Yong Kim: *Studies on Silla Pottery*, Seoul 1960. — This is the first systematic study on Silla Pottery by one of the authors of this book.

2. Apart from the types discussed here, Silla also produced numbers of less attractive wares, probably designed for table use, examples of which have also been discovered from the Heijyōkyu excavation in Nara, Japan. The site of this palace of the Nara period has yielded many types of Sue pottery very similar to those of Silla and often shallow in shape, indicating that they were used in connection with palace festivities.

3. Sueji Umehara: *Shiragi Koga no Kenkyū* (Study on the Ancient Tiles of the Silla Dynasty, Korea), Tokyo 1934.

4. This passage is to be found in *Hsiu-Chung-Chin* which is said to have been written by T'ai-ping Lao-jên, of Sung China. No details are known concerning the author: See: G. St. G. M. Gompertz: *Korean Celadon*, London 1963, p. 45.

5. G. St. G. M. Gompertz, *op. cit.*, p. 46.

6. The translation here is taken from Mr. Gompertz's book.

7. Ken Nomori: *Korai Tōji no Kenkyū* (Studies on Koryŏ Potteries and Porcelains), Kyōto 1944, p. 9 ff.

8. Fujio Koyama: 'Kōrai Tōji Josetzu' (Introduction to Koryŏ Ceramic Wares), in: *Sekai Tōji Zenshū*, Vol. XIII, Tokyo 1955, p. 220.

(The University Prints Series O, Section 1, No. 024), Newton, Mass. 1938.

34. When the damaged Sŏkkuram was discovered at the beginning of the present century, two of the eight Parivaras were missing. They were later discovered among the rubble at the entrance of the ante-room, and the Japanese erected them on each side of the entrance, facing inwards toward the main chamber. Thus, the plan of the ante-room became rectangular with its width greater than its depth. The Japanese thought this was the original plan.—During repair work on the cave temple in 1963, however, the two Parivaras at the sides of the entrance were pulled back to stand on the same line as the three Parivaras on each of the shorter walls so that the eight Parivaras stand face to face in two symmetrical groups. Thus, the plan of the ante-room was changed from a rectangle to a square, with the front completely open. At the same time, a wooden roof with tiles was installed to cover what would otherwise be the open ceiling of the ante-room.

35. *Chōsen Koseki Zufu* (Album of Korean Antiquities), Vol. II, Tokyo 1915, Pl. 166.

36. Heibonsha Co. ed., *Sekai Bijutsu Zenshū* (Art of the World), Vol. VIII, China 2, Tokyo 1956, Pls. 20–23.

37. Recorded bad harvests and uprising of rebels and bandits during the period are as follows: 814 Big flood, 815 Bad harvest and bandits, 816 Bad harvest, 817 Bad harvest, 819 Bad harvest, 820 Bad harvest, 821 Bad harvest, 832 Bad harvest and bandits, 836 Rebels, 839 Rebels, 841 Rebels, 847 Rebels, 849 Rebels.

38. L. Sickman and A. Soper, *op. cit.*, p. 97.

39. Nakagiri dates it to the end of the eighth century or the early ninth century. (I. Nakagiri, *op. cit.*, see 27). However, an original stone throne for the Buddha, apparently of the tenth-century style, is still *in situ* at Kwangju, and the date cannot be pushed back so far as the eighth or ninth century.

PART IV
GOLD, BRONZE AND LACQUER WORKS

1. Chu Kuei, 'Liao-ning Ch'ao-yang Shih-erh-t'ai-ying-tzŭ Ch'ing-tung Tuan-chien-mu' (Bronze Dagger Tombs at Shih Erh T'ai Ying Tzŭ, Ch'ao Yang County, Liaoning), in: *Kaogu Hsuehpao*, Peking 1960–61, pp. 63–71.

Won-Yong Kim: 'Sibidai-yŏngza ui Ch'ŏngdong Tangŏmmyo—Hanguk Ch'ŏngdonggi Munhwa ŭi Kiwŏn Munje' (Bronze Dagger Tombs at Shih Erh T'ai Ying Tzŭ—The Problem of the Origin of Korean Bronze Culture), in: *Yŏksa Hakpo*, No. 16, Seoul 1960, pp. 109–121.

2. For detailed report, see: *Chōsen Koseki Chōsa Hōkoku* (Reports of Surveys of Ancient Remains in Korea) 1922, No. 2, pp. 3–29, Pls. 1–19.—*Chōsen Kobunka Sōkan*, Vol. I, Kyōto 1947, pp. 49–52, Pls. 23–26.

3. *Kaogu T'unghsün*, Peking 1956, No. 2, Pl. 15.—The piece is only identified as a '*Hu fu*' (Tiger Tally).

4. The Ordos region is the southern part of Suiyüan province, in north China, surrounded by the Huangho. Bronzes from the region, known as Ordos bronzes, show mixed Siberian and Chinese elements. Their dates range from 1300 B.C. to A.D. 200. See: A. Salmony: *Sino-siberian Art in the Collection of C. T. Loo*, Paris 1938.—J. Werner: 'Zur Stellung der Ordosbronzen' in: *Eurasia Septentrionalis Antiqua*, 9, Helsinki 1934.

5. K. Hamada: *Keishū-no Kinkanzuka* (The Gold Crown Tomb of Kyŏngju), Kyŏngju 1932.

6. The *Nan-hai Ch'i-kuei Nei-fa-chüan*, describes Koguryŏ as *Kukutesvara* meaning 'Chicken-worshipping Country' in Sanskrit. According to the description, the people of Koguryŏ worship a chicken deity and use cock tails as hat-ornaments. The same remark is made in *Samguk Yusa*, Vol. 4.

7. M. Rostovtzeff: *Iranians and Greeks in South Russia*, Oxford 1932, Pl. XXVI, No. 1.

8. C. Hentze: 'Die Schamanenkronen zur Han-Zeit in Korea', in: *Ostasiatische Zeitschrift*, Neue Folge, IX, Heft 5. Berlin 1932.

9. The author has recently received an unconfirmed account of the discovery of a jadeite deposit in Kyŏngsang Pukdo Province on the northern marginal region of former Silla territory.

10. *Chōsen Koseki Chōsa Hōkoku* (Report of Surveys of Ancient Remains in Korea) 1917, p. 663, Figs. 666–668.—S. Umehara: 'Rashū Hannam-men-no Hōkan' (The Crown from Naju), in: *Chōsen Gakuhō*, No. 14, Tenri 1959, pp. 477–488.

11. Chewon Kim and Moo-byong Youn: *Ŭisŏng T'apni Kobun* (The Ancient Tombs in T'apni, Ŭisŏng-gun, Kyŏngsang pukdo), Seoul 1962. (Report of the Research of Antiquities of the National Museum of Korea, Vol. III.)

12. Government General of Chōsen, *Kokuri-jidai-no Iseki* (The Site of the Koguryŏ dynasty), Plates Vol. II, Seoul 1930, Pl. 119.

13. K. Hamada has pointed out a similar-shaped diadem from

Alexandropol of south Russia. See: K. Hamada: *op. cit.*, p. 36, Fig. 8.

14. The crown now in the P'yŏngyang Museum has not been published. Illustration reproduced from *Umehara Kōko Shiryō* (Umehara Archaeological Card), No. 5132.

15. This is a Lo-lang tomb with an original chamber built of logs. The tomb, excavated in 1916, seems to belong to the early part of the Later Han dynasty (A.D. 25–220). See: *Chōsen Koseki Chōsa Hōkoku* (Report of Surveys of Ancient Remains in Korea) 1916, pp. 664–665.

16. Remnants of a thick hollow gold ring for an earring were discovered in a ruined tomb in P'yŏngyang built with tiles carrying the date of *ying-ho* ninth year (A.D. 353). The tomb is believed to be the tomb of a Chinese residing in the area after the fall of the Lo-lang colony. See: *Chōsen Koseki Chōsa Hōkoku* (Report of Surveys of Ancient Remains in Korea) 1932, Vol. I.

17. Yang Ken, 'Chin-tai Lü-tung He-chin-te Chien-ting Chi Chi Yieh-lien Chi-shu-te Ch'u-pu T'ang-t'se' (Initial Investigation on the Chin Dynasty Alloy of Aluminum and Copper and its Metallurgy), in: *Kaogu Hsuehpao*, Peking 1959. No. 4, Pl. I, Nos. 3, 6.

18. *Chōsen Koseki Chōsa Hōkoku* (Report of Surveys of Ancient Remains in Korea) 1927, Pl. 2.

19. The fact is well testified by the discovery of Han materials in the tombs at Noin-ula. See: S. Umehara: *Kodai Hok-pō-kei Bumbutsu-no Kenkyū* (Studies on Ancient Materials of Northern Origin), Kyōto 1938.

20. See the *Yü Fu Chih* of *Sung Shih* (Annals of Sung).

21. Government General of Chōsen, *Sugihara Chōtarō-shi Shūshū Kōkohin Zuroku* (Illustrated Catalogue of the Sugihara Collection of Archaeological Materials), Seoul 1944, Pl. 5, No. 1.

22. K. Hamada: *op. cit.*, pp. 83–84.

23. For these Koryŏ bells, see: S. Umehara: 'Chōsen-shō Zakki' (Note on Korean Bells), in: *Chōsen Gakuhō*, No. 7, Tenri 1955, pp. 117–140. — Nihon Kōko Gakkai (Japanese Assoc. of Archaeology), *Chōsen-shō Shashin-shū* (Album of Korean Bells), 2nd ed., Tokyo 1923. — Su-young Hwang: 'Koryŏ-jong ŭi Sin-jaryo' (New Examples of Koryŏ Bells), in: *Kogo Misul*, Vol. I, No. 2, Seoul 1960, pp. 3–7; Vol. II, No. 1, 1961, pp. 8–11. — Ryōhei Tsuboi: 'Chōsen-shō Shiryō' (Materials for Korean Bells), in: *Chōsen Gakuhō*, No. 16, Tenri, July 1960, pp. 77–101.

24. Ryōhei Tsuboi: 'Mumei Korai-shō' (Undated Koryŏ Bells), in: *Chōsen Gakuhō*, Combined Nos. 21/22, Tenri 1961, pp. 88–89.

25. Tomio Yoshino: 'Korai-no Raden-sikki' (Lacquer Works of the Koryŏ Period), in: *Bijutsu Kenkyu*, No. 175, Tokyo 1954, May, p. 8.

26. Yoshino, *ibid.*, p. 2.

27. See: Under Gilded Koryŏ ware (Koryŏ dynasty wares) in Part II of this book.

28. Small pieces of crystal or glass with designs painted on one side were used in certain ornamental metal fittings of the Han dynasty. See: *Hakubutsu-Kan Chinretsuhin Zukan* (Museum Exhibits Illustrated), Vol. VIII, Seoul 1936, Pl. 12.

29. The information on the modern lacquer process is based on Mr. Ye's publication. Yong-hai Ye: *Ingan Munhwa-jae* (Masters of Cultural Heritage), Seoul 1963, pp. 221–226.

30. Yong-hai Ye: *Ibid.*, pp. 229–232.

GLOSSARY

ABHAYA MUDRĀ
'Assurance from fear' *mudrā*. Hand lifted; fingers extended and pointing upward; palm to front.

AMITĀBHA
The Buddha who presides over the Paradise of the West. His attendants are the Bodhisattvas Avalokiteśvara and Mahāsthāmaprāpta.

APSARAS
A goddess, a female *deva*.

ARHAT
Lohan in Chinese. A Buddhist monk or saint who has already achieved enlightenment.

ĀSANA
Positions of the legs on Buddhist images.

AVALOKITEŚVARA
One of the Bodhisattvas. Kwan-yin in Chinese. One of the two attendants of Amitābha personifying the latter's charity.

BHADRA ĀSANA
An *āsana* in which both legs are pendant, separate, or with ankles crossed.

BHAIṢAJYAGURU
The Buddha of Medicine.

BHŪMISPARŚA MUDRĀ
'Earth touching' *mudrā*. The right hand points or touches the earth with the palm turned inward.

BODHISATTVA
One who has undergone the severe discipline of Buddhism and will become a Buddha in a future incarnation.

BODHI-TREE
The pipal tree. Gautama attained the Buddhahood under a *bodhi*-tree at Buddh Gaya.

BRĀHMA
One of the *devas* (see *deva*).

CHIAO-TOU
Chinese bronze kettle-ewer form.

CH'I-LIN
Unicorn, a fabulous animal of good omen.

CH'ING-PAI
Bluish white.

CH'ING-TE-CHEN
Kiln or ware named after the town in Chiang-hsi famous as the ceramic metropolis of China from the Ming dynasty onwards.

CHITAN
Ethnically a Mongoloid race, the Chitans established the Liao Empire (916–1125) that once occupied a part of the north China, inner Mongolia and Manchuria.

CH'ŎNGHWA
Ch'ing hua in Chinese; blue and white, painting in cobalt.

CHUNG
Type of Chinese bronze hanging bell.

DEVA
T'ien in Chinese. Former Pagan deities who were converted to Buddhism and became devoted supporters and protectors of Buddhism.

DHARMACAKRA MUDRĀ
'Preaching' *mudrā*, turning the wheel of the law. Hands together in front of the breast; a finger of one hand touches the other hand of which the thumb and another finger are joined at their tips.

DHRTRĀṢṬRA
Guardian of the East.

DHYĀNA MUDRĀ
'Meditation' *mudrā*. Arms are flexed with overlapping hands on the lap.

EKĀDĀSAMUKHA
Eleven-headed Kwan-yin. A Tantric image.

FÊNG-HUANG
Phoenix, a fabulous bird combining the splendour of every feathered creature.

HAO
Literary or artist's name of a learned man.

HSIUNGNU
An Europoid tribe that flourished for some five centuries from late 4th century B.C. to the third century A.D. in the vast area of Mongolia, Ordos and the eastern Turkestan.

JU
Kiln or ware named after Ju Chou, the modern Lin-ju Hsien, in Honan, China.

JUCHEN
Manchus who ousted the Liao and established the Chin dynasty (1115–1234).

KALABINKA
The fabulous bird of Paradise.

KORYŎ-SA
Official dynastic history of Koryŏ period.

KṢITIGARBHA
Ti-tsang in Chinese. A Bodhisattva who preaches and saves all souls in Heaven and in Hell, from the Nirvana of Śākyamuni until the emergence of Maitreya.

KWAN-YIN
See Avalokiteśvara.

KYŎNGGUK TAEJŎN
The official laws and regulations of the Yi dynasty (1392–1910) of Korea, first published in 1471.

LEI
A Chinese bronze form. A jar generally of large capacity similar to the *hu* type, but wide at the shoulder and narrowing towards the foot.

LOHAN
See *arhat*.

LO-LANG
One of the four provinces established by Han China in North Korea in 108 B.C. Though the three other provinces disappeared soon afterwards, Lo-lang remained prosperous until the fourth century A.D.

LUNG-SHAN
The type-site of the late Neolithic culture of China that follows the Yangshao stage and precedes the Shang period, partially coinciding with the latter.

MAEBYŎNG
In Chinese *mei-p'ing;* Prunus vase; vase with wide shoulder and contracted neck suitable for displaying a single branch of prunus blossom.

MAHĀSTHĀMAPRĀPTA
Bodhisattva. Shih-chih in Chinese. An attendant of Amitābha personifying his wisdom.

MAITREYA
A Buddha as well as a Bodhisattva, who has attained Buddhahood but is waiting in the Tuṣita Heaven to emerge as the Saviour after 5.6 billion years from the Nirvana of Śākyamuni.

MANDORLA
The almond-shaped back panel of a Buddhist image.

MAÑJUŚRĪ
Bodhisattva of wisdom. An attendant of Śākyamuni.

MUDRĀ
Positions of hands and fingers in Buddhist images.

NIEN HAO
Year designation. A *nien hao* was adopted at the beginning of each reign, and in some cases changed several times during its course. It is thus not the name or title of an emperor.

PAEKCHA
White porcelain.

PARIVARA
Eight attendants of the four Guardians.

P'ING-T'O
A lacquer-working technique in which designs cut out in gold or silver are plastered on the wet surface of the lacquer and a layer of lacquer is then applied above it; the lacquer surface is then polished until the metal design is exposed.

SAGI
Ceramic ware.

SAKRA-DEVENDRA
One of the *devas*. Also called Indra.

ŚĀKYAMUNI
The Sage of the Śākyas, the commonest title of Gautama Buddha.

SAMANTABHADRA
The Bodhisattva of universal benevolence. An attendant of Śākyamuni.

SAN KUO CHIH
The official history of the Three Kingdoms (220–280) of China, compiled by Chen Shou.

SARĪRA
Relics or ashes of Buddhas or saints.

SHENG
A musical instrument.

SHŌSŌ-IN
An old treasure house in Japan. It was originally the storehouse of the Tōdaiji temple in Nara. It houses hundreds of treasures mostly of the eighth century. The best known among them are more than 600 pieces belonging to the Emperor Shōmu (d. 756) and dedicated to the Temple after his death.

STŪPA
Pagoda.

SŪTRA
Buddhist scriptures.

T'AO-T'IEH
Glutton motive. It is commonly, composed of the bodies and detached limbs of *k'uei* dragons.

TEMMOKU
Black ware.

TING
Kiln or ware named after Ting Chou in Ho-pei, China.

T'O
Type of Chinese bronze bell, to be held in the hand.

TOU
A Chinese bronze form, hemi-spherical bowl raised on a high stem with a spreading foot. Usually with a cover which may be inverted for use as a separate vessel.

TRIBHANGA
Thrice-bent posture with the hip thrust sideways and the head held erect.

TSUN
A generic name for ritual wine-vessels, applied especially to those which cannot be placed in a recognized class.

UṢṆĪṢA
The protuberance on the skull of Buddha.

VAIROÇANA
First Dhyani Buddha, and recognized by some sects as the spiritual or essential body of the Buddha-truth, all-pervasive like the light of the sun, as the Chinese name Ta-jih suggests.

VAJRA-PĀṆĪ
A fierce protector of Buddhism holding in his hand the Vajra thunderbolt.

VARA MUDRĀ
'Bestowing' *mudrā*. Hand dropped; fingers extended and pointing downwards; palm to the front.

VIRŪDHAKA
Guardian of the South.

YANGSHAO

A village in Honan, China which is the first Neolithic site discovered iu China characterized by painted pottery. The name now represents the Neolithic, painted pottery culture of China.

YING CH'ING

Shadowy blue, misty blue; a characteristic pale blue glaze of certain Sung and later wares.

YONGJAE CH'ONGHWA

Collection of essays by Sŏng Hyŏn (1439–1508). Yongjae is the literary name of the author.

YÜEH

Kiln or ware named after Yüeh Chou, the modern Shao-hsing, in Chê-chiang (Chekiang) province, China.

BIBLIOGRAPHY

Academy of Arts, Republic of Korea, ed.: *Hanguk Yesul Ch'ongnam* (General Survey of Korean Arts), Seoul 1964.

The Arts Council, ed.: *An Exhibition of National Art Treasures of Korea*, London 1961.

H. S. CHIN: *Kyŏngju ŭi Kojŏk* (Ancient Remains in Kyŏngju), Seoul 1957.

Chin-Tan Hakhoe, ed.: *Hanguk-sa* (The History of Korea), Vols. I–VII, Seoul 1959–1965.

Chōsen Sōtokufu (The Government General of Korea), ed.: *Chōsen Koseki Zufu* (Album of Korean Antiquities), Vols. I–XV, Seoul 1915–1935.

Chōsen Sōtokufu, ed.: *Bukkoku-ji to Sekkutsu-an* (Pulguksa and Sŏkkuram Cave), Seoul 1938.

Chōsen Sōtokufu, ed.: *A Royal Tomb 'Kinkan-Tsuka' or The Gold Crown Tomb at Keishū and its Treasures*, Seoul 1924–1927 (Special Report of the Service of Antiquities, III.)

Chōsen Sōtokufu, ed.: *Chōsen Koseki Chōsa Hōkoku* (Report of the Survey of Antiquities of Korea), Seoul 1916–1938.

Chōsen Sōtokufu, ed.: *Chinretsuhin Zukan* (Museum Exhibits Illustrated), Vols. I–XVII, Seoul 1918–1941.

P. A. ECKARDT: *Geschichte der Koreanischen Kunst*, Leipzig 1929.

G. FUJISHIMA: *Chōsen Kenchiku Shiron* (History of Korean Architecture), Tokyo 1930.

R. FUJITA: *Chōsen Kōkogaku Kenkyū* (Archaeological Studies on Korea), Kyōto 1948.

G. ST. G. M. GOMPERTZ: *Korean Celadon*, London 1963.

K. HAMADA: *Keishū-no Kinkanzuka* (The Gold Crown Tomb of Kyŏngju), Kyŏngju 1932.

K. HAMADA and S. UMEHARA: *Shiragi Koga no Kenkyū* (Studies on Silla Roof Tiles), Kyōto 1943.

R. HEINE-GELDERN: 'Weltbild und Bauform in Südostasien', in: *Wiener Beiträge zur Kunst und Kultur-Geschichte Asiens*, Bd. IV, 1930, S. 28.

W. B. HONEY: *Corean Pottery*, London 1947.

W. B. HONEY: *The Ceramic Art of China and other Countries of the Far East*, London 1944.

H. B. HULBERT: *The History of Korea*, Seoul 1905.

H. IKEUCHI: *T'ung-Kou, I*. The Ancient Site of Kao-Kou-Li in Chi-An District, T'ung-Hua Province, Manchoukuo, Tokyo/Hsin-Ching 1938.

H. IKEUCHI and S. UMEHARA: *T'ung-Kou, II*. Kao-Kou-Lian Tomb with Wall Paintings in Chi-an District T'ung-Hua Province, Manchoukuo, Tokyo/Hsin-Ching 1940.

CH. KIM, A. B. GRISWOLD and P. H. POTT: *Burma Korea Tibet*, London 1964. (Art of the World Series.)

CH. KIM: 'The Stone Pagoda of Koo Huang Li in South Korea', in: *Artibus Asiae*, vol. XIII, 1/2, Ascona 1950.

CH. KIM: 'Two Old Silla Tombs', in: *Artibus Asiae*, Vol. X, 3, Ascona 1947.

CH. KIM: *Two Old Silla Tombs, Ho-U Tomb and Silver Bell Tomb*, Seoul 1947.

CH. KIM: 'Masterpieces of Korean Art in America', in: *Artibus Asiae*, Vol. XX, 4, Ascona 1957.

CH. KIM: 'Treasures from the Songyimsa Temple in Southern Korea', in: *Artibus Asiae*, Vol. XXII, 1/2, Ascona 1959.

CH. KIM: 'Han Dynasty Mythology and the Korean Legend of Tangun', in: *Archives of Chinese Art Society of America*, Vol. III, New York 1948–1949.

CH. KIM: 'Kannonji to Seitō hakken no Sariyōki' (Kameunsa and Reliquary of sarīra of its western pagoda), in: *Mizue*, No. 720, Tokyo, Feb. 1965.

CH. KIM and M. YOUN: *Kam Eun Sa*. A Temple Site of the Silla Dynasty, Seoul 1961. (Special Report of the National Museum of Korea, Vol. II.)

CH. KIM and M. YOUN: *Ŭlsŏng T'apni Kobun* (The Ancient Tombs in T'apni, Ŭisŏng-gun, Kyŏngsang pukdo), Seoul 1962. (Report of the Research of Antiquities of the National Museum of Korea, Vol. III.)

CH. KIM and G. ST. G. M. GOMPERTZ: *The Ceramic Art of Korea*, London 1961.

W. Y. KIM: *Early movable Type in Korea*, Seoul 1954.

W. Y. KIM: *Studies on Silla Pottery*, Seoul 1960.

W. Y. KIM: 'An Early Chinese Gilt Bronze Seated Buddha from Seoul,' in: *Artibus Asiae*, Vol. XXIII, 1, Ascona 1961.

W. Y. KIM: 'Hanguk Pulssang ŭi Yangshik Pyŏnch'ŏn' (Stylistic Evolution of Korean Buddhist Images), in: *Sasanggye Monthly*, Nos. 91, 92, Seoul, Feb., March 1961.

W. Y. KIM: 'Hanguk Munhwa ŭi Kogohakchŏk Yŏngu' (Archaeological Studies on Korean Culture), in: *Hanguk Munhwasa*, Vol. I, Seoul 1964.

W. Y. KIM: 'Hanguk Misulsa Yŏngu ŭi Isam Munje' (Topics from History of Korean Art), in: *Asea Munje Yŏngu* (The Journal of Asiatic Studies), Vol. VII, No. 3, Seoul 1964.

W. Y. KIM: 'Kodai Kankoku no Kondōbutsu' (Gilt Bronze Buddhist Images of Ancient Korea), in: *Mizue*, No. 719, Tokyo, Jan. 1965.

W.Y.KIM: 'Kodai Kankoku no Sekibutsu' (Stone Buddhist Images of Ancient Korea), in: *Mizue*, No. 721, Tokyo, March 1965.

Y.U.KIM: *Hanguk Sŏhwa Inmyŏng Sasŏ* (Dictionary of the Names of Painters and Calligraphers in Korea), Seoul 1959.

Y.S.KOH: *Hanguk T'appa ŭi Yŏngu* (Study of Korean Pagodas), Seoul 1948.

Y.S.KOH: *Chōsen no Seiji* (Korean Celadon), Tokyo 1939.

Y.S.KOH: *Koryŏ Ch'ŏngja* (Celadon of Koryŏ), Seoul 1959.

Y.S.KOH: *Hanguk Misulsa Mihak Nonch'ong* (Essays on Korean Art History and Esthetics), Seoul 1964.

A.KOIZUMI: *Rakurō Saikyō Tsuka* (The Painted Basket Tomb of Lo-lang), Seoul 1934.

Korean Studies Guide, Berkeley and Los Angeles 1954.

F.KOYAMA, T.OKUDAIRA and A.TANAKA: *Chōsen Tōki* (Korean Pottery), Tokyo 1946.

K.B.LEE: *Kuksa Sinron* (New History of Korea), Seoul 1961.

Masterpieces of Korean Art, Boston 1957.

E.McCUNE: *The Arts of Korea, An Illustrated History*, Rutland, Vermont and Tokyo 1962.

Ministry of Education, Republic of Korea, ed.: *Kukbo Torok* (Korea's Treasures—Registered National Treasures of Korea), Vols. 1–5, Seoul 1959–1961. (1: Bells and Buddhist Instruments, Ceramics, and Archaeological Materials; 2: Books and Calligraphy; 3: Buddhist Images; 4: Monuments in Stone; 5: Stone Pagodas.)

Munhwa Kyoyuk Pub.Co., ed.: *Sege Misul Chŏnjip* (Art of the World), Vol.II: Korea & Ancient Far East, Seoul 1962.

I.NAKAGIRI: 'Shiragi Chōkoku Oboegaki' (Notes on Silla Sculpture), in: *Chōsen Gakuhō*, No.29, Tenri 1963.

National Museum of Korea, ed.: *Misul Kogohak Yong-ŏ-jip, Kŏnch'ukp'yŏn* (Korean Vocabularies in the Field of Art, Archaeology, and Architecture), Seoul 1955.

K.NOMORI: *Kōrai Tōji no Kenkyū* (Studies on Koryŏ Potteries and Porcelains), Kyōto 1944.

T.OBA: *Keishū Nanzan no Busseki* (Buddhist Sites on Mt. Namsan), Seoul 1940.

T.OBA and K.KAYAMOTO: *Rakurō Ōkō Bo* (The Tomb of Wang Kŭang of Lo-lang), Seoul 1935.

S.ODA: *Chōsen Tōjishi Bunkenkō* (Bibliography on History of Korean Pottery), Tokyo 1936.

C.OSGOOD: *The Koreans and their Culture*, New York 1951.

SECHANG OH: *Kŭn Yŏk Sŏ Hwa Ching* (Sourcebook of Painters and Calligraphers of Korea), Seoul 1928.

E.O.REISCHAUER and J.K.FAIRBANK: *East Asia, The Great Tradition*, Boston 1960.

Riōke Hakubutsukan Shojōhin Shashinchō (Album of the Yi Household Museum Collection): *Butsuzō no bu* (Buddhist Sculpture), Kyōto 1929; *Tōjiki no bu* (Pottery and Porcelain), Kyōto 1932; *Kaiga no bu* (Paintings), Kyōto 1933.

Riōshoku (Yi Household): *Chōsen Kohun Hekigashū* (Collection of Mural Paintings of Korea), Seoul 1916.

B.ROWLAND Jr.: 'A Study of Style and Iconography in Oriental Art', in: *Art in America*, Vol.XXIX, July 1941, No.3, p.115.

T.SAITŌ: *Chōsen Kodai Bunka no Kenkyū* (Studies on the Ancient Culture of Korea), Tokyo 1943.

T.SAITŌ: *Chōsen Bukkyō Bijutsukō* (Studies on the Buddhist Art of Korea), Tokyo 1947.

T.SAITŌ: 'Shiragi Kasō Kotsutsubo Kō' (Studies on Urns of the Silla Dynasty), in: *Kōkogaku Ronsō*, N.2, Tokyo 1938.

T.SEKINO: *Chōsen Bijutsu Shi* (History of Korean Art), Kyōto 1932.

T.SEKINO: *Chōsen no Kenchiku to Geijutsu* (Architecture and Art of Korea), Tokyo 1941.

T.SEKINO, S.YATSUI, S.KURIYAMA, T.OBA, K.OGAWA and T.NOMORI: *Rakurōgun Jidai no Iseki* (Archaeological Researches on the Ancient Lo-lang District), Seoul 1925–1927.

T.SEKINO, S.YATSUI, S.KURIYAMA, T.OBA, K.OGAWA and T.NOMORI: *Kōkuri Jidai no Iseki* (Archaeological Researches on the Ancient Koguryŏ District), Seoul 1929–1930.

Sekai Tōji Zenshū (Ceramics of the World), Vol.XIV: *Richōhen* (Yi Dynasty Wares), Tokyo 1956.

Sekai Tōji Zenshū, Vol.XIII: *Chōsen Kodai Kōraihen* (Korea: Early Period and Koryŏ Period), Tokyo 1955.

L.SICKMAN and A.SOPER: *The Art and Architecture of China*, Harmondsworth 1956.

S.SUGIYAMA: *Chōsen Kenchikushi Kenkyū Hōkoku* (Research Report on Korean Architecture), Kyōto 1949.

Y.H.TOH: *Anak Samhobun Palgul Pogo* (Report on the Excavation of Tomb No.3 in Anak), P'yŏngyang 1958.

R.TSUBOI: 'Mumei Chōsen-shō Shiryō' (Materials on Korean Buddhist Bells without Inscription), in: *Chōsen Gakuhō*, No. 21/22, Tenri 1961.

S.UMEHARA: *Chōsen Kodai no Bunka* (Culture of Ancient Korea), Kyōto 1946.

S.UMEHARA: *Chōsen Kodai no Bosei* (Tomb Structure of Ancient Korea), Kyōto 1947.

S.UMEHARA: 'The newly discovered Tomb with Wall Paintings of Kao-Ku-Li Dynasty', in: *Archives of Chinese Art Society of America*, Vol. VI, New York 1952.

S. UMEHARA: 'Kankoku Keishū Kōhukuji-to Hakken-no Shari-yōki' (The Reliquary discovered in the Pagoda of the Hwangbok-sa Temple, Kyŏngju, Korea,) in: *The Bijutsu Kenkyū*, No. CLVI, 1, Tokyo 1950.

S. UMEHARA and R. FUJITA: *Chōsen Kobunka Sōkan* (Selected Specimens of Ancient Culture of Korea), Vols. I–III and following, Kyōto 1947.

L. WARNER: 'Korean Grave Pottery of the Korai Dynasty', in: *Bulletin of the Cleveland Museum of Art*, Vol. VI, 5, April 1919.

M. YAMADA: *Chōsen Tōjiki no Hensen* (Evolutions in Korean Pottery), Tokyo 1939.

M. YANAGI: *Chōsen to Sono Geijutsu* (Korea and her Art), Tokyo 1922.

P. D. YI: *Kuksa Taegwan* (Outline of Korean History), rev. ed., Seoul 1958.

T. YOSHINO: 'Kōrai no Radenki' (Shell-inlaid Lacquer Ware of the Koryŏ Dynasty), in: *Bijutsu Kenkyū*, No. 175, Tokyo, May 1954.

GEOGRAPHICAL MAP

△ = mountains
○ = places

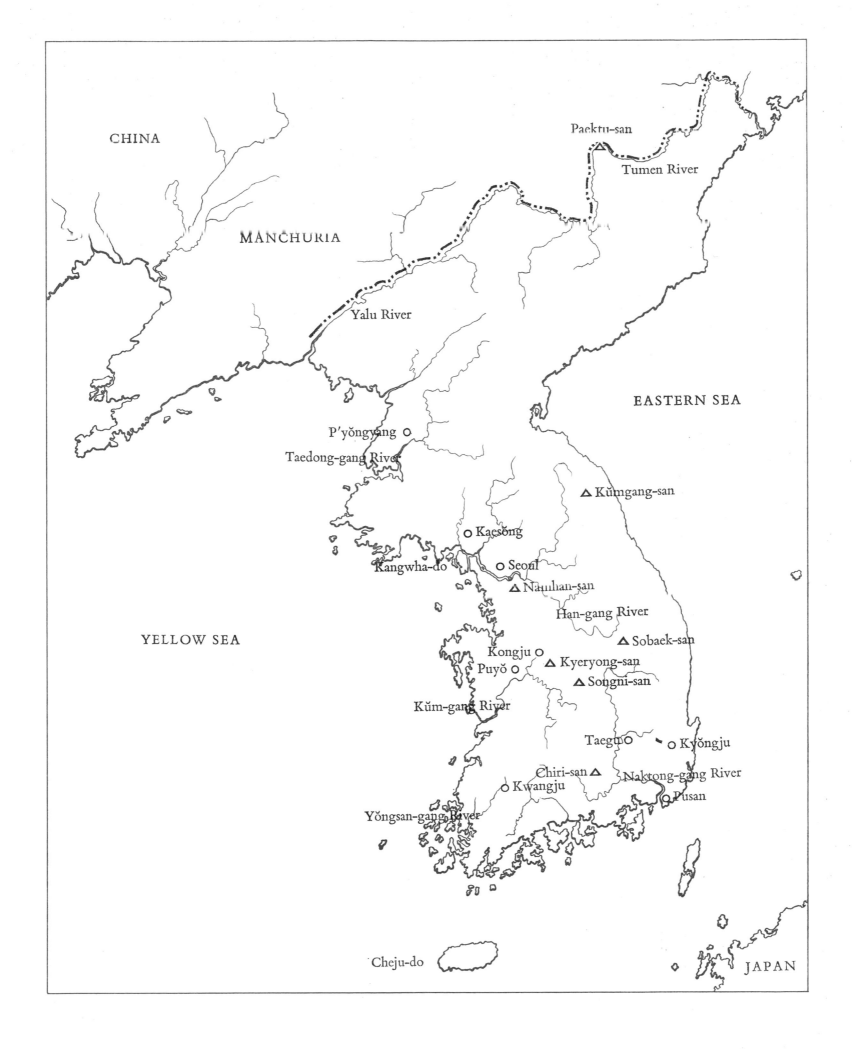

CHINA

MANCHURIA

Paektu-san

Tumen River

Yalu River

EASTERN SEA

P'yŏngyang ○

Taedong-gang River

△ Kŭmgang-san

Kaesŏng ○

Kangwha-do   ○ Seoul

△ Namhan-san

Han-gang River

YELLOW SEA

△ Sobaek-san

Kongju ○

Puyŏ ○   △ Kyeryong-san

△ Songni-san

Kŭm-gang River

Taegu ○   ○ Kyŏngju

Chiri-san △   Naktong-gang River

Kwangju ○   ○ Pusan

Yŏngsan-gang River

Cheju-do   JAPAN

ART-HISTORICAL MAP

o   = places
△   = mountains
◻   ━ temples

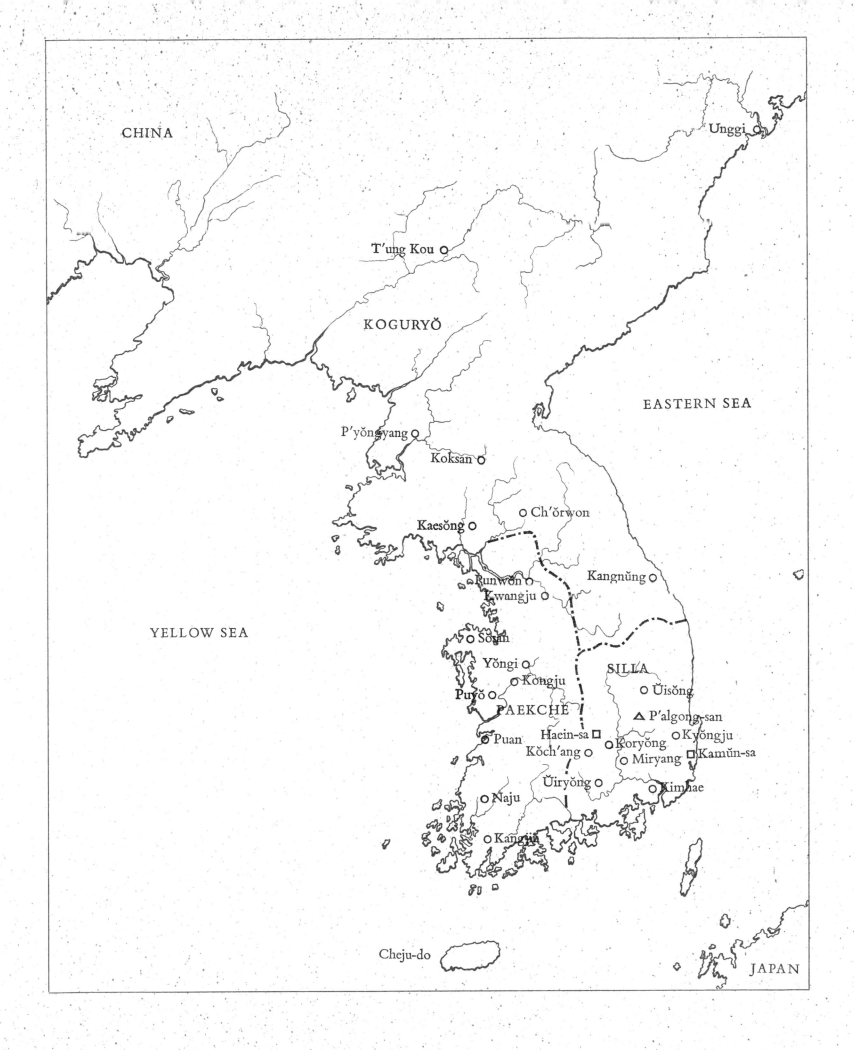

CHINA

Unggi○

KOGURYŎ

T'ung Kou○

EASTERN SEA

P'yŏngyang○

Koksan○

Ch'ŏrwon○

Kaesŏng○

Kangnŭng○

Kunwŏn○
Kwangju○

YELLOW SEA

Sosan○

Yŏngi○

SILLA

Kongju○

Ŭisŏng○

Puyŏ○

PAEKCHE

△P'algong-san

Haein-sa□

Kyŏngju○

Puan○

Koryŏng○

Kamŭn-sa□

Kŏch'ang○

Miryang○

Ŭiryŏng○

Kimhae○

Naju○

Kangjin○

Cheju-do

JAPAN

COMPARATIVE CHRONOLOGY

	KOREA		CHINA	JAPAN
	HISTORICAL EVENTS	ARTISTIC MANIFESTATION		
B.C.				
	Pre-Ceramic Culture		Sha-Yüan Culture	
3000				Jōmon Culture
			Yang-Shao Culture	
2000			Lung-Shan Culture	
	Neolithic Age	Comb-Pattern Pottery	Ca. 1550 The Shang Dynasty (ca. 1550–1050)	
1000			Ca. 1050 The Western Chou Dynasty	
800			770 The Eastern Chou Dynasty	
700				
500	Bronze Age	Plain Pottery Dolmen		
400			403 The Warring States (403–221)	
300	Iron Age			Yayoi Culture (ca. 300 B.C.–A.D. 300)
200			221 The Ch'in Dynasty (221–206)	
			202 The Han Dynasty (202 B.C.–A.D. 220)	
	108 Fall of the Wei-man Ch'ao-hsien			
	Establishment of the Lo-lang Colony (108 B.C.–A.D. 313)			
100				

	KOREA		CHINA	JAPAN
	HISTORICAL EVENTS	ARTISTIC MANIFESTATION		
100	57 Kingdom of Silla (57 B.C.–A.D.935) 37 Kingdom of Koguryŏ (37 B.C.–A.D.668) 18 Kingdom of Paekche (18 B.C.–A.D.660)			
0 A.D. 100		Kimhae Pottery		
200		Silla Pottery appears	220 The Three Kingdoms (220–280)	
300	313 Fall of the Lo-lang Colony		316 The Sixteen Kingdoms (316–439)	The Yamato Court Kofun Period (ca. 300–500)
		357 The Tomb of Tung Shou near P'yŏngyang with mural paintings		
	371 King Sosurim (371–384), Koguryŏ 372 Arrival of Buddhist Monk Shun-tao from Chin (350–394), China Beginning of Buddhism in Koguryŏ 384 Arrival of Buddhist Monk Malananda from Eastern Chin (317–420) Beginning of Buddhism in Paekche 391 King Kwanggae-t'o (391–413), Koguryŏ			
400		Tomb of Kwanggae-t'o (391–413)		

	KOREA		CHINA	JAPAN
	HISTORICAL EVENTS	ARTISTIC MANIFESTATION		
400				
		415 Inscribed bronze vessel from Ho-u Tomb, Kyŏngju		
	427 Capital of Koguryŏ moved from T'ung-Kou to P'yŏngyang		439 The Six Dynasties (439–589)	
	475 Capital of Paekche moved from Hansŏng to Kongju			
500				
	514 King Pŏbhŭng (514–540), Silla			
	528 Beginning of Buddhism as an official religion in Silla		531 The Sui Dynasty (531–618)	
	538 Capital of Paekche moved from Kongju to Puyŏ	539 The 'yŏn-ga' dated gilt bronze Buddha, Koguryŏ		
	540 King Chinhŭng (540–576), Silla			
				552 Asuka Period (552–645)
	562 Fall of Tae-Kaya by Silla			
		Extensive Construction of decorated Tombs in Koguryŏ		
600	612 Sui Army attacks Koguryŏ			
	613 Sui Army again attacks Koguryŏ		618 The T'ang Dynasty (618–907)	
		634 Construction of Punhwang-sa Temple, Silla		

	KOREA		CHINA	JAPAN
	HISTORICAL EVENTS	ARTISTIC MANIFESTATION		
	645 Repulse of the T'ang Army by Koguryŏ			645 Taika Reform (645–649) Nara Period (645–794) Hakuhō (645–710) Tempyō (710–794)
	660 Fall of Paekche 661 King Munmu (661–680), Silla			
	668 Fall of Koguryŏ Unification of Korean Peninsula by Silla The Great Silla Dynasty (668–935)			
		673 'Kuei-yu' inscribed Buddhist stelae		
		679 Construction of Sach'ŏnwang-sa Temple		
		682 Construction of Kamŭn-sa Temple		
		689 'Chi-chou' inscribed Buddhist stelae		
		692 Construction of Stone Pagoda at Hwangbok-sa, Kyŏngju		
700	702 King Sŏngdŏk (702–736)			
		706 Dated *sarīra* case with two gold Buddhist images from the Hwangbok-sa Pagoda		
		720 Pair of stone Buddhas of Kamsan-sa with inscription		
		725 Casting of the Sangwŏn-sa bronze bell		
		751 Construction of Pulguk-sa Temple and the Sŏkkuram Cave Temple		

	KOREA		CHINA	JAPAN
	HISTORICAL EVENTS	ARTISTIC MANIFESTATION		
		771 Casting of the Pongdŏk-sa bronze bell		794 Heian Period (794–1185) Kōnin Period (794–894) Fujiwara Period (894–1185)
800				
		858 The iron Buddha of Porim-sa Temple 865 The iron Buddha of Top'ian-sa Temple		
	892 Rise of rebel Kyŏnhwŏn in South-western Korea			
900	901 Rise of rebel Kung-ye in Central Korea		907 Fall of the T'ang The Five Dynasties (907–979) 916 Liao (Chitan) Dynasty (916–1125)	
	918 The Koryŏ Dynasty (918–1392) 919 Capital established at Kaesŏng 935 Surrender of Silla		960 The Sung Dynasty (960–1280)	
	993 Three invasions by the Chitans (993–1018)	993 Proto-Celadon vase with 'Sun-hwa (ch'un hua) 4th year' inscription		
1000				
		1010 Casting of the Ch'ŏnhŭng-sa bronze bell Ca. 1050 Rise of true Koryŏ Celadon		

	KOREA		CHINA	JAPAN
	HISTORICAL EVENTS	ARTISTIC MANIFESTATION		
1100			1115 The Chin (Juchen) Dynasty (1115–1234)	
			1125 Fall of Liao	
1200				1185 Kamakura Period (1185–1392)
	1214 King Kojong (1214–1259)		1206 The Yüan (Mongol) Dynasty (1206–1368)	
	1231 First Mongol invasion			
	1232 Second Mongol invasion			
	Evacuation of Koryŏ Government to Kanghwa Island			
		1234 Use of movable metal Types to print 'Sang-jŏng Ye mun'		
	1235 Third Mongol invasion	1236 Completion of Wood blocks of *tripitaka*		
	1239 Surrender of Koryŏ to the Yüan		1279 Fall of the Sung Dynasty	
	1281 Yüan-Koryŏ expedition to Japan			
1300				
			1368 The Ming Dynasty (1368–1662)	
		Ca. 1390 *Punch'ŏng* and White Porcelain produced		
	1392 Fall of Koryŏ			1392 Muromachi Period (1392–1573)
	The Yi Dynasty (1392–1910)			
	1394 Capital moved from Kaesŏng to Seoul			Ashikaga Shōgunate

	KOREA		CHINA	JAPAN
	HISTORICAL EVENTS	ARTISTIC MANIFESTATION		
1400	1403 Opening of the Government Printing Office (Movable types) 1424 Integration of various Buddhist sects into two main sects 1443 Invention of Korean Alphabet by King Se-jong (1419–1450)	Beginnings of first Yi Blue-and-White Porcelain		
1500		*Punch'ŏng* Pottery at its zenith		
	1592 The Imjin Japanese (or Hideyoshi) Invasion (1592–1598)	*Punch'ŏng* declines		1573 Azuchi-Momoyama Period (1573–1614)
1600	1623 King Injo (1623–1647) 1627 First Manchu Invasion		1616 Rise of the Manchus The Ch'ing Dynasty (1616–1912)	1615 Yedo Period (1615–1867) Tokugawa Shōgunate
	1636 Second Manchu Invasion Surrender of King Injo (1623–1647)		1644 Fall of the Ming Dynasty	
1700				

	KOREA		CHINA	JAPAN
	HISTORICAL EVENTS	ARTISTIC MANIFESTATION		
1800		1760 Painter Kim Hong-do (1760–?)		
	1864 Prince Regent Taewŏn-gun (1864–1873)	1884 Closing of the official Punwŏn Kiln		1867 Meiji Era (1867–1912)
1900	1894 Sino-Japanese war in Korea			
	1904 Russo-Japanese war			
	1910 Annexation of Korea by Japan			
	The Government General of Chōsen (1910–1945)		1912 Fall of the Ch'ing Dynasty	1912 Taishō Era (1912–1926)
				1926 Shōwa Era
			The Republic of China	
	1945 The Republic of Korea			

INDEX

278

This book was printed in the workshops of Benziger & Co. A.G., Einsiedeln. – The illustrations in four colour offset were executed by Imprimeries Réunies, S.A., Lausanne. – The heliogravure reproductions were executed by Braun & Cie. S.A., Mulhouse-Dornach. – The halftone blocks were made by Process Engraver Schwitter, Ltd., Basel. – The binding is by Van Rijmenam N.V., 's-Gravenhage. – Lay-out by Irmgard Loeb, Basel, after a design by André Rosselet, Auvernier (Switzerland).

Printed in Switzerland